Pastoral Helmsmanship

The Pastor's Guide to Church Administration

Rodney A. Harrison
Jeffrey A. Klick
Glenn A. Miller

What Others Are Saying

"I highly recommend this new book to you. As a pastor for over 30 years, I assure you this kind of work is needed. It contains personal experience with practical wisdom. There are many things one learns in seminary, but there are many that only the practice of pastoral ministry can teach. This book contains wise counsel and seasoned wisdom in practice. I commend it to you."
 Frank S. Page
 President and Chief Executive Officer
 Executive Committee, Southern Baptist Convention

"Helmsmanship suggests that someone is at the wheel, guiding, protecting, and keeping the destination in view. That is what a pastor must do, and the author's Rodney Harrison, Jeffrey Klick and Glenn Miller have given a well-rounded orientation for new pastors – and also mature ones – of how to guide the church without being a dictator and without surrendering to a laissez faire attitude."
 Elmer Towns
 Co-Founder and Vice President
 Liberty University, Lynchburg, Virginia

"Practical help from experienced ministry leaders – people who lead real churches, not model churches that don't really exist – is the strength of this very helpful book. These men write from their perspective as practitioners, but also from a vantage point seasoned by training hundreds of other young leaders. They know the pitfalls to avoid, the problems that undermine effectiveness, and the strategies for handling difficult people. Learn from their wisdom and avoid debilitating ministry leadership mistakes."
 Dr. Jeff Iorg
 President, Golden Gate Seminary

"I love it when practitioners (who also think deeply) write books from successful experience. But this is no 'sample of one.' *Pastoral Helmsmanship* is written in community and is stronger for it. My own estimation of the volume comes down to this — will I use a good bit of the material therein? Answer — you bet. After you read it you will think similarly."
 Dr. Matt Friedeman, Professor of Evangelism and Discipleship,
 Wesley Biblical Seminary

"There are no easy ministries! Ministry is challenging and fulfilling, satisfying and frustrating, recognized and ignored, uplifting and depressing. *Pastoral Helmsmanship* is full of all those extremes and yet points to the incomparable calling that resides in the heart and soul of every minister who has received the compelling assignment from God to proclaim the Gospel of Jesus Christ. That call may express itself in many different ways, but however that may be, there is incredible joy and anointing that God gives to those He calls. These pages will point out the dangers that lie ahead, but also the blessings and incomparable joy that come along the way. Read these pages to your benefit and to the blessing of those you will serve."
    Jimmy Draper
    President Emeritus LifeWay

"Rodney Harrison, Glenn Miller, and Jeff Klick have set sail once again with another great work for the Kingdom of God! You will not be disappointed with *Pastoral Helmsmanship*. Join the authors as they help you set your sails toward church revitalization and a renewed spirit of pastoral leadership. This is a must-have book placed on your study desk so you can learn from it daily."
    Tom Cheyney
    Founder & Directional Leader
    Renovate National Church Revitalization Conference

"*Pastoral Helmsmanship* is chock-full of practical advice that every minister urgently needs. I encourage every pastor and church staff member to keep *Pastoral Helmsmanship* close at hand. It will prove a steady guide for the practical, administrative, and logistical issues that stymie so many ministries."
    Dr. Jason Allen
    President, Midwestern Baptist Theological Seminary

"*Pastoral Helmsmanship* is filled with practical administrative tips, born out of the years of experience of its authors, but the real benefit of reading this book is not merely learning how to do pastoral administration in our 21st century context; It is in being immersed in the deep love for God and His people that you will encounter on every page."
    Jim L. Wilson, Director of the Doctor of Ministry Program
    Golden Gate Baptist Theological Seminary

"*Pastoral Helmsmanship* should find a place on every pastor's bookshelf as a much-consulted reference. The writing is accessible, the principles are encouraging, and the illustrations are excellent. I like the quotes to highlight each chapter heading and the Questions to Ponder that draw the reader into personal application of the principles. I highly recommend this book to every pastor!"
    J. Mark Fox
    Pastor, Antioch Community Church, Elon, NC
    Adjunct Professor at School of Communications, Elon

"In these days of cultural turbulence, the Church needs steady leadership. *Pastoral Helmsmanship* is full of insight from experienced leaders that will give pastors the tools needed to faithfully steer their congregations into safe harbor."
    Dr. J.R. Miller, Professor at Southern California Seminary

"From bow to stern, *Pastoral Helmsmanship* offers a stimulating and instructive 'pastor's guide.' From pastors in training to pastors in turmoil our authors, seasoned shepherds all, are on board to assist us in unraveling the maze of relational and administrative elements required for effectual pastoral ministry. And all this while never losing sight of God's purpose of navigating the church safely to its eternal harbor."
    Eric Burd, President, Household of Faith Fellowship of
    Churches Pastor, Vancouver Household of Faith Community
    Church

"As a professional who has served scores of churches over the past 20 years and as a church officer and board member, I have seen a consistent need for a comprehensive but practical resource for pastors to use in understanding, conducting, and overseeing church administration. *Pastoral Helmsmanship* provides valuable insights, tools, and solutions to the pastor in the challenging world of church administration."
    John A. Parrish, MBA, CPA, CFE
    Partner, Keller & Owens, LLC

Scripture Translations:

The Holy Bible, English Standard Version (ESV) Copyright © 2001 by Crossway Bibles, a division of Good News Publishers

New International Version (NIV) Copyright © 1973, 1978, 1984 by International Bible Society

New American Standard Bible (NASB) Copyright © 1960, 1962, 1963, 1968, 1971, 1972, 1973, 1975, 1977, 1995 by The Lockman Foundation

King James Version (KJV) Public Domain

Holman Christian Standard Bible (HCSB) Copyright © 1999, 2000, 2002, 2003, 2009 by Holman Bible Publishers.

Revised Standard Version (RSV) Copyright © 1946, 1952, and 1971 the Division of Christian Education of the National Council of the Churches of Christ in the United States of America.

Disclaimer:

Nothing in this book is intended to constitute or replace legal advice but is given as general information. Any legal or tax issues addressed are done with the understanding that those issues should be discussed with competent professionals. In addition, the web links referred to within the text were all working when the book was published. Given the fluid nature of the internet, some may no longer be functional.

Copyright Information:

No part of this publication may be reproduced, stored in a retrieval system, or transmitted in any way by any means—electronic, mechanical, photocopy, recording, or otherwise—without the prior permission of the copyright holder, except as provided by U.S.A. copyright law. Requests for permission should be made in writing.

Copyright © ICM Publishing, 2014, Expanded Edition 2015
Copyright ©Rodney A. Harrison
Copyright ©Jeffrey A. Klick
Copyright ©Glenn A. Miller
All rights reserved

Contents

Section One - The Pastor

Introduction   2

1. Tempered by the Storm   7

2. Vision: The Navigating Chart to Your Final Destination   17

3. Personal Time Management   27

4. Balancing Ministry and Family   35

5. Occupation Hazards of the Ministry   47

6. Pirates and Landlubbers: Identifying Troublemakers before they Sink the Ship   61

Section Two - The Pastor and Administration

7. Building the Right Crew: Recruiting the Right Paid and Volunteer Staff   73

8. Motivating the Crew; Navigating Staff Attitudes and Actions, and when to throw Jonah Overboard!   87

9. The Bounty: How to Handle Incoming Funds with Integrity and Accountability   103

10. Sailing with the Right Provisions: How to Handle Expenditures   117

11. Staying Accountable to the Owner: How to Properly Budget and Report the Finances of the Church   141

12. Barnacles, Sails and Swabbing the Deck: Facilities Management: 157

13. Icebergs, Hurricanes and Torpedoes: Risk Mitigation   169

14. Navigating the Legal Waters of Ministry   183

Section Three - The Pastor as Helmsman

15. Understand Yourself and the Crew:
    None of Us Work Alone   193

16. When Mutiny is in the Air: Conflict Resolution   205

17. The Belly of the Ship: Delegation, Committees
    and Volunteers   227

18. The Calm after the Storm: Leading through
    Change Management   239

19. Mutiny Mitigation: How to Lead
    an Effective Meeting   257

20. Eight Navigation Tips   267

21. Enjoying the Journey: Final Thoughts from
    Seasoned Sailors   277

Section Four - Resources

Treasure Chest: Helpful Articles   282

Samples, Suggested Reading, Websites   312

Acknowledgements:

Special thanks to my wife, Julie. For over thirty years she has been a gentle current of encouragement to me in fair weather and a sea anchor during the season of storms. I also wish to express my appreciation to my father, Byron Harrison, a seasoned sailor in the waters of academics, administration, churchmanship, and family, whose examples I have sought to faithfully follow. (Rodney)

Thank you Lord, for the gift of my bride Leslie, who has weathered the storms of ministry alongside me, my children, Andrea, Sarah, and David, who give me a right to speak in the gate, and to my ten grandchildren, who are all a delight to my often weary soul! (Jeff)

I am very grateful to the Lord for my family and for the joy of being able to serve churches and ministries across the theological spectrum to further the work of Christ's Kingdom. (Glenn)

Special thanks to Chris and Ben Miller for their efforts in helping us complete this project in a timely fashion. Your diligence is greatly appreciated!

Dedications:

To the students being equipped for the journey of a lifetime, this book is dedicated to you as you prepare to take the helm. (Rodney)

To all the pastors who labor diligently for the Lord in relative obscurity, your eternal reward from Him will be great, and many will call you blessed. (Jeff)

To my Dad — immigrant, retired Air Force, pastor and church planter — the hardest working guy I know. (Glenn)

Section One
The Pastor

Introduction

"I wonder if there are any icebergs ahead?" the Captain of the Titanic might have mused.

    Pastoral Helmsmanship is much more than a book about church administration; it is about effectively navigating in the increasingly complex world of ministry. Combined, the authors have over a century of administration experience. More importantly, they each hold to an unwavering commitment to God's Word and an uncompromising conviction of God's love for His church. This book will provide the reader with the biblical foundations and practical application points to faithfully navigate the church with which you have been entrusted.

    The title of the book stems from the Greek word "kubernesis" which is frequently translated as "administrates, governs or manages." The context of this word is the administration or management of the local church. Join us on a journey of first century discovery as it relates to "church" and "administration."

    In Matthew 16:18, Jesus says, "I will build my church (*ecclesia*)." Later, in the book of Acts, written in the first century, the early church leaders continued to borrow this Greek word, *ecclesia*, to describe what had clearly become something new and different — not just a sect of Judaism. For first century Romans the word *ecclesia* simply referred to the calling of the citizens of a Greek town out of their houses by the herald's trumpet to summon them to assemble.[1]

Introduction

We can easily imagine a calling out of the local citizens to hear or discuss the latest news from Rome. As the citizens (who were all male) gathered together in close proximity, non-citizens, including many merchants, slaves, and women would gather within earshot to hear what was happening.

It is fascinating that the Holy Spirit chose to appropriate *ecclesia* rather than several other potential terms to describe the church such as συναγω (sunago), which means to gather together or assemble, or επισυναγωγη, (episynagoge) which means to assemble or come together, as found in Hebrew 10:25.

As pastors and church leaders, we must understand that the church is truly a gathering of citizens (believers) whose home is not of this world. It also helps to realize that some, if not many, who gather with us during the week to hear and see what the church is doing may not be "citizens"—much like those non-citizens who eavesdropped upon the Greek gathering of citizens. Moreover, like the early citizens of Rome, the purpose of the gathering is to share, hear, and repeat the message that has been delivered to the church.

At first, the local church didn't have any discernible leaders. However, as the church matured God gave her missionaries and prophets, evangelists and pastors. Of course, that also created a new challenge for the church, as her leaders were now identifiable and potentially vulnerable to harassment and persecution.

This potential persecution may help one understand why Paul, just before instructing Timothy to appoint elders in the churches, exhorts Timothy to:

> **First of all, then, I urge that entreaties and prayers, petitions and thanksgivings, be made on behalf of all men, for kings and all who are in authority, so that we may lead a tranquil and quiet life in all godliness and dignity.**
> **(1 Timothy 2:1-2 NASB)**

---

[1] Fenton John Anthony Hort, "The Christian Eccledia: A Course of Lectures on the Early History and Early Conceptions of the Eccledia" (Macmillon & Co, London, 1914), 6.

Paul understands that the church, this young and vulnerable gathering of the called out people, will need a season of political favor and tolerance. It may be that the principle of this "first of all" exhortation is less about us praying for political leaders and those in authority above all others than it is the apostle's realization of that practical need—appointing qualified leaders. This will only be successful if God provides the church with divine favor among the kings and those in authority long enough for the church to mature sufficiently so that it would not perish when the times of hardship would come. In this book we, the authors, will never jettison a clear understanding that:

Unless the LORD builds the house, they labor in vain who build it; unless the LORD guards the city, the watchman keeps awake in vain. (Psalms 127:1 NASB)

Paul prepares Timothy for an administrative task of leadership selection and development with a "first of all" plea for prayer so that his work will be successful. In the same way, the pastor must also recognize the "first of all" prayer priorities of the church.

Today, the church continues to be a gathering of the called out ones—those who have been adopted into God's family by faith through grace. Like those who gathered in the first century, the church today faces both real and potential threats. Those threats are greatest in times of discord or change, which is where a foundational understanding of the word "kubernesis" comes into play. Of Latin origin, the word means to steer or pilot a ship. As with all scripture, the Holy Spirit inspired the writer to use a word that perfectly articulates the provision God provides the church—those skilled in administration or governing the church.

In the first century, the pilot (kubernesis) of the ship was also called the helmsman. It was his job to steer the ship and interpret the soundings in order to ensure the ship was not subjected to unnecessary dangers or run aground. As such, the helmsman's skills were put to the test during times of transition such as going into and out of port and times of storms. Although the helmsman frequently

Introduction

accomplished his task with skills that were almost second nature, the reality is that he was ultimately under the command of the captain. The helmsman was always second-in-command, never first. So it is with God's church. Christ is the Head, and the helmsman (pastor) is under His authority and command.

It has been our observation that many pastors do not see themselves as administrators. Today, a significant number of medium and large churches employ "Church Administrators" who provide the day-to-day oversight of the myriad of planning and logistical needs of the church. It is our belief that even in the largest of churches the pastor is never able to abdicate the role of pastoral helmsmanship. It is imperative that the pastor understand this last statement. The pastor in his role as overseer (Gk, *episkopos Acts 20:28 et. al*) is required to provide oversight of the local church. Even in churches that employ staff administrators, the role of overseer requires administrative skills and personnel sensitivity by the pastor.

At the same time, we are aware that a majority of pastors feel they are ill equipped for the task of administration. In Thom Rainer's article "10 Things Pastors Wish They Knew Before They Became Pastors," five of the ten issues will be covered in this book.[2] And yet, most pastors are fortunate to have one course on administration during their seminary training. In fact, at a vast majority of seminaries, it is possible to complete one or more graduate programs without a course in administration. In the Pulpit and Pews series, the book *Pastors in Transition* sums up the problem well by noting,

> **"Recommendation 1: Seminaries should do more to prepare their students for the practical aspects of ministry."[3]**

However, preparing for the realities of the pastorate is not just a problem or need for the seminaries. We also recognize that a number

---

[2] Thom Rainer, "10 Things Pastors Wish They Knew Before Pastoring," Thomrainer.com, http://thomrainer.com/2013/03/09/ten-things-pastors-wish-they-knew-before-they-became-pastors/ (accessed January 23, 2014).

[3] Dean R. Hoge, Jacqueline E. Wenger, "Pastors in Transition: Why Clergy Leave Local Church Ministry," (Wm. B. Eerdmans Publishing Co, 2005), 202.

of pastors are called to ministry with no formal administrative training. Like the early church leaders, many are called from the marketplace to the ministry. It is our goal to provide pastors and church leaders a solid foundation for navigating the church regardless of their educational or experience level.

In that light, the book is designed to be used either as a textbook or a quick reference handbook. While most will want to read the book from cover to cover, please feel free to jump to the chapter or topic that interests you, or that you need the most.

We pray that the Lord would guide you in your role as helmsman for the part of the Kingdom where you serve. The Lord will build His Church, and He will not fail. Together we are a part of that process and for this truth, we are eternally grateful.

1 Tempered by the Storm
Never trust a sailor that does not limp.

All of us have a story to tell, including victories to revel in and defeats to regret. Each of us has arrived at where we are by the road we traveled — or, in light of our book's theme, the seas we have sailed. Along our journey we have encountered storms. Some were fierce; others simply rocked our boat a little. Each encounter changed us. Shaped us. Tempered us. Our story will not be your story exactly, yet they are similar. Perhaps this small window into each of our lives at a personal level, will help you see that we have been there. We know and understand. You are not alone in your storm. There is hope, and it rests in Jesus.

Rodney

This story requires setting the stage. On December 31, 1999 I was one of several adult volunteers from our church attending the Anaheim, California venue of YouthLink 2000, a multi-national, multi-city millennial celebration for youth. Among the 20 or so high-schoolers from our church was my 13 year old daughter. Around 8:00 pm, one of the speakers challenged the youth to embrace the new millennium by "giving your all to Jesus." He continued by challenging the youth to be sure their lives had been given to Jesus.

My response was, "yep, I've done that." Next, he challenged those present to give their education and future careers to Jesus. "I've done that too," reflecting on the call that took me from a career in health care administration to church planting. Then he challenged his listeners by reminding them that most would someday be married, and to commit your marriage and future spouse to God now. "Done that too," was my response. The next challenge was to commit their future children to the Lord. Again in my mind I said, "Check, we've done that." But this time, it was as if the Lord was saying, "No, you have not." I recall thinking, "Of course I have. We even had dedication services for each of our three children." However, there was only a silence from God.

For the next several hours, I wrestled with God. At one point, I said to Him (silently, of course), "God, my children are yours. Everything is yours." Unexpectedly, I sensed a response from God saying (again, silently), "You've not given her to me." Next to me was our second child, my oldest daughter. "But God, I have given her to you. You can take her to the mission field, you can let her be a pastors' wife; you can do whatever you want; just don't let her be hurt." The silence and sorrow that followed was broken by a thunderous roar of tens of thousands of youth yelling "ten, nine, eight, seven…" I recall crying out loud, "She's yours, God, yours no conditions, she's yours!" as the countdown reached one. As the crowd erupted in "Happy New Year" and "Welcome to the New Millennium" I hugged and kissed my daughter, who was unaware of the battle that had been raging.

A few minutes later, an invitation was given for the youth who had made decisions that evening to come forward. One of the first at the front was my daughter, who responded to God's call to be a missionary to her peers, no matter what it took or where it took her.

In my mind, I envisioned my daughter going to some third world, Muslim nation. However, the path God chose was something no one could anticipate.

On a bright March Sunday afternoon, I was returning from preaching at a small Baptist Church near Bakersfield, California. When I arrived in Porterville, about 1 hour north of the church, it was already 6:30 pm. Since the evening service at my home church was almost over, I drove directly home. When I arrived at our house, I noticed the front door was open. Where I lived, that was not a good sign. I parked on the curb and walked to the front door. "Is anyone in there?" No answer. I peered in, looking for signs of a robbery. The television, VCR, and video games were there. I walked inside, looking in the kitchen. The microwave and small appliances were all where we had left them. I went to the garage, where I had a collector car and a multitude of tools. Everything was as I had left it. Confident that no-one was in the house, I walked through the hallway to the bedrooms. It was then that I heard sobbing. As I called out, I tried the door, which was locked. After several pleas, my daughter finally opened the door, crying out, "I don't know what to do. I'm sorry, I don't know what to do." In the minutes that followed, I found that my precious daughter had been sexually molested earlier that evening at a church event. The perpetrator threatened her and the family with bodily harm if she said anything. She was so hurt and scared; she ran the four miles from the church to home without telling anyone. Thus began a journey of pain, grief, grace, love, and forgiveness.

As a father, I had once said, "If people hurt me, I don't care but if they touch my daughter, I'll kill them." Those words came to mind as my daughter clung to me in the hallway. Instead of revenge, I remember praying with her Romans 8:28. At the end of the prayer, I asked God to help us to love and forgive the man who did this horrible act, and to make wise decisions in the coming days.

The first decision was to call the police. The next was to contact the church. As a church leader, one often forgets that the storms come not only to the church, but to our families. Jesus told his followers, "In the world you will have tribulation" (John 16:33). James reminds us, "Count it all joy, my brothers, when you meet trials of various kinds, for you know that the testing of your faith produces steadfastness" (James 1:2).

Over the next several months, on a daily basis I would need to ask God for the strength to love and forgive the man who violated our daughter. I also continued to trust God to fulfill what I was claiming as a promise, to "…cause all things to work together for God, for those who love him, those called according to His purpose" (Romans 8:28).

Four months later, my daughter was at Centrifudge, a summer camp experience for youth. Almost immediately, she noticed a girl who did not participate in the camp activities. A conversation something like this ensued:

> **My Daughter**: Hey, why aren't you joining us for the activities?
> **The Girl**: I don't want to be here!
> **My Daughter**: Then why did you come to camp?
> **The Girl**: You wouldn't understand!
> **My Daughter**: Try me, I might.

The girl had come to camp to escape the pain of being a victim of sexual abuse. Camp was a one week break in the cycle of fear and pain. As the girl and my daughter became friends, the opportunity to share Christ grew. I'll never forget the phone call from my daughter that Friday, as she shared how her new friend had accepted Christ.

Three months later, my daughter and I drove 400 miles to participate in the baptism of this girl and her mother, who had also become a Christian. On the drive home, my daughter asked, "Dad, do you think there are many other girls like us?" My recent research showed that nearly one in four girls is sexually abused by the time they finish high school. "Yes, I'm afraid that there are many girls like you, and most are going through this alone and without Christ." The next day, my daughter put up an index card on the high school bulletin board.

> **"Girls, been hurt and abused? Need someone to talk to? Starbucks, 6:00 am. Thursday."**

That Thursday morning as I drove my daughter to the Starbucks next to the High School she said, "Dad, what if no one shows up?" My response was immediate, "Even if no one is there, I'm so proud of you for being willing to use your experience to help others." To our surprise, over 20 girls responded to that first meeting. Over the years, my daughter has used this experience as a platform for sharing the gospel with multitudes who would never have heard the message of hope from a pulpit.

God also used this experience in my journey, teaching me that love and forgiveness are not dependent on me or deserved. Through Christ, I was able to love and forgive the man who did this to our daughter. Sadly, he took his own life in 2010. As a result, I now understand how David could lament Absalom's death despite his actions.

As with the other authors, we have all been through the storms. This is just one of many we have endured, but it is the one that has taught me the most about the weathering of the rough seas. Learning forgiveness is a key component in ministry survival.

Glenn

Things could not have been going better. Before coming on staff, my wife and I had been active members and volunteers at our local church for five years. My good friend, the Youth Pastor, was promoted to Senior Pastor, and he asked me to leave my comfortable, secure seminary administration position and go on staff at the church as their church administrator. So off I went!

In the next five years the church grew from 600 to 1,200 people. We added a new addition, remodeled almost all of the older buildings, and landscaped the grounds to a prideful condition! The school had grown from 100 to 200, we had 3,500 people at our annual July 4th patriotic celebration, we were in the middle of a four million dollar capital campaign, and several of us had just returned from speaking at a pastor's conference in Benin West Africa. I had just turned 40 years old and purchased a nice new house; we had lots of friends at the church, were active in small group ministry, — life was good.

Well, you can already feel it coming — things were going too well. The leadership became increasingly uncomfortable with my style and pace, and they decided that it was time for me to go. At that juncture, I lost the job that I loved, the church that I helped build, nearly all of our friends, and our home group — basically everything. Turning 40 at the same time was fun, thus greatly enhancing the whole mid-life crisis thing.

So, now what, God? I have followed you this far: are you going to leave me stranded now? It was the darkest time in my life. It felt like I was completely abandoned. I had worked hard, achieved great things for God, and there I was — alone, unemployed, churchless, and with few friends.

I had felt for some time that God was pushing me toward a full time ministry that would serve churches through accounting and administrative services. We had started a small company several years before and had a few church clients. And, while I believed this was God's ultimate plan, I was not yet ready to take the risk and follow God's leading; instead, I first took an Ishmael diversion (substitute my plan for God's). I bargained with God that I would go on staff at one last church, help them out for a few years, and THEN follow His call. I was hired just one month later at a large church and life was good, sort of. My start date was two months out and by the time it arrived, the senior pastor I was going to be working for was fired, and they decided they didn't really need me! Oooops!

So there we were, now totally out of money, no résumés out, and no prospects on the horizons. I went to see a counseling friend of mine and he assured me we would get through this! Bold statement! He was a lot more confident than I was. He recommended that I go home and make a list of 10 people to contact and tell them about our new, expanding ministry to churches. I did not think I could do it. Sadly, and in tears, I went back to my home, went into my basement office and began making a list of people to call. Before I could finish that list, the first three people on the list called me wondering if I had any time to help them! It was truly a miracle. To this day, I never finished the list, and never finished calling the people on it.

Today, 15 years later, my wife and I own and operate a multi-million dollar accounting and consulting ministry that has 25 employees and has served over 1,000 ministries to date and is still growing. The moral of the story — listen for His voice and follow it. While men may fail us or even treat us unjustly, God never fails us. Follow His path, for His ways are higher than ours! Amen.

Jeff

I never thought I would be a pastor. My dream was to be a corporate executive or president of a national firm. At twenty-three, this dream seemed in reach. H & R Block had taken a chance on a young man and placed me in charge of 32 taxes offices. My territory ranged over Missouri and Kansas with a few scattered offices in Nebraska and Iowa.

Setting net profit records, exceeding efficiency goals, and living on coffee was the life for me. When asked by my supervisor what my corporate goal was, I quipped back, "To take your job," and I meant it. He knew it as well and smiled.

There are two words scattered in the Bible and they are sprinkled in our lives as well, and they change everything – **"But God."**

After three years of living my dream, God asked, better stated, required me to quit my job and assist a friend in managing his inner city remodeling company. There was no doubt about the direction, simply about my obedience. After a major struggle in prayer, my wife and I chose to follow the Lord's clearly revealed plan for us even though we didn't know where it would lead.

In previous years we had learned some of the cost of disobedience - we helped split a church by waging a subversive war against the senior pastor. The price paid was huge in hurts, wounds, slaughtered sheep, and sin. About six months later God graciously spoke to our hearts and brought conviction. We went back to the pastor and the other church members and asked for forgiveness and grace was extended. As the Lord would have it, this pastor ended up working on the same staff with me many years later, but that is a story for another time.

While attempting to enjoy working in a job that was not part of my dream, I noticed a request for help with some bookkeeping in our church's weekly announcement bulletin. I mentioned to a staff member that I would be glad to assist with this until they found someone and thought little about it after that. But God, (there He goes again,) had other plans.

Pastoral Helmsmanship

Meetings were called, phones rang off the hook, and decisions were made that I knew nothing about. Apparently a twenty-six year old, Associate of Arts holding guy, was a hot commodity for this church. The church was dealing with major growth pains and they wanted someone to become the first administrator. This church had grown from 150 members to 1,100 in a very short time and was in need of organizational help. For some reason, they thought I was an answer to prayer.

My bride and I met with the leaders the following Sunday and they made me an offer I couldn't refuse. "How would you like to make half of what you are making now, and work harder than you ever have in your life?" went their sales pitch. Who could refuse? We sold our new car, moved out of our new duplex, and began to relive the dream I thought was lost.

Coffee flowed. Meetings were plentiful; budgets, planning, hiring, firing, building additions, fund raising, pressure, stress, and deadlines. It just didn't get any better than this, even in corporate America! God had returned me to my dream job and even better - in the Church! What could possibly go wrong?

For eleven years we built, organized, categorized, prioritized, systematized, and any other word you can think of to ride the waves of growth. The church grew to 3,500 Sunday morning attendees. Our network of churches exploded with growth and ministry life was good. We had money, fame, and hosted the best speakers and music groups; we were "it" in our town and region.

Over those same years, I became the senior pastor's right hand man. I served as a deacon, then as an elder, and always as part of the executive committee that actually made all of the decisions. This was a pretty heady time for a young man. Seminars were attended, degrees and training was acquired, and life seemed perfect. But God...was not finished yet in His refining process.

The senior pastor had a problem that no one knew about. Like so many successful men before him, he led a secret life of immorality. One day, he just left town with his book editor and chaos ensued. Meetings were called, discussions lasting into the morning hours were had, and decisions were being made. Council was sought, but ignored, and my dream world came crashing in around me. A very good friend, a co-elder approached me and said, "Jeff, you need to resign, you do not have a prayer here." I was clueless as to what he meant, though I shouldn't have been.

When the senior pastor runs off with a woman, someone has to pay for that choice. I was elected. For the next three months, meetings were endured, my personal life was scoured looking for evidence of sin or hidden knowledge of the affair, and my reputation was trashed. Falling from being considered to replace the senior pastor as his successor I soon became the administrator from hell. Quite a drop, and way too rapidly to adjust to the pressure. I guess it is sort of like a deep sea diver that surfaces too quickly; illness and death can follow.

Death did follow, at least death to my dream again. After a few months, even I understood that it was time for me to move on, so after seeking counsel, I resigned. My mind was reeling and my heart was broken. My family was in even worse shape. From a natural perspective, our lives were ruined. But God was not finished! He rarely is.

As we wandered around from church to church, people would come up to us and ask us where we were going to attend the next week. Confused, I would ask why they wanted to know. They would say, "Oh, you are our pastor and we had been praying for you to get fired for years so you would go start a church." "Thanks a lot," I thought, though didn't say it out loud.

Months later, after making sure it was okay with those in the previous church we began a new work. Through tears and heartache, we planted a completely new type of church. Out of the ashes of destruction something good was birthed. God is like that. We recently celebrated our twentieth anniversary of this church plant and I marvel at God's grace and plan.

"But God," are some incredible words. God is redemptive and has a plan. God really does have everything under control even when it seems all is out of control. Out of the death of a vision, something better was birthed. Through pain, heartache, disappointment, and betrayal, God brought a dream back to life. Better than I thought possible. Why was I surprised? He is after all, the God of

Resurrection. Jesus excels at calming the fiercest of storms; He calmed mine, and He can and will calm yours.

Each of us has a story that somewhere includes, a "But God." This is not a new understanding but an ancient one. Few say it clearer than Joseph did:

> **As for you, you meant evil against me, but God meant it for good, to bring it about that many people should be kept alive, as they are today. (Genesis 50:20, ESV)**

The unexplained pain and heartache in your life can and will become the ashes that fertilize God's redemptive plan. The wounds will heal, and God will redeem, because He is like that. God does not fail and His purpose will be accomplished, regardless of sin, man, or wickedness.

We trust that this glimpse into our lives has encouraged you. We know that many of you are going through trials, or you will sooner than later. God is no respecter of persons — He was faithful to redeem each one of our lives and situations, and He will do the same for you. In fact, He will do more than any of us can even think and ask, and that is a promise from the One who cannot lie.

Questions to Ponder

1. What storms has God used to place you in a position to hear and heed His voice?

2. Identify your own "But God" moments. How can these memories serve you in the coming days?

3. Which verse speaks to you the most today—Romans 8:28, Genesis 50:20 or another verse?

2 Vision:
The Navigating Chart to Your Final Destination

We don't know where we are going, but we are making excellent time in getting there.

The church was in the midst of the 1960's Jesus Movement. Members regularly used their gifts, talents and abilities to share and communicate the Gospel. One member painted a pastoral scene behind the baptistery, with the words of Proverbs 29:18 "Where there is no Vision, the People Perish" (KJV). Over the years, the members slowly moved away for a multitude of reasons; graduation from college, marriage, new jobs. The once vibrant church was running just a handful of people when a former member, the man who had originally painted the mural, was in town on a business trip and decided to visit his former church.

Following a lifeless worship service, he headed over to the baptistery to see if his mural, which was now covered by a drape which covered the unused baptistery, was still there. Peering in, he saw once beautiful artwork was now faded. What he noticed most was that the paint had chipped away over the W in the Proverbs passage. The verse now appeared to say, "here there is no Vision, the People Perish."

Vision is akin to the purpose for a ship. For the purpose of this book, we understand that the God-given vision can also be described as the mission or purpose for the church. Vision serves as the point we fix our eyes upon so that our leadership and efforts are always helping to move the church and members in the right direction. However, the myriad of books on this subject—both sacred and secular—often serves to confuse rather than clarify. To help you understand vision, at least from our perspective, here are our vision stories.

Rodney

A few years after yielding to God's call to ministry service, I believe the Lord placed upon my heart and mind the desire *to be used up by God*, meaning, there was no turning back. Could something this short be a vision? For me, it was a start. First, it was necessary to validate the vision. Does Scripture support the vision? The somewhat uncomfortable answer was, "yes." God has every right to use me—His creature and creation—fully and completely. Every vision will be unique, whether it is a congregational vision or a personal vision. However, the vision must align with and never contradict Scripture.

Another aspect of vision is that it often begins with or is compatible with the words "to be" or other similar phrases. Why? Because vision is future oriented. It guides us where we will be going and who we, as a church or individual, will become. At this point, my vision was somewhat unclear, but it was enough to get started on the right journey.

For the first couple of years, following the vision simply meant I was to direct my energy and efforts to the things of God. This meant leaving a comfortable career and home and heading to seminary to be trained. Later, it meant leaving the new-found comforts of ministry in the South for the pioneer areas near the Canadian border. Over time, God expanded the vision to include the "reduction of the unchurched population." From that point on, my goal was to be involved in church planting efforts that were primarily evangelistic and/or church revitalization efforts that were reclamation ministries. Both involved being used by God to reduce the unchurched population.

When the opportunity came to pursue a calling in academics, at first I felt this was inconsistent with what God had laid upon my heart, and I said "no" to the invitation. However, I soon realized that the Lord was expanding the vision in a way that both were compatible and complementary to the vision. Today, the institution I serve has become one of the preeminent centers for church revitalization. Students coming to our school seek to serve the church by being willing to be "used up by God" through radical missions, revitalization, and a biblical understanding of the doctrine of theodicy (why God allows suffering.)

For thirty years the vision has guided decisions related to family, finances, and time. As noted, over the years the vision has expanded and gained greater clarity, and yet it serves the same purpose of providing focus and purpose. Paraphrasing an old credit card commercial, I would challenge every pastor with this thought: Vision, Don't Lead the Church Without It.

Jeff

Gene (not his real name) called me and wanted to get together for lunch. "I want to pick your brain," he said. Little does Gene know that there really is not much to find there, but I will go along with him for the fellowship and the meal. Most pastors love to talk and eat, so that is perhaps why so many pastors struggle with weight issues, but I will leave that rabbit trail unexplored.

Gene had heard the "call" to pastor a church. Excitement was in his voice and dreams flowed from his mouth between bites. Phrases like: "I want to change the city for Jesus," and "I can't wait to start preaching!" bubbled out.

When a young pastor contacts me (like Gene), and wants to discuss the ins and outs of ministry, I always begin with their vision. I ask open-ended questions like:

- What drives you? What has God spoken to you about vision?
- What do you want to impart to those that God adds to you?
- If you could open up people's minds and place something inside of them what would it be?

- Where are you going and can you explain it?
- What burns in your heart and spirit that you can't wait to share with others?
- How do you know this vision is from God?

These questions should at least be considered before attempting to lead others. We do not have to know everything but we should at least know what our passion and vision is. Gene did not. Gene just wanted to preach. While commendable, Gene will probably not make it long term as a pastor without a vision. If people do follow Gene, they will most likely become frustrated because he does not know where he is going.

Vision is freeing and confining at the same time. Vision defines where we are heading. Like railroad tracks, vision allows us to move along smoothly. Trains do not move well without tracks - and neither do pastors without a vision. The train speeds along on smooth tracks. Yet, when derailed it stops, and often crashing causing great noise and damage. A pastor without vision is akin to a train off the tracks.

What is your passion? What is burning in your soul? What comes out when you share with others? What is going to define you, and help you evaluate how you are succeeding in doing it? Vision.

> *"Without a vision the people perish or run unrestrained," so states Proverbs.*

> *"With a vision people are saved and run in a proper direction," so states Jeff.*

Vision defines us. Vision guides and directs our efforts. Vision brings clarity to the cloud of confusion, and helps cut through the plethora of opportunities chasing too few minutes. Vision is foundational and critical. So what is yours?

My vision is different from yours, and yours will be uniquely your own. God did not create duplicate people. If God has called you, then He has placed within you a vision that only you can fulfill. What drives your thoughts and burns within your heart? What always ends up coming out in your messages regardless of the text preached? No matter the verse or book, eventually you end up here. Mine deals with the restoration of the family and the practical aspects of how it is worked out in our daily walk with Jesus. Yours could be evangelism, discipleship, youth, missions, the lonely, helpless, poor, rich, singles, history, or any number of issues. Each of us is different. We are all unique expressions of Christ, and we will reflect His calling differently. The Shepherd inspires and places His vision in His under-shepherds uniquely.

For me, vision brings clarity and freedom. In one respect, a church is not different from household solicitations. I receive calls, emails, and yes, even snail mail every week from those that "feel led" to minister to my church family. In addition, many would invite us to join them in their service to the planet...or at least want to enjoy our money helping them. While the validity of these requests is not necessarily the issue, the fitting into our vision clearly is.

Our church has a specific vision that we believe God has led us to follow. The freedom to refuse to participate in everyone else's vision is gained because of the vision we possess. If someone asks us to invite him or her into our service, it is a simple matter to see if his or her vision aligns with ours. If not, then the answer is no. If yes, then the answer is maybe. After prayer and discussion, we will consider the event or giving opportunity and our participation. It may be something we do, and it may not be, but having a clear vision makes these decisions much easier. Having a vision does not mean you never step outside of it and partner with or give to someone else, but it does mean that the bulk of your decisions are much clearer and easier to make.

If we want people to follow us, we must have some general idea of where we are heading. We must have an idea of how to get there and how to make corrections when we swerve off the plan. As I mentioned, our vision is primarily focused on the restoration of the family to health. Our desire as a church body is to learn how Christianity is supposed to be lived out day by day in a very practical manner, beginning in our homes. Our vision is clear and measurable.

This vision is expounded in eleven points called cleverly enough, "Our Vision Statement." While we are not doing everything in our statement every day, this is one of our founding documents, and it includes guiding principles that we attempt to follow. For example, one of our goals is to help marriages. We desire to see a reduction in the divorce rate among believers and to see a husband and wife grow together in oneness in Christ. Therefore, I will often teach a message that has some points centered on how a particular Scripture actually makes a difference in a godly marriage. I will not teach a marriage seminar every week, but every week the vision is reinforced somehow or someway.

Everything we end up doing at our church will be filtered through the vision. If something is contrary to the vision, we will not do it. If something enhances our calling and vision, we most likely will. The issue is not a matter of whether the potential activity or ministry has a valid purpose, the issue is, does it enhance or reinforce our vision.

In practice then, every sermon, activity, printed documents, event, and whatever else takes place in our church body should tie back somehow to the vision, or we should question if the action fits into what God has called us to accomplish. Vision is freeing.

If you are a pastor who is reading this, what does it all mean to you? What if you were hired into a church or onto a staff that already has a strong vision in place and perhaps their vision is not yours? This does not mean that your vision has to die. Maybe your vision can be repackaged or slowly adopted over time. Of course, it is easier to start a church than to take over one, but the vision is still critical either way.

When I was hired at the large church, my vision was still being formed. I was clearly the low man on the organizational chart. As I served and gained experience, my right to share and speak grew. Eventually I was added to the elder board and I served on the Executive Committee that made all of the day-to-day decisions. This greatly enhanced my ability to share the vision God had given me. The vision deepened, and the leadership warmed to many of my ideas and concepts. As the years rolled by it became time for me to move on and start my own church. This opportunity came in a package that I did not want or expect but God was still ruling and directing.

In 1993, through a series of painful events shared in a previous chapter, I resigned my position at this large church and sought the Lord regarding what I should do next. It became apparent that we were to begin a brand new work with a fresh vision, and we did so two months later. God works in interesting ways, and this book is an example of His efforts. Now, twenty years later we are still walking in that vision. What's yours and are you walking in it?

Glenn

I daily work with pastors and churches that struggle with issues that on the surface appear to be process or task oriented, but in reality, are rooted in the lack of vision or a wrong vision. The danger of a lack of vision has been well articulated above; however, the wrong vision will have similar devastating results.

"Vision hi-jacking" is a term used to describe what happens when a church or pastor either does not have vision clarity, or, during a season of crises or change, the vision is changed by one who has the voice of a vocal minority. Like an airline hijacking, vision hijacking endangers the people, takes them where they don't want to be, wastes resources, and creates fear and confusion.

Uncorrected, vision hijacking can result in death and destruction. Vision is always validated by scripture and by others. It helps if those "others" are godly men and women, not the malicious and malcontents. Vision provides the ultimate purpose for the church to exist. Too often, vision is perceived as being forged in a series of meetings lead by consultants and guided by workbooks. The results are often not clearly understood, and much to-do is made about being sure that everyone is using the proper terms such as vision, purpose, mission as defined by goals, objectives, values. There may be value in such processes, but when the results do not truly drive the direction of the church, it is likely that true vision does not exist.

In the mid 1980s a vision was born in my heart to offer accounting and payroll services to help churches and nonprofit organizations improve their record keeping and reporting, enabling them to spend less time on administration and more time ministering. Over the years, the process by which the vision is being fulfilled has changed several times. The essence of this vision is summed up in these words, "Miller Management Systems brings order out of chaos." That vision, which was born in my heart for a business, is now the driving force behind this book, showing once again that when God provides a church or individual His vision, it will show itself in a multitude of ways unimaginable at the time the vision is originally received.

Is the Vision Unchangeable?

Another issue many pastors face is trying to change or modify their vision in an established church. One day I (Jeff) had lunch with a pastor serving in a denominational church. The pastor was really struggling with where he was in the implementation of his vision. The pastor had a heart to make a significant change in the direction of his church, but he just did not see how it was possible. The pastor uttered a sentence that I have not been able to forget:

> *"Our church is so much in debt that if we make a change, and we lose one family, we will go under."*

My heart broke for the man, but I did understand his dilemma. Churches sometimes are trapped in debt. Pastors become fearful of offending those that pay their salary or are large givers. Money is important, and while we are not to love it, we sure have a hard time living without it. So do churches. This is a sad reality that many pastors face — the tension between preaching and teaching the truth, verses running the risk of offending those that pay the bills.

If we are to be pastors of integrity, then we must teach the truth in love. Ultimately, God is our source of provision, and we cannot allow any other to take His place. That does not mean, however, that we should not use wisdom and prudence in our efforts to implement the vision we embrace. We need to be aware of the financial pressure and walk carefully when we share hard truth.

If we need to make changes to the churches' vision, we should proceed prayerfully and carefully. We must invest the time to win the hearts, minds, and confidence of those we lead. Our leadership team, boards, and key people must be won over to our point of view. If we are really hearing from the Lord with the change we have in mind, He can change people's point of view.

Here is a truth that I have learned that might help:

The decision reached is often not as important as the process used to reach it.

Maintaining our key relationships is important. A divided church will not stand and it is far better to slow down on change than to ram it down someone's throat. God is not in a hurry, and we should not be either. If what we think needs changing is from God, then we will have the wisdom and grace to help bring others along. If we only face resistance on every front, perhaps we need to lay it down and wait. It is much more palatable for those who follow us to make five degree turns rather than ninety degree ones.

Personal Vision

The personal vision of many in Scripture may be revealed through what God said about that person. I (Rodney) can imagine David's vision as "to be a man after God's own heart." Moses' vision may have been "to be a friend of God." Paul's vision might be "to preach the Gospel to those who have not heard." Personal vision has also been a part of many great Christian leaders. Billy Graham's vision, "Proclaiming the Gospel of the Lord Jesus Christ to all…and equipping others to do the same" continues to guide the organization he established. In the same way, we might be able to grasp a sense of the personal vision of some of the great Christian leaders from their writings and teachings. I can imagine Charles Spurgeon's as, "To work as if all depended on me, and pray as if it all depended on God." For D.L. Moody, it might have been, "To be the man that shows the world what God can do with a man fully consecrated to him."

Personal vision can serve as the filter by which major decisions such as changing churches, implementing major changes, continuing one's education, or adding staff are considered. Although vision is not a substitute for prayer, fasting, seeking wise counsel, gathering facts, and searching God's Word when making decisions, vision informs and guides, helping to provide clarity as to your call and purpose.

Although not every person will go through the following process, we have found that these steps are useful for those desiring clarity of personal vision.

Step 1: Write down your call to ministry.
Step 2: Put into writing what you are passionate about.
Step 3: What is your life verse or favorite passage of Scripture?
Step 4: What would you like to be doing in five to ten years?

After you have gone through this process, spend time in prayer, asking God to reveal His purpose and plan. Be patient, as often times the process is as important as the outcome.

Questions to Ponder

1. Does your church have a clear vision or mission statement that is guiding your church and impacting your decisions? If so, is it future oriented, scripturally grounded, and congregationally understood?

2. Do you, as a church leader, have a personal vision statement? If so, write it down. If not, what steps might you take to gain clarity of vision?

3. Do you know of a church or ministry that has been a victim of "vision hijacking." What were the visible results?

3 Personal Time Management
I don't have time to get organized.

The old story is told of the farmer that began his day with the intention of plowing the south forty. As he was heading towards the tractor, he noticed the front porch step was broken. On the way to get the hammer and board to repair it he saw the gate needed to be fixed so it hung squarely. While working on the gate the observant farmer saw how untidy the tool shed was. As the farmer was organizing the shed, he saw a hole in the fence, the horses needed brushing and the barn door needed painting. As the farmer went through his day, he accomplished many tasks; however, the south forty was never plowed.

Many days it is easy to drive to work, or if we office at home, walk into our little space, sit down, and stare blankly at our desk or computer screen. We think, "What was it I was supposed to be doing today again?" The phone rings, someone pops their head in our office and asks the dreaded question, "Can I talk to you a minute?" We know two things instantly - one, it will not be for a minute and two, it most likely involves something bad. The pastoral life is anything but boring and many times is extremely busy.

Pastors, like the farmer above, are always faced with too many tasks for the hours allotted. If we lose sight of what is important we will end up busy but not necessarily accomplishing what really is a priority. We can watch our ministry, marriage, and family slide away by not focusing on what should be accomplished.

Our prayer and study times drift into quick snippets of rushed grasping for something clever to say on Sunday, instead of seeking the Lord for His direction and purpose. Our wife and children simply become housemates and strangers because we are overwhelmed with the demands of ministry. If we fail to manage our time, we will be victims of everyone else's emergencies. We must serve, but we should serve with a plan, not simply haphazardly. There is a famous poster you have probably seen that states:

Lack of prior planning on your part does not constitute an emergency on my part.

While I wish that humorous statement was true, the tyranny of the urgent is always with us. We must learn to prioritize and choose wisely between competing needs. We are stewards over our time as well as over our money and therefore we must learn how to best use this gift from God.

Through proper planning we will not lose sight of what God calls us to accomplish through demanding busyness. Time management is really a misnomer, for we all have the same amount of time available to us. What we need is schedule management.

One common system is the ABC system, but it really does not matter which one you use; just *use* one. This one is simple and effective. The ABC system entails two five to ten minute blocks of time at the beginning and ending of each workday. At the start of a day, simply list out everything that has to be accomplished, or the projects you are working on. It does not matter how long the list, just write it all down. Your list might look something like this:

Personal Time Management

To Do List

- 3 Hospital visits
- Sermon Prep
- Staff/Elder Meeting Prep
- Prayer
- Exercise
- Illustration research
- Home repairs
- Facility cleaning
- Correspondence
- Planning
- Budget review

Your list will look different, but that is not the point. The main point is to capture what you believe needs to be accomplished. Writing it down (or capturing it electronically in your device) helps to visualize and remember throughout the day. As we age, our memory is about as long as a pencil, or notepad, or smart phone, so write it down or you will lose it.

After you write down everything you can think of you know you have to do, the next step is to place a letter by each task as to their relative importance. A's should be the most important; this means "I have to get this done ASAP," type tasks, or those tasks that if left undone will cause great damage. B's are important but not critical, meaning, no one is going to die or be overly angry if the tasks do not get completed. C's are those tasks that I would like to finish or do but they really are not that important or most likely, time intensive. I know what you are thinking; "All of my tasks are A's!" Trust me, they are not. The hardest part of this exercise might be assigning the true value of the task!

After you complete your evaluation of what needs to be accomplished, your list might look something like this:

Pastoral Helmsmanship

To Do Today
Priority

- 3 Hospital visits — A
- Sermon Preparation — B
- Staff/Elder Meeting Prep — A
- Prayer — A
- Exercise — B
- Illustration research — C
- Home repairs — C
- Facility cleaning — A
- Correspondence — C
- Planning — B
- Budget review — B

As you place the letters by the tasks, a picture of what you need to focus your time on should come into focus. Decide to work on the A's as much as you can. Next, spend time on the B's. Without a visual aid, most of us typically work on the C's because they tend to be accomplished quicker, easier, and we often enjoy doing them. We sometimes swap short-term gratification for investing in what matters the most.

We all want to feel like we accomplished something with our day, so we tend to gravitate to the easier, not as important tasks. In truth, how much pain and heartache could have been avoided if we had focused on what really mattered instead of what simply felt good to do? By forcing ourselves to prioritize our tasks, we are assigning a value to what *needs to be* finished, or at least worked on because it is important. If we let the important tasks fall to the wayside because we spent our limited time on the unimportant, or at least the not as important tasks, we will regret it.

The principle is to spend your best time on the A's, then the B's and if there is time, finish a few C's just so you feel better. If some of the A type tasks are long, involved ones, like writing a book or completing a budget, then spend some quality time each work day on the project. Putting off the task will never help you complete it, but tackling it a little bit each day will. Eating an elephant is no small task, but it can be accomplished — one bite at a time. Hard tasks, important ones, typically take great effort and diligence to complete, and therefore we put them off. We must not if we wish to be excellent stewards. Establishing the importance of the task will force us to at least consider working on it rather than gravitating to the easier jobs.

This list is intended to assist, not restrict. We should find freedom in organizing our day and time, not a legalistic bondage. Most of us, if we were really honest, probably spend less time doing what we should do and more time doing what is easier. Good stewardship demands that we change this.

Here is a real benefit of the program. As you prepare to end your workday, take out your list again and review it. Scratch off what is finished and reprioritize what is left to do. Perhaps your list looks like this at the end of the day:

To Do Today
<u>Priority</u>

- ~~3 Hospital visits — A~~
- ~~Sermon Preparation — B~~
- ~~Staff/Elder Meeting Prep — A~~
- ~~Prayer — A~~
- Exercise   B
- Illustration research   C
- ~~Home repairs — C~~
- ~~Facility cleaning — A~~
- Correspondence   C
- Planning   B
- Budget review   B
- Call the city planner
- Schedule staff follow-up meeting
- Fix car
- Replace office supplies
- Talk to Bob

Life happens and interruptions are a normal part of our world. Very few of us will have a finished list at the end of our day, and rarely will the final list look like the one we began the day with. There will be tasks added and perhaps deleted due to changing circumstances. Priorities and pressures will change the importance of some of the jobs we wrote down, so we must adjust. This technique is a tool, not a straightjacket.

After spending a few minutes writing down what we accomplished and what else was added to our list, we go through our list again assigning letters to the tasks that are still unfinished, then we lay it down and walk away. Congratulations! Tomorrow is almost planned for us. When we hit the office in the morning, we take out the list, and begin to work on the A's rather than waste time trying to remember what it was we needed to do today.

The ABC system helps us prioritize what is really important and builds in a to-do list. This system, or some derivative of it, has worked for millions of people. It may not for you, but what do you have to lose by trying something different? Maybe the south forty will actually be plowed if the farmer makes a list. Maybe your day will go better and smoother if you do. Whatever system you end up using to help plan your day, the key to productivity is to use it.

As long as we are considering how we spend our time, let's touch on another often overlooked issue. As leaders we must learn to delegate and empower others, and we will develop that concept further in a later chapter. For now, let's turn our attention to a thought shared by Andy Stanley in his book, *Next Generation Leader*, regarding the concept of focusing on our strengths. While reading this book, one truth Andy shared hit home in a new way:

There are others that love to do what I hate doing.

What a novel thought — someone may actually enjoy the tasks that I dread. In fact, they will not only enjoy it, but also do a much better job than I ever could. Why should I struggle and hope to achieve being mediocre when there is probably someone out there that would excel? This leads to a challenge — will we let go of tasks that we are only marginally good at, and empower others to assist us or to perform them? How much time could be saved and invested in a better fashion if we did this? Why should we struggle and endure a task we hate when someone else would love it?

If we will focus on what God has gifted us to do, and if we will walk in the vision we have, we will accomplish more for the Kingdom. We will be able to invest our limited time in what we are good at and leave the other tasks to those that do them better and would be thrilled to do what we dread.

I (Jeff) have a friend of mine that said something like this to me one day as he was observing my feeble attempt at mudding sheetrock: "Pastor, why don't you go study or read a book and I will attempt to fix what you have done here." My buddy was an excellent carpenter and could do almost anything handyman wise. I on the other hand am very good at demolition, but not so much on fixing or building. While I could have continued to throw mud on the wall, the end result would not be anything near what my friend would produce. I had to make a hard choice — I could choose to allow my pride to be hurt or I could realize that he was correct. I went and read an excellent book that proved to be mutually satisfactory to all involved.

Learning to invest my limited time in what I am good at is important to implement. We all have strengths and also weaknesses. To become a good manager of our time, we must learn to use it wisely. Part of effective time stewardship is acknowledging the truth that everyone else already knows — we cannot do everything, nor should we.

Personal Reflective Administration Time

Every pastor and leader should build into their schedule reflective time. Pushing papers, phone calls, board meetings, and everyone else's crises will choke out deep thinking if we let it. Praying, planning, and preparing should be a part of our routine. In our world quiet time, reflection time, and just thinking time is almost unheard of.

Social media, technology, and unlimited access to resources can make us informed and busy but also drain us of imagination, deep thought, and vision. Jesus often withdrew to lonely places for reflection and prayer. We should follow His example.

Failure to provide time for developing and deepening our relationship with our Lord, will eventually take a serious toll. If we cheat ourselves out of this time, our ministries will probably be less effective and even suffer harm. Perhaps a personal retreat is in order to refocus, think undistracted and drink deeply from God's Word.

Questions to Ponder

1. How could I increase my effectiveness in being a steward of the time God has given to me?

2. If I am hesitant to implement some sort of time management system, why is that?

3. Thinking about those around me, to whom could I delegate tasks that I am mediocre at?

4. What practical choices could I change in my personal behavior to assure that I am being a good steward of time?

5. When was the last time that I had a block of time just thinking and waiting on God to speak? Have I lost track of what God has called me to do, and how do I get it back if I have?

# Balancing Ministry and Family
Dancing on the edge often leads to cuts on the feet.

Somewhere between Matthew 10:37:

Whoever loves father or mother more than me is not worthy of me, and whoever loves son or daughter more than me is not worthy of me. (ESV)

and Ephesians 5:25:

Husbands, love your wives, as Christ loved the church and gave himself up for her, (ESV)

along with Ephesians 6:4:

Fathers, do not provoke your children to anger, but bring them up in the discipline and instruction of the Lord. (ESV)

resides the balance of the pastor's life. There is a healthy tension between serving our Lord with all of our heart, soul, mind and strength and taking care of the family that He has given to us.

Are we to burn out for Jesus giving everything to ministry, or are we to live with our wives in an understanding way so our prayers are not hindered as Peter chides us in 1 Peter 3:7? Are these boundaries mutually exclusive, or can the pastor work within them?

We are called to faithfully discharge the duties of the ministry in obedience to our Lord's commands. And, we are to take care of our families to be an example to the flock according to His other commands. Quite a tension, and much easier to write about than to put into practice.

Perhaps the issue is not really an "either or" type problem but a "both and" type of one. Either ditch is still a ditch off the main road. We can sell out to ministry and be unfaithful at home. We can excel at home and fail as a pastor. Neither is acceptable in God's Kingdom. Many times neither choice is that clear.

Our ministry walk is similar to our personal walk with the Lord, not always a straight line, but three steps forward and two back. Or, as the writer of this Proverb states:

For the righteous falls seven times and rises again, but the wicked stumble in times of calamity. (Proverbs 24:16 ESV)

In most cases, there will be times when we fail on both fronts. Life is not perfect. People do not die at convenient times, nor do they enter the hospital on our schedules. Rarely do emergencies happen during normal working hours, but they almost always seem to happen during a family meal time or on a day off.

How do we navigate the waters of family and ministry? We need the Scriptures, the Holy Spirit and grace. We need to communicate clearly with both our families — the one at home, and the one we serve as pastor. The pastor's life is unique and both the church family and our personal one need to understand the challenges.

The Personal Family Side

Unlike most career choices, the family is intimately involved in the ministry. They have no choice. Even if your spouse and children do not want to be, they are. From being considered a non-paid staff person to being expected to maintain a pristine, perfect lifestyle, the family is impacted by the pastor's profession.

It is typically not stated, but the pastor's spouse is considered part of the package when the pastor is hired. Counseling duties, administrative and organization supervisor, perhaps de facto decorator and chief bottle washer, the spouse is expected to be involved. So are the children. If any of them can play the piano and run the nursery — even better. All of course at no pay.

Beyond the expected, often unstated workload of the family members of the pastor, is the pressure put on the family to live up to unrealistic standards. Since pastors are expected to be super spiritual saints, the family must be equally strong. The pastor and their spouse must never quarrel and the children must be shining examples of near-perfection.

The expectation from some people is that the pastor and their family just sit around singing hymns and praying all day. The pastor's family is viewed many times under a microscope, and sometimes it gets annoying under that glare.

What would be considered completely out of line in the business world seems to be just perfectly fine in the Church. Most people that work in Corporate or Blue Collar America would not dream of ever attacking or criticizing a co-worker's family. I wish that could be said for the House of God. Like any other person, it really is hard to remain in a sanctified condition when someone is saying mean hateful things about your spouse or child. At times, we would like to do unto others what they are doing unto our family, but that is another story, and not very Christlike.

We can, however, do a few things if we are under this pressure regarding our spouse and children. First, be upfront during the hiring process or whenever beginning a new pastorate. Explain what your spouse and children will and will not do. If they want to be involved, great! If not, that should be equally fine. If it is not fine, then further discussion should be held up front, not as you are leaving in hurt and anger. Second, deal with offenses as they arise and do not just ignore them. It is very easy for your spouse or children to slip into bitterness. We must teach them how to forgive, how to confront, and how to walk on in grace. This will need to take place early and often in the ministry.

The Scripture tells us to "Know well the condition of our flock," and that includes the ones under our own roof. We must allow time for venting, discussing, and open, honest communication to take place. We must foster an environment where we can freely share what is going on in our own hearts.

Spouses and children will hear details of people's lives that are not common knowledge and they will need help in learning how to process it all, not to mention the fine art of confidentiality. There is a burden in ministry of knowing details of people's lives that few others know. Our family members must be trained on how to deal with this knowledge. Since many of the issues that pastors deal with involve problems, it is an ever present temptation for the pastor's family to become jaded toward the church.

PK Jokes and Family Problems

Sadly, many "PK" jokes are true. Children of the pastor are sometimes ignored and offered on the altar of ministry, and this becomes obvious by how they behave, or probably better stated, misbehave. Ministry can become addicting and wise pastors will not allow it to take over their life. God gave the pastor a family and He expects it to be taken care of. The pastor's family is a part of the church and should be entitled to quality time.

Consider these passages about the qualifications for an elder/overseer/pastor for a moment before we move on: (Emphasis added is ours)

> The saying is trustworthy: If anyone aspires to the office of overseer, he desires a noble task. Therefore an overseer must be above reproach, the husband of one wife, sober-minded, self-controlled, respectable, hospitable, able to teach, not a drunkard, not violent but gentle, not quarrelsome, not a lover of money. **He must manage his own household well, with all dignity keeping his children submissive, for if someone does not**

know how to manage his own household, how will he care for God's church? He must not be a recent convert, or he may become puffed up with conceit and fall into the condemnation of the devil. Moreover, he must be well thought of by outsiders, so that he may not fall into disgrace, into a snare of the devil. (1 Timothy 3:1-7 ESV)

If anyone is above reproach, the husband of one wife, and his children are believers and not open to the charge of debauchery or insubordination. For an overseer, as God's steward, must be above reproach. He must not be arrogant or quick-tempered or a drunkard or violent or greedy for gain, but hospitable, a lover of good, self-controlled, upright, holy, and disciplined. He must hold firm to the trustworthy word as taught, so that he may be able to give instruction in sound doctrine and also to rebuke those who contradict it. (Titus 1:6-9 ESV)

It is interesting that of the many qualifications required for leadership the primary one expounded upon is family related. It is as if God knew that a pastor whose family was out of order could not keep the church in an orderly fashion either, (sarcasm intended). While the pressure to be perfect from others is over the top, the requirement from God to be in order is not. A pastor whose home is not functioning well is not able to stand with complete authority and ask that their followers should have their home in order. Those who live with us reflect what they are seeing and learning in the home. We teach as much by what we model as by what we say.

Lest we become overly discouraged with these verses, a process is implied and not perfection. "Manage his own household" does not mean there are never any problems, it means that the pastor is aware of them and doing everything within their power to deal with them. There are no perfect parents — only a perfect Heavenly Father. If memory serves me well, God also had some disciplinary issues with His first two children. We will always have relational issues to deal with; we just need to make sure we take care of them before they get out of control and cause damage to the Church.

The home is a wonderful testing and proving ground for servant leadership. Marriage and child training will give us insights on how to help others in these arenas.

We did an informal survey one time in some of our social media world asking pastors what percentage of their time was spent in marriage/family counseling. The results were about as expected — the vast majority of it dealt with this topic. Dysfunction runs rampant in many homes, and the pastor's home should not be among them.

As pastors, we are leaders, and leaders walk ahead. Our families provide a wonderful training experience for us to learn how to help those following us. Wouldn't it be a great goal to have all those PK jokes turned into wonderful examples to follow instead of being a source of mocking?

We are to lead and pastor the church, and that church includes our families. If we fail here, our creditability will take a hit, for our Christianity should make the most difference within the relationships that are closest to us.

We need to invest quality time in our family to assure that our ministry is not discredited by our marriage failing or our children rebelling. Sinful people can and will make sinful choices, and these are beyond our control. However, we must be diligent to invest in our spouse and children to not provide additional opportunities for failure. We need to be pastors at home, as well as in the church we serve.

The Church Family Side

We are called to a glorious ministry that includes a life of service to the Body of Christ. Our schedules are unique and so are the demands placed upon us.

While we are to be faithful spouses and parents and to invest wisely at home, we also are called to be faithful to the God-given task of serving as pastors. We serve our Lord in this calling and we are to be diligent and industrious, not lazy and unfaithful.

How do we invest at home and also fulfill the demands of ministry? While there are no easy answers, there are principles that we can follow.

We must explain to our spouse and children the time demands of ministry. Communication is important to help our family catch a pastoral vision. There will be times when schedules are messed up, ball games are missed and days off are interrupted. That is simply a part of the pastor's life. Sharing this reality with the spouse and children is important to help prepare them *before* it happens.

God expects us to be faithful in our calling, and we must model this to our family. God expects them to be faithful as well in their callings, and they will learn it best from observing your words, attitudes and behavior.

We need to be careful with our words and attitudes towards those under our care. Our family will catch how we really feel. Do we enjoy the ministry or simply endure it? Are we delighted that we are called to be a pastor, or are we grumpy every time the phone rings? Do we really believe that what we do has eternal value? Our family will know the truth regardless of how we may answer those questions.

We are called to serve and lay down our lives and our schedules for those under our care. Our families are important, but not more important than walking in obedience to the calling we have received from our Lord. We will stand before the throne of God someday and give an account of what we did with the talents we were given. This includes how we led both of our families.

When we are at home we need to be engaged at what is going on at home. We need to use the time we have wisely. We do not ignore our spouse or children, but love them as commanded by our Lord. We also realize that there will be many times when we must serve our other family, the Church one. We need to seek the Lord regarding balance between both ministries. We are not to neglect either for the sake of the other.

Our families are temporal, so are our marriages. We are told to lay up treasure in heaven and to invest our time in eternal matters. Pastors have an advantage over other people because much of our work primarily focuses on the eternal realm. We can devote hours to prayer, studying the Word of God and helping people. In most instances we are paid to do so!

We are not to neglect our families because of ministry, but we are not to neglect ministry because of our family. Most of the time we are not forced to do so. We can take vacations, days off, and lead a fairly normal life. But if a medical doctor is on emergency call for physical health issues, and their family learns to deal with it, shouldn't a pastor's family be trained to accept the eternal, spiritual life and death nature of our calling?

We are called to be faithful in discharging our duties in the ministry and the home. There will be times when our spouse and children will have to receive less time than normal; it is the nature of our calling. After the emergency (funeral, crises counseling, mission trip, etc.) passes, we should adjust our schedule to allow for some make-up time with the family.

Peter, after writing about husbands, and wives, servants and sufferings, gives direction to pastors and leaders in these verses:

> **So I exhort the elders among you, as a fellow elder and a witness of the sufferings of Christ, as well as a partaker in the glory that is going to be revealed: shepherd the flock of God that is among you, exercising oversight, not under compulsion, but willingly, as God would have you; not for shameful gain, but eagerly; not domineering over those in your charge, but being examples to the flock. And when the chief Shepherd appears, you will receive the unfading crown of glory.**
> **(1 Peter 5: 1-4 ESV)**

We may not know what the unfading crown of glory is, but it sounds like something worth earning through our labors. We are commanded to shepherd the flock willingly, eagerly, and by being an example to them. We invest in our family and we serve the Church. They are not mutually exclusive, nor should one cheat out the other. Both are necessary, and we will give an answer to the Great Shepherd regarding how we lead each of them.

Not to be overly critical of our fellow pastors, but there is a tendency to whine, an expectation to be honored or esteemed, and even a temptation to be lazy. Ministry life is often unsupervised and

Balancing Family and Ministry

there are seasons when there is little ministry to accomplish. No one is beyond being tempted to laziness. The church we serve should not be viewed as interference to our lives and schedule, but a gift from our Heavenly Father.

Consider the following story. The church plant failure was a surprise. The pastor was a gifted preacher and had a track record of success in his previous career. His age: mid-30's, his family: a wife and two children., His academic preparation and his church planting aptitude scores all suggested the new church should thrive. When I (Rodney) met with him, he stated the problem was a lack of people in the church willing to be trained as leaders. After some time of reflection, I asked the pastor to describe his evening schedule. The conversation went like this:

> **Monday is my day off. Tuesday night I go to soccer practice with Timmy. Wednesday night I have Bible study at the church. Thursday evenings I go to karate practice with Rebecca. Friday night is my date night with Sarah. Saturday is family night. Sunday we have church.**

The issue here, of course, is that the pastor did not have time available to develop leaders. When questioned, the pastor quickly defended his schedule by stating, "I was modeling the importance of putting family before work."

One frequently hears pastors and others teach, "God first, Family second, Career third." What we don't realize is that these words are the mantra and teaching of Mary Kay Ash, founder of Mary Kay Cosmetics, and are not in the Bible. Scripture speaks of sacrifice and the prioritization of the things of God, not balance and comfort. Perhaps a quote from Oswald Chambers is more appropriate:

> Your priorities must be God first, God second, and God third, until your life is continually face to face with God and no one else is taken into account whatsoever.[4]

---

[4] My Utmost for His Highest 1992 - "The Price of the Vision" July 13

In Luke 14:15-23 one reads of the parable of the King's banquet. The invitation was taken lightly by those first invited due to fields, farms, and family. In Luke 9:59-62, Jesus extends an invitation to two potential followers. Both seemed on the surface to desire to follow Christ but put personal priorities and family concerns first. What is significant is that Jesus deemed these men unfit for the kingdom of God. These passages, and others, remind us that putting off the matters of God to focus on our career or our family may not be a wise choice.

Instead of making a three tiered list that is both simplistic and unsupported in Scripture, consider God as the pivot that everything else balances upon. When we start to tilt too far in one direction or another, the proper response is to refocus on God.

As a minister, we must give consideration to the when and where of leadership development. In one church, we had many young families, most of which did not grow up in church. Leadership development was critical, and time was precious. The solution in this situation was to have the leadership meetings on Tuesday at 10 pm at a local coffee shop. This allowed the young men time to be with wife and family and tuck in kids before the weekly leadership meeting. The meeting place was far more centralized than the church building, so the drive time was 10 minutes or less for everyone. Your solution for leadership training will be different. However, the Great Commission task of "making disciples" is a pivotal decision.

Every job has its downsides and frustrations, and being in the ministry is intense sometimes. However, so is fighting fires, stopping crime, teaching in a classroom, and working on Wall Street. There is the spiritual warfare dimension of ministry and we are not downplaying that burden, but many people serve in stress filled occupations and do not whine about it. We should excel in gratitude for the ministry, not in complaining about how hard it is.

Finally, pride is an ever-present temptation in the ministry. We will address this issue more in another chapter, but we must not let the praise of others inflate us to a dangerous place. James Dobson is credited with saying, "The problem with being on a pedestal is a step in any direction is down." We should be very careful about stepping up on that perch in the first place.

Questions to Ponder

1. Have I allowed the ministry to choke out my God-given responsibility to shepherd my family? If so, how?

2. Have I allowed my family to become an idol that is in competition to serving the Lord with all my heart, soul, mind and strength? If so, how?

3. After reflecting over my schedule, what would the Lord ask me to change?

4. Is there anything in my schedule that I will not review? If so, why?

5. What steps can I implement to remain in balance between my personal and church family?

5 Occupational Hazards of the Ministry

Why do we need armor or a sword if we are not in a serious battle? Ephesians 6:11

The pastor looked ashen and near death when his friends carried him into our prayer room. I (Jeff) did not know him, but it was clear his time of departure was close. The dying man whispered into the ear of my senior pastor something those of us standing nearby could not hear. The two men locked gazes and then my pastor said, "I forgive you, and so does Jesus." The man on the stretcher began to weep. After they left, my pastor shared what the man said. This pastor had committed adultery many years earlier in his career. Unable to find the strength to confess before, now as he faced death, he had to unload on someone. He desperately needed someone to forgive him.

Bankers, lawyers, and construction workers can confess to adultery and keep their jobs. Pastors typically lose theirs. The burden of this unconfessed sin had been a yoke around this dying pastor's soul for decades and he needed release. We prayed he found what he was seeking before he met his Lord.

Every career choice has occupational hazards and the ministry is no different. A carpenter can cut off a finger if he is not careful no matter how skilled he may become. More than one master electrician has been killed by not paying attention, and many older pastors quit because they allow some of these emotionally charged rascals to take them out.

What follows are some of the common hazards encountered in ministry: discouragement, depression, immorality, cynicism, pride, greed, and the lust for power or control. Many of these are running rampant among clergy and the devastation to the Church is huge. When a shepherd chooses to step into immorality (notice I did not say fall), the sheep are often slaughtered. When a shepherd becomes cynical, finding joy becomes difficult, their family suffers, and the pastor is tempted to become uncaring. If a pastor is motivated by or succumbs to the temptations associated with money, greed, or power, destruction soon follows.

The first area to examine is the nearly constant battle with discouragement and even depression that often invades the life of the pastor.

Discouragement/Depression

Biographies of the prince of preachers, Charles Spurgeon, reveal that he often had to be confined to his bed because of depression. Are you kidding me? Spurgeon? I (Jeff) read in one of those biographies that a main reason for the depression was that he did not feel like his life was making any difference. Oh come on, I have twenty of his books on my shelf! Not making a difference? No one, not even Spurgeon is immune to the dangers of ministry. Perhaps his emotional battle was chemical or even physically induced, but regardless of its source, many pastors struggle with being discouraged. In fact, read this verse carefully and notice Paul's transparency:

> **For we do not want you to be unaware, brothers, of the affliction we experienced in Asia. For we were so utterly burdened beyond our strength that we despaired of life itself. (2 Corinthians 1:8 ESV)**

Did Paul actually write, "despaired of life itself" in that verse? No matter how you examine this verse, it seems that Paul was clearly struggling emotionally and did not want to live any longer. Depression can do that to the strongest people, even godly heroes. Paul was overwhelmed, burdened beyond his strength, and wanted everything to end.

People can say mean, hateful things. Often unintentional, words can crush us. Sometimes, the lack of affirming words can hurt us. Most pastors strive to teach, preach and minister in excellence, yet often this work is overlooked or unappreciated. A "good sermon preacher" comment can carry us for a week while silence or "you must not have had much time to work on your message today preacher" can set us up for a really rough Monday.

We all want to know that our lives matter and a pastor's work is hard to evaluate properly. How much time is enough time for prayer, service, sermon preparation, etc? How do you measure the impact of a sermon, hospital call, or prayer time? There is not a great deal of closure in the ministry for the work is never finished. Some pastors struggle to see the value of what they have given so much of their heart and soul towards. Discouragement follows.

In addition to the normal highs and lows of ministry, there is the spiritual component of warfare. The enemy of our souls hates what we do and will do whatever is necessary to discourage the work. Unless we take up the armor of God and the shield of faith, we will be defeated by the fiery darts of discouragement.

A certain amount of adrenaline crash is normal after each message, major event, or tense meeting, but allowing this crash to lead to depression or long term discouragement will cripple us. We must build outlets for stress, forge relationships to encourage us, and allow people access to our thinking to help us through this battle. We need people to pray for us and with us to help us overcome the drive to quit.

There are physical, mental, emotional and spiritual reasons for discouragement and depression. We must be aware of the dangers of not dealing with this hazard of ministry. Our families, friends, preaching, and church can suffer harm if we ignore it or allow it to disable us.

Open up to someone. Get a physical. Talk to someone close to you and get some help if you struggle with these issues. The problem will not simply disappear. What would you tell someone who came to you for counsel regarding these hazards? Perhaps following our own advice here would be wise.

Immorality

Almost from the beginning of time immorality has been a major problem. Examples of multiple, competing wives, sexual violence against women, incest, seduction, and prostitution can all be found in the Holy Bible. Sex and the battles that surround it are not foreign concepts in God's Holy Word. The book in the center of the Bible is a passionate love story, and Hosea was told to marry whom again? The wisest man of the Old Testament wrote several chapters about the consequences of moral failure, and he should know; he had 1,000 women in his harem and, apparently, a huge sexual addiction.

"Men and women are different," scream the headlines as if that is some new revelation. Ask any child over the age of five, and he or she could tell the experts that much. Many pastors spend a significant amount of their time in marriage counseling, and a good deal of it ends up focusing on immoral behavior of some sort. Sadly, adultery, pornography, lust, and immorality of all kinds are rampant in the body of Christ. Given these facts, why do we act surprised that pastors commit sexual sin?

Unless you live in an information vacuum, you will have known personally or read about multiple pastors and high profile Christian leaders who have given into sexual temptation. Some have run off with another person's spouse and many have simply ruined their ministry through addictions to pornography. The destruction caused by their moral failures is huge. Churches have closed their doors, and new believers have walked away from Christianity. Marriages have been ripped in two, and young people have mocked Christ. Failing morally is an almost constant danger to the pastor, and we are foolish if we do not take precautions against this scheme of our enemy.

So, what can we do about it? An excellent question and we have a few thoughts about it. First, as pastors, we need to understand that our enemy would love to destroy us. The devil hates godly, effective pastors, and he has a horrible plan for your life. If we fall, not only do we do damage to our families and our ministry, but all those that look to us will be shaken. Take out the head and the body will be killed. We have a bull's eye on our back, so we need to be on guard. We need to take precautions, and we need accountability if we hope to finish strong.

Next, we need to set up clearly defined, unmovable boundaries or, if you prefer, rules of engagement. Here are several that I (Jeff) use that you can borrow if you wish:

- I will not meet, drive, or be alone with a woman that is not my wife or daughter, never, nada, no way, not happening.

- I will refrain from frontal hugs and touching of other women — side hugs only and then just quickly. I do not need to feel her breasts against my chest and she does not need to feel my arms around her. Sorry, warning, mayday, mayday, flee from immorality! My passions are too strong, and who knows what the woman may be feeling. I would rather appear aloof and cold than to get into an immoral mess.

- I do not counsel a woman alone. In over thirty years of counseling I have had only one woman become angry at me for not meeting alone with her; most thank me for it.

It is simply too easy for the protection aspect of men to kick in when a woman pours out her heart. I need someone else there, preferably my wife. Even better is to follow the Biblical guidelines explained here:

> **Older women likewise are to be reverent in behavior, not slanderers or slaves to much wine. They are to teach what is good, and so train the young women to love their husbands and children, (Titus 2:3-4 ESV)**

Men are attracted to women, and women are drawn to men. These are undeniable truths, and we ignore it to our own peril. Men and women who are not married to each other need to be careful about spending large quantities of time together. Bonding can happen quickly, and un-bonding is very difficult. If I have to counsel a female, I make sure there is glass in the office door, or better yet, leave it open so everyone can see. I would much rather err on the side of caution than walk through the trauma of immorality.

We are told by Paul to flee immorality (1 Corinthians 6:18), and I take him at his word. If I can avoid the temptation, that is more likely to be successful than overcoming it in the heat of the moment. By not placing yourself or the other person in question into that type of situation in the first place, you have already taken a good step to not ending up in a moral failure.

With the proliferation of pornography, the battleground for moral failure has expanded. Every sports program on TV seems to find the cheerleaders, and just about any product sold needs a shapely young woman to sell it. Surfing the web without protection and purpose is an invitation to disaster. "Idle time is the devil's workshop" could not be truer than the pastor that simply goes out to surf the web to waste time. With one stray click of a mouse, sexual enticement can be found. Do we really need to go there? Will feasting on those images help our sermon preparation or ministry gifts? Will our sensitivity to the Spirit increase if we fill our minds with those pictures?

Men need to control what they look at, and women to think about how what they are wearing impacts men. We need self-control and the fruit of the Spirit to reign in our lives. Immodesty and immorality are not fruits of the Spirit but lead to destructive deeds of the flesh. We are not to give the devil any place in our life, and what we allow our eyes to feast upon is a big opportunity for our foe.

For some practical ideas regarding the computer, I would suggest making sure your computer screen is visible to anyone walking by the door. Just knowing that someone can come in and instantly see what's on your computer screen will help provide some incentive to be more careful. There are many content type filters available for the internet, and installing one would be wise.

Men also need to be careful with their flirtations just like the women need to be careful with how they dress. Most studies show that men are attracted by what they see and women by what they hear and feel. As pastors, we are in a position of influence, and we must be careful what we say and do. God will hold us responsible for our actions and even our intentions, so we must walk carefully in this arena. Those pastors that take advantage of the sheep sexually will pay a dear price.

For an exercise read Proverbs chapter 2, 5, 6, and 7 and notice the patterns, decisions, and consequences in the texts. Solomon explains in these chapters the dangers of seduction and moral failure. "So you will be delivered from the forbidden woman," "Her steps lead to hell," "Can a man carry fire in his chest and not be burned?" and "As an ox goes to the slaughter," paint a scary picture of the cost of moral failure.

If we, the pastors, give into moral failure, we will tarnish the Lord's reputation, crush our spouse, children, and grandchildren, shake the faith of many of the sheep under our care, and give the enemies of Christ reason to blaspheme. The cost is high, and there are no rewards worth this price tag. If you are already involved in an improper relationship, then leave it now. If you need help, get it today. Quit your church, break your computer, or move out of town if necessary. Whatever you need to do to get free is worth whatever the price tag is for that freedom. Do not be ignorant or deceived, you will be found out and the enemy will torment you until you repent, like the dying pastor we met in the opening of this chapter. The only way out is confession and renouncement of the sin. Freedom can be gained by repenting and changing your behavior. If you are trapped, then run to the Lord and find release.

In our current environment, the homosexual attraction is also becoming a trap and temptation for many in ministry. Establishing a clear Biblical view towards this behavior will help and provide a measure of protection. The above principles still apply even in same-sex temptations, and the solution does as well — repent, seek help, and run into the arms of Jesus.

There are multiple books available that share even more help in the battle against sexual immorality. Please see the resource section at the end of this book for a listing of some of them. The bottom line is that many pastors destroy their ministries, families, and future by not being on their guard against this foe of immorality. Please do whatever is necessary to avoid becoming the next statistic.

Cynicism

While there are many dangers we could develop for those serving in the ministry, we have chosen these few because they are so prevalent. Many pastors have given into sexual temptation and fallen, and probably even more have simply quit caring and given up because of frustration.

I (Jeff) know two good brothers, slightly older than me, that are both resigning from their church. While that in itself is not a big deal, for they both were in their sixties, what bothered me are the words they used in their announcement. Insightful phrases flowed out of them,
"I am sick of pastoring," and "I am so glad to be away from all these people." I understand their thoughts for working with people can be a real pain; however, we must not end our ministries in a state of cynicism. Words like, "hate," "disgust," and "completely frustrated," often creep into the speech of the retiring pastor, and that is sad.

Pastoring involves working with people and as we all know, people are, well, people. The Scriptures use words like, "hard hearted, dull, stubborn, divisive, and unloving" to describe God's children. Often, pastors are on the receiving end of people's hurtful words and stubborn resistance. It is easy to become frustrated, and while some frustration is normal and even healthy, allowing it to move over into cynicism is not.

Cynicism is usually defined with words like, "mistrust," "jaded" and "scornful," and these typically refer to the motives of others. When a pastor slips into this mindset, they are on shaky ground. We are told by the Great Shepherd to love the sheep, lay down our lives for them, and serve them. We are not to hate them, mistrust them, or run away from them. People can and often will hurt us, but we must watch our attitude and reactions to their actions. We are not discrediting or denying the temptation to become cynical, just reminding us that we must resist it.

The reality of the frustration of working with imperfect people will never leave. We are not perfect, and neither are those under our care. We are sometimes slow to change, and so are they. We resist the Lord's discipline, and so do others. We can be stubborn and unkind, and so can the sheep. Only Jesus is perfect, and the rest of us are a work in progress. Sometimes it takes years for a truth to become part of our understanding and actually work its way into our daily lives. The same is true with those under our leadership.

A reality of leadership is that we often see something from God sooner and clearer than those that are following us. We will have a passion for a vision or truth that few others will. If it were the other way around, they would be the leaders and we would be following them. Since we may see a truth quickly, we are tempted to become frustrated with others that do not see it as soon or as clearly as we do. I believe that is why patience is both an attribute of love and a fruit of the Spirit. We must bear with one another in love.

The 8% Reality

Let me (Jeff) share a theory that I have that has helped me over the years in my battle against cynicism. I call this theory "The 8% reality." We are all familiar with the parable of the sower and the seeds told in Matthew 13, and most pastors have probably taught on it a time or ten.

We also know that the point of a parable is typically singularly focused and contains one primary interpretation. However, there are often many applications to the parable that we can glean, and this is one I use to help me deal with frustration. I hope it will help you as well. This is not meant to be theological in nature, but illustrative!

We know that Jesus said that the sower sows the seed, and how it lands on various types of soil. 75% of it produces nothing, and 25% finds good soil and produces a crop. Even within this 25% that produces, there is a difference ranging from 100% full production down to around 33%, or to use the Biblical terms, "some a hundredfold, some sixty, some thirty." What I glean from the math is that even within the good soil there is a difference in fruit bearing. Great observation, so what does this have to do with fighting cynicism?

One cause of cynicism is the fact that we feel like we pour our hearts out, invest our time and emotional energy into people, and they just do not get it. No matter how clearly, passionately, or frequently we explain our vision; it is rejected or not completely implemented. Herein lays the point of my 8% theory.

The truth is that 75% will probably not ever get it. Even within the 25% that do buy into the vision there will be a variance to the degree of implementation. In fact, just about 8.33% will understand all of it. 75% of the seed produced nothing, and only 25% of the good soil produced a crop. (Disclaimer: I am not a math major so I round up or down as it is convenient for my theory.)

The reality is that there will be a small percentage of people that buy into our vision completely, and these are represented by the 25% seeds that land on the good soil. Within those that are attracted to our vision there will be a further division. Some people will understand it and walk it out 1/3, and some 2/3, and a small group, say 8%, will be completely on board with the vision. (Okay, I know that 25% divided by 3 is not exactly 8%, but see disclaimer above).

No matter how anointed we may be, regardless of how passionately we share our vision, there will always be a bunch of folks that simply do not get it, nor do they want it. God has assigned to each of us a realm of influence and that will be limited. Within this realm, there will be varying degrees of acceptance from those that follow us, and to expect otherwise is a sure way to end up being cynical. One key to fighting cynicism is to make sure that we are investing in the 8% a significant amount of our time and emotional resources.

Sometimes it is easy to spend a vast amount of time in useless arenas. By that, I mean outside of our vision and gifting. For the record, no person is useless, and no one is outside of needing help and instruction, but part of what we need to learn is what *is* our arena and what is it that God has called us to do. Jesus taught the crowds but He primarily invested Himself in the twelve. Jesus also seemed to even narrow that down to the three closest to Him — James, Peter and John. We all have crowds, leaders, and those closer to us. May we invest wisely the limited time we have.

Pride, Greed, and Control Issues

In addition to immorality and cynicism, pastors can fall into these three hazards. Pride involves having an overinflated image of our self and often leads to both sexual failure and becoming hard-hearted. Many of the big name leaders that have fallen will say something like, "I felt like I was above the rules," or "I didn't think the rules applied to me." Pride was allowed to take up residence in the heart, and sin and destruction followed.

> **Likewise, you who are younger, be subject to the elders. Clothe yourselves, all of you, with humility toward one another, for "God opposes the proud but gives grace to the humble." (1 Peter 5:5 ESV)**

Peter echoes James' words (James 4:6) and adds, "all of you." This all of you, includes pastors. If we want grace in our lives, we must watch out for pride. God does not need us to accomplish anything. God can, and has removed others that began to think they were indispensable to the Kingdom. We are given grace to serve and die to ourselves, not to inflate our egos or self images.

One definition of humility that is easy to grasp is:

Humility - having the arrogance knocked out of you.

What a wonderful picture. Life has a way, and we are pretty sure God makes sure it does, of deflating us. If we refuse to humble ourselves God will make sure we are humiliated. We must come to the place where we realize that He is God, and we are not. There cannot be two captains, and lordship is an exclusive term.

We must lead people to the Lord and not to us. Yes, we lead, but we are not the final destination; Christ is. We serve and lead because God has graciously allowed us to. If we have special gifts and talents, they are on loan from our Creator, and He expects us to use them for His glory not ours.

Greed is another sin that can impact anyone. The Scriptures state:

> **No one can serve two masters, for either he will hate the one and love the other, or he will be devoted to the one and despise the other. You cannot serve God and money. (Matthew 6:24 ESV)**

> **For the love of money is a root of all kinds of evils. It is through this craving that some have wandered away from the faith and pierced themselves with many pangs. (1Timothy 6:10 ESV)**

Many pastors are underpaid, and the temptation to love money is a constant danger. The Scriptures are full of warnings about wealth and living for what is temporal. God is not opposed to money or wealth, but Jesus is the One who placed serving His Father and money in opposition. We cannot serve both, but we will choose one.

Greed will never be satisfied. When asked how much wealth is enough, the rich man replied, "just a little bit more." Like lust, the fire of greed will never say enough. God is the ultimate Source of our provision. Every good gift comes from His hand. We are told to love God with all of heart, soul, mind, and strength. We are told to seek His Kingdom first and foremost. While money is a tool to be used, it is never a god to be worshipped. Pastors must guard against greed, the unhealthy pursuit of wealth, and pride associated with success.

Pastors can also become power happy control freaks. We are called to serve, not dominate. There is only one Lord, and we are not Him. We are under shepherds serving at the pleasure of the Great Shepherd. We tend God's sheep. We feed God's flock, but they are His sheep, and we must be careful how we treat them. A reading through Ezekiel 34 should send up many warning flags regarding how a shepherd treats the sheep. God will not tolerate for long those shepherds that abuse His flock.

We learn to lead through grace, humility, and service, not through manipulation, power plays, domination and excessive control. Servant leadership is what Jesus modeled, and we should follow His example.

We have briefly examined discouragement, immorality, cynicism, greed, pride, and excessive control that are all hazards faced in the pastoral ministry. There are others of course, but for now, let's end our thoughts on these dangers pastors face with a Scripture that can help tremendously:

O LORD, my heart is not proud, nor my eyes haughty; Nor do I involve myself in great matters, Or in things too difficult for me. (Psalm 131:1 NASB)

God has not asked us to solve all the problems of the world or His Church. In fact, He said Jesus would build the Church, and we are quite sure He will do an excellent job. When someone asks about a denomination or a controversial issue raging in the national spotlight, a good response includes Psalm 131:1 quoted above. The truth is that we can do nothing about it and usually no one involved is asking our opinion. We cannot carry the weight of it, and we are not the ones charged with fixing it. Jesus is, and He will do just fine. Our role is to pray for these matters before the One who can and will actually do something about them.

God has given each of us a realm of influence, and He expects us to do the best job there that we can. Our understanding of this reality should be freeing. It releases us to stay focused on what our Lord has asked us to do for Him in building His Kingdom. Of course, we can see the problems, and we can pray, but worry, fear, doubt, and frustration over them not a options. Jesus can and will make His Bride ready for His return. In the meantime, we are called to be faithful, diligent, watchful, expectant, and to invest in those that are following the vision God has given us. If we do these things for His glory, these hazards may knock on our heart's door, but we will be simply too busy to answer it.

Questions to Ponder

1. After thinking through the hazards mentioned in this chapter, have I made myself vulnerable to the enemy in some way?

2. Am I walking in moral purity in my dealings with those of the opposite gender?

3. Have I slipped over into cynicism somehow? If so, what can I do about it?

4. If someone followed me around all day and listened to my words, what would they reveal about my heart attitude?

5. Do I struggle with pride, the love of money, or control issues? Why or why not? What would those closest to me say about these hazards?

6 Pirates and Landlubbers:
Identifying Troublemakers before they Sink the Ship

Sometimes the first mate really is the problem.

Antagonists are individuals who on the basis of non-substantive evidence, go out of their way to make insatiable demands, usually attacking the person or performance of others. These attacks are selfish in nature, tearing down rather than building up, and are frequently directed against those in a leadership capacity. Kenneth Haugk, in *Antagonists in the Church*[5]

In baseball, it has been said that timing is everything. Several years ago, one of the larger Baptist churches in our region called me (Rodney) as interim pastor. Originally, the congregational survey indicated the people did not want an interim. Therefore, for five months the church used pulpit supply. However, a developing conflict in the church convinced leadership it was time for an interim pastor.

Pirates are the antagonists and troublemakers who thrive on times of change. Landlubbers are members who are often unregenerate or otherwise unqualified for membership, but nevertheless, show up in our churches. This chapter will deal with both antagonists and

---

[5] Kenneth Haugk, Antagonists in the Church, (Augsburg Publishing, 1988)

troublemakers, along with scriptural insights that will help you deal with these members before they sink your ship.

On my first Sunday as interim pastor, a member invited me to lunch. During lunch, he asked many probing questions regarding my beliefs, including my impressions of the staff and church leadership. This is what Kenneth Haugk called, "The Instant Buddy Flag." In the next two months, five other "Red Flags" as identified by Haugk, became apparent. Based on my understanding of antagonists, I was able to make adjustments in my communication style and approach with this person. Haugk correctly writes, "For too long congregations have been places where antagonists can operate with success." As I reflected back upon the congregations and conflicts I have been observed in as a pastor, denominational leader and seminary professor, the misplaced acceptance of bad behavior has taken an immeasurable toll upon many of these ministries. In most of these cases, the "kernel of truth" behind the antagonist's claims or concerns is the reason the ungodly behavior is never dealt with appropriately.

Understanding the behavior, characteristics and dysfunctions of problem makers is like having an intelligence photograph of the troublemaker's game plan. Awareness of God's Word as it relates to bad behavior in the church gives hope amidst situations that often seem hopeless.

Unchecked, antagonists will make leading the church an impossible task.

Why do we have Antagonists in the church? Because *they are in the world.* The problem with antagonists in the church is that they leave in their wake...
- broken lives
- broken dreams
- discouraged, apathetic people.

Kenneth Haugk noted 20 red flags of an antagonist. Based on my experience, I added one and have provided some short comments and modifications to his list of twenty.

1. *A previous track-record of antagonistic behavior in the church.* This is why knowing the history of the church is paramount for new pastors.
2. *The Parallel track-record...* a track record of bad behavior outside of the church, such as in the workplace or community.
3. *The Nameless Other Flag...* "There are lots who feel like me", "everyone feels you should resign", "no-one supports the change."
4. *The Instant Buddy:* The first to take you to dinner, visit your office, ask for an appointment.
5. *The Predecessor-downer:* Denounce your predecessor and build you up syndrome.
6. *Gushing* (and often premature) *praise for your leadership*
7. *Asking "I gotcha" questions:* "What version of the Bible do Baptists use?", "What is the church's position on Calvinism" or "What is the bible's position on eschatology?"
8. *Overly Smooth and Charming:* Be aware of wolves in sheep's clothing.
9. *The Church Hopper:* "Finally, I found a church (or pastor) I can believe in."
10. *Lies:* Little lies are common.
11. *Aggressive methods:* Over-the-top, unethical or combative means to get their voice heard.
12. *The Flashing $$$ sign:* Rich antagonists love this one.
13. *The Note Taker:* Take notes during pastoral visits, the song service, the coffee-hour or other inappropriate times.
14. *The Portfolio:* Developing a "case" with "proof" of wrong-doings that shows evidence of a long-standing plan.
15. *Cutting Comments:* Saying things at times or places to cause great pain.
16. *The Different Drummer:* Always seeking to start new policies, change things, or do it their own way.
17. *The Pest:* Always calling, emailing, texting. Take note: If they are always calling you, they are calling others!

18. *The Cause*: Calvinism, Politics, Multi-level schemes, KJV only, etc.
19. *The School of Hard Knocks*: Little formal education, but have gone through many struggles. Tend to brag about "their school."
20. *The Poor Loser*: When the church votes differently, the antagonists will get mad *and* get even.
21. *Start at the Top*: Instead of following the chain of authority in a minor matter, antagonists frequently go directly to the pastor, chairman of deacons, board of elders, bypassing the established chain of command.

Two more kinds of "trouble-makers" in the church that are often left unidentified, and yet, left unchecked, can cause untold damage.

1) *Unregenerate Members* Acts 8:12f (Simon); Revelation 3:20 (note the invitation is given to members of the church).
2) *Those called to ministry*...and said, "*No*" to God's call. Often, there is reluctance due to the cost, which might include having to go back to school, relocation, a significant cut in income, family concerns and a perceived lack of ability. However, the call brings with it a passion. Often, the call is ignored, but the passion is still present. Thus, a typical pattern results in something like this:

> *Those called as a pastor become a deacon or elder*
>
> *Those called as missionaries becomes the church mission leader*
>
> *Those called to education ministry become Sunday School Directors*

Those who fail to embrace the call seem destined to illegitimately live out the call through functionally similar roles in the local church, often undermining legitimate leaders in the process.

While pastoring a church plant in Northern Minnesota, the chairman of Deacons, Fred (not his real name), invited my wife, Julie and me, to his home for an informal meeting at 2:00 pm. Upon my arrival, I discovered that the rest of the members had been invited to this meeting at 1:00 pm, so when we arrived, the foundation for change—meaning my departure as pastor—had been laid. We weathered the meeting, which focused on my management of the church. However, my heart was so broken that I drafted a letter of resignation that night.

After the evening service, Fred and I agreed to meet for breakfast at 6:00 am to follow-up on the previous day's debacle. My plan was to submit my resignation, giving two weeks' notice and taking two weeks of unused vacation. At 4:00 am the phone rang. My grandmother, who lived two time zones away in California, mixed up the time change, and thought she was calling me at 8:00 am. However, God's timing being perfect, this call resulted in a life-changing learning experience. My grandmother's first question was, "Rod, how are you?" The reality was that I was as low as I had ever been since surrendering to the ministry call. Despite that, I said, "I'm OK." She then said, "That's good, because I was worried about you. You see, on Saturday I had a minor stroke, and I've been in the hospital. This morning I woke up and realized I forgot to pray for you yesterday. You know I have prayed for you every day since your mother was carrying you. But yesterday, I failed to pray, and I was worried for you."

Upon hearing these words, I realized that this experience was not a personality or process conflict, it was spiritual warfare. For the record, management problems can't be spiritualized, and spiritual problems can't be managed; both are distinct. Two hours later I met with Fred. The conversation went something like this:

Rod: You know, that was a painful meeting yesterday. However, I realized that I may not know the congregation as well as I thought. So let's start with some basics. Fred, what is your story? Tell me a little about yourself, your upbringing, your salvation and what you desire for the church.

Fred: I was raised in a Christian home in Louisiana. We were church goers, and during a revival meeting I went forward to give my life to Christ. Not long after that I was baptized, and became active in the church. In college I was active in collegiate ministries on our campus. That's where I met Claudia. We were married right after college. After going to seminary, I completed my graduate degree at LSU...

Rod: Hold it; you went to seminary in Fort Worth?

Fred: Yeah, I did 20 hours there.

Rod: What for?

Fred: I thought God had called me to be a church planter. At the time, to be appointed as a missionary pastor one needed 20 hours of seminary, so I took enough classes to be appointed. However, our assignment was on an Indian Reservation that was pretty tough. When Claudia saw the living conditions, it was too much for her, so we returned to Louisiana and I completed my degree at LSU.

Fred was one of several "trouble-makers" I have encountered who were called to ministry, and said "no" to the call of God. I later learned that Fred and his family had made a habit of joining new churches, where he always became a deacon, and the pastors eventually always left. However, this time, with the knowledge of what was happening, I was able to put the problem into a new perspective. Not only was leaving the wrong choice, it would have provided Fred with another notch in his belt. Instead, in a loving and caring way, I was able to help Fred return to the point of his spiritual departure. Today, Fred is a church planter/pastor, serving the same mission agency he had once abandoned.

With an understanding of the "Red Flags" of an Antagonist and "Two Trouble-Makers," now let us turn to what Scriptures says. First, we must:

1) **Identify**
   a) Romans 16:17 - I appeal to you, brethren, take note of those who create dissentions and difficulties, in opposition to the doctrine which you have been taught. (RSV)

2) **Confront**:
   a) Acts 13:9-10 - Then Saul—also called Paul—filled with the Holy Spirit,... said, "You son of the Devil, full of all deceit and all fraud, enemy of all righteousness! Won't you ever stop perverting the straight paths of the Lord? (HCSB)

   b) 1 Timothy 5:20 - Publicly rebuke those who sin, so that the rest will also be afraid. (HCSB)

3) **Avoid**
   a) Romans 16:17 - Avoid them

   b) 2 Tim 2:16-17 - Avoid such godless chatter, for it will lead people into more and more ungodliness, and their talk will eat its way like gangrene: such men are Hymenaeus and Philetus;(RSV)

Notice that in these passages Paul calls these proven antagonists out by name. Somehow, many members in the church consider it inappropriate to identify, confront or call out those who are causing dissention in the body.

Another problem stems from a misunderstanding of Matthew 18. Some minimize the importance of this passage. Due to the additions of chapters and verses, we tend to start at verse 15. However, verse 14 is a critical transition, pointing out the life and death implications to those who are "little ones" when a church fails to address a brother's sin or offense.

In the same way, it is not the will of your Father in heaven that one of these little ones perish. If your brother sins against you, go and rebuke him in private. If he listens to you, you have won your brother.

Pastoral Helmsmanship

But if he won't listen, take one or two more with you, so that by the testimony of two or three witnesses every fact may be established. If he pays no attention to them, tell the church. But if he doesn't pay attention even to the church, let him be like an unbeliever and a tax collector to you. (Matthew 18:14-17 HCSB)

Another challenge for pastors and leaders is the limited understanding of the discipline passages. For many, Matthew 18 is all the Bible says about discipline. As seen above Romans, Acts, 1 and 2 Timothy, Gods Word has much more to say about the problem. In addition, some passages relate specifically to problems related to leadership:

> **1 Timothy 5:19** Don't accept an accusation against an elder unless it is supported by two or three witnesses. (HCSB)

At the quarterly church business meeting, a question was asked of the pastor. After his response, Bob, a charter member of the church, stood up and yelled, "That's a lie. In fact, you're nothing but a big liar. The only reason you are the pastor is the fact that your father is a big wig in the denomination (which was not true)." Bob's rant continued for about one minute, during which time he brought additional accusations of fiscal mismanagement and academic preparedness. Based on 1 Timothy 5:19, and with a clear understanding of the church by-laws, the pastor asked if there was one or two more who could speak to these accusations. Silence. The pastor then asked the church to discipline the member on the grounds of 1 Tim 5:19, the motion carried, and the member was disciplined, thus removing his rights of membership.

A week later, the pastor met with the former member. During this meeting, it was discovered that Bob had joined the church in an unorthodox way. Instead of the normal process for membership, he had the church clerk add his name to the roster of charter members. No one caught, or at least commented on Bob's name being on the list, and so without the requisite testimony of a profession of faith, believer's baptism, and confessional agreement, Bob was counted among the membership of this church.

When faced with difficult members, the wise pastor will take the time to meet with them and hear the story of their spiritual journey. You might just discover a story similar to the ones in this chapter.

Questions to Ponder

1. How has your church created an anti-antagonist environment? Identify specific policies or actions that minimize the possibility of antagonists causing damage and disunity.

2. Do church documents such as the constitution or bylaws clearly and faithfully address the Biblical process for church discipline, including those passages that protect leadership from false accusations?

3. When reading about the unregenerate members and those called-to ministry and said "No" to the call, did one or more names come to mind? If so, what do you plan to do about this awareness?

4. Did the fact that Paul identified proven antagonists by name surprise you? Would it surprise members in your church?

5. When reading the 21 Red Flags of an antagonist, did one or more persons come to mind with more than four red flags? If so, think about how you might deal with these people in the future.

Section One Summary

In this first section we wanted to provide you with some tools to assist you personally. We shared briefly about our own journeys, discussed a way to help with the handling of your time, delved into the tension between family and ministry, exposed some of the hazards encountered in the ministry, and ended with a discussion on dealing with difficult people.

In Section Two we will move into some very practical matters of administration — hiring and firing of staff, budgeting, financial integrity, reporting, facilities management, and how to navigate around the risks and legal icebergs that try to shipwreck every church.

Section Two
The Pastor and Administration

# Building the Right Crew:
Recruiting the Right Paid and Volunteer Staff

It is better to hire well than fire well.

Sooner than later most pastors will be faced with the hiring process. A secretary might be required, perhaps a music, youth or children's leader, or a custodian. Each of these additions to the church staff requires prayer, wisdom, and multiple practical considerations.

As ministry expands, so do the demands upon the pastor's schedule. Moving from a solo pastor to a multiple pastor situation can be daunting. Even adding clerical and support staff changes the dynamic of relationships and the flow of ministry.

Every person is important, and working together in the ministry, while often viewed as glorious from the outside, can be messy and painful to those on the inside. Good procedures can help limit problems. So can understanding some basic objectives and tools before offering a position to someone.

The principles in this chapter can be applied to volunteers as well as paid staff. We will provide a much more detailed explanation and tools for working with volunteers in chapter seventeen. For our purposes here, the most effective way to find the right person for the need is important whether they receive a paycheck or not.

Pastoral Helmsmanship

As the workload increases, the need for help intensifies. Spending enough time before the hire considering several important criteria will greatly reduce the pain of hiring the wrong person. Sometimes that happens regardless of how careful we may be, but on many occasions, good planning, interviewing, and goal setting, could have helped avoid the termination later on.

Before letting anyone know what you are thinking, spend some time prayerfully considering the need. One reason to do this is that many times people will hear of a potential opening and offer their services to fulfill that need. They may be good intentioned, but unqualified, or not the person you wanted. Proper timing and preparation in clearly defining the need can limit hurt feelings and potential rejection.

Christians are interesting job candidates. For example, placing something like, "Job opening, Pastor's Secretary wanted," in the church bulletin will potentially unleash a great deal of activity, much of which is unwanted. Six people may respond to the advertisement proclaiming that, "God told them they were to have the job." Now what do you do? If one of them is qualified for the position, you still have five others that you will have to tell them they "missed God's voice." They will most likely believe you did and hurt feelings will be unavoidable.

It is far better to pray, plan, create a clear job description, and interview knowing what you are looking for, then to simply let the need be known. In fact, it may become clear who should fill the need, without even advertising after you have spent the time preparing.

When considering hiring someone for your staff or ministry team, think about the title of the job. Titles do mean a great deal. For example, Associate Pastor implies carrying out some of the pastoral duties, whereas Pastor's Assistant does not. The first person needs to be a pastor and the second one does not. Accountant implies something different than a Bookkeeper. Maintenance means something beyond Custodian. Titles add clarity to the job expectations from both sides of the desk — the hiring side and the applicant's side.

After determining the title of the position, consider what skills are needed? A Music Minister should have extensive training whereas an

Assistant Music Minister will need less. What job are you looking for them to fulfill? What are the expectations involved? What would you like them to be able to accomplish from the beginning, and what would you allow time for them to learn? The skill set is important for expectations and results achieved.

What type of characteristics are you looking for in this person? Do they have to be a leader? Do they need to be organized and possess communication skills? What people skills do they bring? A bookkeeper might be able to put their head down and work all day with very little interpersonal contact; the receptionist cannot. What about the attitude they possess? Are they upbeat or sour? While often hard to tell in an interview, the attitude they possess will impact those they contact...including you.

Each staff person interacts with others and represents the ministry. What is the prospective candidate saying by how they smile, dress, speak, and interact?

The Ministry Description

After spending some time thinking about the personality traits and skill set you desire, the details of the job must be clearly spelled out. While writing these details down may seem tedious and unnecessary, they are vitally important. Having a written ministry description provides both the employer and employee the opportunity to discuss what is expected. These documents provide a benchmark after employment to determine if the job is being performed in agreement with what was discussed during the hiring process.

If you fail to write down what was discussed, this can potentially lead to a misunderstanding later on. Your understanding of what you thought you communicated is left open to your interpretation. Their understanding of what they thought they heard might be different than yours. By having the ministry description written down, both memories will function better as the issues are discussed at a later date.

In the ministry description we recommend that you include at least the following:

- **Position Status**: Part time, full time, seasonal, as needed, summer, etc
- **Employee Classification**: Pastoral, Specialist, Administrative, Supervisory, Support, Physical Plant, Clerical, Volunteer, etc.
- **Regular Work Hours**: Overtime, Bonus, Comp Time (comply with Wage and Hour Regulations)
- **Accountable to:** The person to whom this position reports directly to for supervision, direction, coaching, reviews, and evaluations
- **Accountable for:** The people they will be accountable for
- **Position Overview:** A general overview of expected areas of focus
- **Overview of responsibilities:** List basic areas of focus, not the daily detail of the position
- **Budget authority:** Make sure they understand their authority and limits
- **Evaluation:** Let them know how and when they will be evaluated, then you must follow through
- **Conduct:** Again, let them know what is expected of them by working for the ministry. Include anything expected outside of the normal business hours.
- **Short term goals:** 90–120 days to help bring clarity to an often confusing time when first beginning a new ministry position.

There is always more to discuss but certainly not less to assure that the issues are covered in sufficient detail. For sample ministry descriptions please turn to the appendix under the resource section.

Recruiting Possible Candidates

God has the right person prepared for the position. Our job is to find them. We must spend time praying and seeking God's will on each hire. Every person added to the ministry team brings positives and negatives, skills and problems. Only Jesus was perfect, and every other human is not. What we are looking for is the best possible fit for each need.

If you are having a difficult time finding people to fit the need, consider some of the following:

- Survey your current contacts, friends, pastors, etc.
- Think about where potential employees would find your position of need - Newspaper, social media, announcement sheet, etc.
- Ask the leaders in your group for suggestions or recommendations.
- Spread the word via social media contacts asking for referrals. Consider offering a finder's bonus for the best referral.
- Expand beyond your personal circles to magazines, denominational headquarters, other pastors etc.

The need and position trying to be filled will determine how far and wide your search spreads. Regardless of where your search may take you, be patient. It is better to wait and perform due diligence before the hire, than to rush it and wish you would have slowed down.

Remember: we hire our own problems

There are pros and cons regarding hiring someone you know or from within the organization. The benefits are that you know the person. You most likely are aware of some of their strengths and weaknesses. You probably already know their depth of support for the ministry and maybe they have already been assisting in some way.

The negatives or risks of hiring someone you know is that you know the person. You know their weaknesses. You might have to fire or discipline them someday and potentially ruin the relationship, and you might be accused of hiring your friends which amounts to cronyism.

The advantages and disadvantages of hiring someone from within the organization or a person you know must be weighed, but there are issues to be evaluated when you consider hiring from the outside as well.

From the positive point of view, an outsider can infuse new energy and enthusiasm to the organization. New people can bring fresh ways of looking at procedures and bring an entirely different set of experiences to the team. These can also be seen as negative if there are territorial issues or an affinity for the status quo.

The risks of hiring someone from the outside are the learning curve regarding their strengths and weaknesses, unfamiliarity with the personality quirks, and skill level. Can their track record be verified? Can their references be counted on to be completely honest given the legal issues of our day?

There are pros and cons to every hire. There are risks associated with every personnel move. We pray, wait for direction, clearly define the need, and then begin the search.

The Interview

Wherever we may find the possible employees from, eventually we will have a conversation regarding the position to be filled. Depending on the position needing to be filled, it is highly likely that an application will be filled out, or résumé will be sent in.

From both or either of these forms, a great deal of information can be gleaned.

- Were the forms filled in correctly?
- Is the résumé messy or neat? Attention to detail, or not, will reflect on the type and quality of job performance.
- How organized is the information presented?
- Is it relevant to the ministry description you prepared?
- Does the résumé show initiative? Self-starting?

- Are there leadership skills demonstrated?
- Is there creativity in the presentation of the résumé?
- Is it accurate, complete, or spotty?

The résumé or application is the first impression the job seeker is presenting to you as the potential employer. How much effort did they put into it? How careful and concerned were they over making an excellent impression? If the person didn't care enough to do well in this initial offering of their services, how well with they do if you hire them?

Assuming you find a few possible candidates from the résumés or applications offered, then an interview should be established. How many candidates need to be interviewed? The answer is; it depends. How important is the job ministry position being filled? How many excellent résumés were there? How much time do you want to spend to find the right person for the job? One or two may be too few, whereas six may simply muddy the waters. Spend as much time as necessary to find the best candidate to fulfill the ministry description.

Before scheduling an interview you need to think through some of these questions:

- Who should be involved in the process?
- How many interviews will be conducted?
- When and where should the interview(s) take place?
- Will the interview be in person or on the phone?
- Will the interview be one-on-one or by a team?
- If a team is involved, does everyone involved clearly understand the criteria for the hire? The core questions asked?
- Are there other aspects to the selection process (e.g., preaching, participating in a children's class, taking a skill test, completing a drug screening) prior to the selection being finished?

Good questions are a key to the interview process. The best questions are those that are referred to as open-ended type questions. Asking questions that can be answered, "Yes" or "No" typically does not offer much insight into the person. Whereas questions such as, "What did you learn from that project?" or "What would you do differently next time?" will allow a larger view into the personality and skill set of the person.

As you prepare your questions, avoid having all the questions be ones they are likely prepared for. It is usually helpful to throw them off the script to see how they respond. Questions such as, "What is your second greatest weakness?" and "What would your worst friend say regarding your personality?" will often open some interesting avenues to explore.

In most interviews you are exploring how the candidate will perform the job, and how they will fit into the team. Developing questions that are specific to the ministry description will help with the former goal and general, open ended questions will help with the latter goal. Questions that begin with "how," "why," and "what" will typically open the way for good communication.

- What did you learn from your previous experience?
- How would you proceed in this situation?
- Why did you take that action instead of the other choice?
- What do you think about efficiency?

There are questions that we cannot ask based on current Federal Discrimination laws. These include:

- Marital status
- Parental status
- Age
- National Origin
- Race or Skin color
- Criminal record
- Disability

Because you are hiring for a ministry position, you may inquire regarding religion or creed, whereas in the public sector, you may not.

The person interviewing will be naturally nervous and that should be expected. We should attempt to put them at ease and let them know exactly the process that will be followed. Clear communication will help release some of the natural tension.

During the interview we should eliminate disruptions so we can provide our undivided attention to the person. We should confirm the ending time so the parameters are set. We want to make the applicant as comfortable as possible so we can conduct the best interview to help meet the need. We and our ministry are being interviewed, as well as the candidate.

Studies have shown that body language is a large part of communication, so we should observe and take notes. How open is the person to the questions being asked? Some nervousness is to be expected, but are they overboard? How about eye contact? While not completely accurate, we must learn to trust our instincts in this process. Making a bad hire is worse than making no hire.

If multiple candidates are being considered, take plenty of notes. Each person will be considered not only in light of their skill set regarding the position we are attempting to fulfill, but also in comparison to the other applicants.

After reviewing the résumés and your notes from the interviews, it is time to make a decision. Finding the right person for the job is important to assure a mutually beneficial relationship. As you prayerfully consider each person here are five "C's" to consider:

- **Competence** - Do they have the necessary skills (or the ability to be trained in them) to be effective in the position?
- **Character** - Do they have the character to do their job with integrity over the long haul?
- **Chemistry** - Do they have the chemistry with you, your team, and the organization to be an effective team player?
- **Commitment** - Do they have a commitment to your mission, vision, and core values?
- **Calling** - Are they called to serve with you and your organization?

The applicant may be a wonderful person, they may be likeable and would do an okay job, but if they don't possess these five traits; it might be wiser to keep looking.

If you are satisfied that you have found the right person, this person meets all of your criteria, the team has agreed, and you have a confirmation from the Lord, then you are ready to make an offer. However, before you do, there are still a few matters to attend to:

- Thoroughly check all references asking good questions and listening for any qualified hesitant answers:

    1. How do you know _____.
    2. How long have you known them?
    3. What can you tell me about their strengths?
    4. What can you tell me about their weaknesses?
    5. Explain the job and ask . . . is this something they would be good at?
    6. Why did they leave your organization? (if applicable)
    7. Would you rehire this person? (if applicable)
    8. What else could you tell me that would help me discern whether or not we should hire this individual?

- Follow up with the previous employer to assure accuracy regarding the timing and reasons for their departure. Ask them if they would rehire, but realize that most former employers have to be very careful in what they share.

- Consider having the individual take a DiSC or Myers Briggs personality assessment.

While the time invested in these procedures may seem extreme, they really don't have to take that long. The importance of every hire will come into clearer focus if termination action becomes necessary later on. Spending sufficient time and effort *before* the hire can save a great deal of pain *afterwards*.

When you are sure you have the right person for the job, then the final stage begins — making the offer for employment.

This is obviously one of the most difficult parts of the "matching" process. You do not want to under or over employ someone, nor insult them with your offer, and you don't want to lose your best choice over a few thousand dollars. But how do you know what to offer? Here are some factors to consider when assembling the compensation package:

- **Education level** – education matters. It speaks to ability, fortitude, lifelong learning, and can lead to a more global perspective.
- **Relevant experience** – experience matters. Relevant experience really matters!
- **Proven, tangible skills** – find ways to prove their skills through their résumé or other outlets such as hobbies or volunteer work.
- **Proven track record of success** – the key word here is proven. Don't rely on what they think should happen, but rather what they've already accomplished. Although it is true that people change, grow and improve, there is no better way to predict the future than to look at the past.
- **Salary of comparable positions in the local market** – what the local market pays for similar positions is relevant and important. What they make at a different job at a different organization is not as relevant. There are multiple organizations that publish church salary surveys including the National Association of Church Business Administrators and The Church Law and Tax Store for example.
- **Level of impact the staff member is likely to bring to the organization.** This one is important. How much are they likely to help the organization meet its mission?

Each one of these factors ought to be a part of the final compensation package. Every organization will attach different weights to these criteria and that is fine. Just be sure to do a good job measuring the criteria for the potential candidate.

One very potentially sticky issue is how you know you are not offering more or less than you should in comparison to the applicant's expectations? That is a good question and it only has one answer — Ask. Find a way to get a feel for their expectations, the range they are expecting or some kind of measurement before the offer is made. In this way you are more likely not to over or under employ, or insult the potential employee. If their expectation is more than 10-15% different than yours, you may want to reconsider your offer.

In addition, you have to consider why is there such a difference, high or low? Perhaps they are in error, or perhaps you need to do more homework, but under or over employing can lead to unsuccessful employment relationships. Be careful and be open in the communication process. This is the time to discuss these issues with candor and to make sure that both parties are satisfied with the final pay package agreed upon.

If you have made the offer and it has been accepted, congratulations! Your ministry potential has just increased and you have begun a journey of growth.

Every journey has a beginning and most have an end. In the next chapter we will look at employee motivation and what to do when it becomes evident that the employment must conclude.

Questions to Ponder

1. Has the time arrived to expand the ministry through adding personnel? How do you know?

2. What are the most important attributes you are looking for in the person(s) you hire? Why?

3. Thinking back on previous hiring experiences in your life, what do you wish was performed differently? What was enjoyable?

4. How will you know that God wants you to hire the individual you finally settle upon? Is this person a true match to your organization?

5. How will the hire impact the current relationship aspects of your ministry? Does this person really possess all 5 C's and if not, why are you hiring them?

8 Motivating the Crew:
Navigating Staff Attitudes and Actions, and when to throw Jonah Overboard

How do I tell you your time has come to a close?

In the previous chapter we provided many factors to consider, as well as tools to assist you in hiring people to work alongside you in ministry. While it would be ideal that those who are hired would never need motivating, we all know that simply is not true. In addition, sometimes it becomes obvious that the employment relationship needs to be terminated. In this chapter we will help you walk through both of these challenging processes.

Even after making an excellent hire following all of the best techniques, employees (and volunteers) can lose motivation. Many begin well, with an excellent attitude, and over a period of time, finish horribly with a rotten taste in their mouth toward you and the ministry. How does this happen? More importantly, can we limit or avoid it altogether?

Every person is a unique expression of God's creative genius. Each one has differing needs, and a unique mental makeup. This makes a one size-fits all method impossible. There is, however, one truth regarding employees that is universal:

People don't care how much you know until they know how much you care.

As the employer, we must let those who work for us and alongside us know that we care for them. We value them as persons and not simply as a tool to accomplish a task. We must be willing to invest the time needed to understand who it is that works for us, and what it will take to keep them engaged and motivated. We are after all, working for the Master to accomplish His business.

One motivation tool we would like you to consider is what we call the "Equity Theory." This theory attempts to explain some of the difficulties in the workplace in terms of the perceived inequities employees face. These inequities may be real or simply something that is perceived, but they often have a direct effect on motivation.

A few common areas of equity can be defined by:

- Amount of work accomplished = Amount of pay/benefits received
- Years of service = respect of opinions and judgment or level of autonomy
- Quality of contribution = corresponding good reviews, raises, and promotions
- Emotional effort invested = a corresponding level of appreciation
- Loyalty shown = loyalty received

When a real or perceived inequity is held by the employee, i.e. their investment is perceived as greater than their return, certain negative behaviors can occur. For example:

- Hard work results in getting additional worked dumped on the employee without appropriate appreciation. The employee can decide that the trade off is simply not worth it. It would be better to be less productive.

- Unfair or unequal treatment of another staff person often leads to discouraged workers. If the praise, rewards, or success is not determined by production but favoritism, why bother?

As stated previously, every person is unique. While this is true, there are trends that are associated with certain groupings or generations. What was true and certain as a motivation in one generation often changes dramatically in the next.

For example: the definition of success to those born before 1945 was financial security, lifetime employment and a gold watch received upon retirement. Those born in the next generation, commonly referred to as Baby Boomers, understood that to be successful meant to have more toys, the corner office, and the opportunity to make many lifestyle choices.

Those born after 1965, called, Generation X, viewed success as a lifetime of being employed, and achieving personal happiness. Those born after 1982 simply viewed success as the accumulation of wealth. This information is important when considering the generation your employee is part of as it directly relates to motivating them.

Perhaps clearer is a generational comparison specifically related to motivation. The first generation valued family security, their children having more than they did, and a pleasant retirement. The Boomers wanted enough money to enjoy their lifestyle, to create a company that would last, as well as an early retirement. The "X'ers" wanted challenging work, lifetime learning, and short term payoffs for their work. The current generation would just like some stability!

Being aware of the social trends generationally will help determine how someone may view motivation. In addition, education levels, family environment, birthplace, personal values and their current family situation all will play into their motivation needs.

Creating an Environment for Success

No one likes to work in a demotivating environment. As leaders we have a great deal to say and do regarding the work environment.

We directly affect how employees feel about their job and how they stay motivated. Or not.

If we want to create a de-motivating environment:

- Provide cautions, guarded, excessively formal communications
- Make sure you squash all disagreements
- Make sure you fail to share information, creating a secretive feeling
- Always conduct poor, ineffective meetings
- Set unclear and unrealistic goals
- Set low commitment levels for the team
- Make sure to misuse each team member's strengths and talents
- Certainly do not give feedback through performance appraisals

No one, of course, would want to implement that list of procedures on purpose, but have we inadvertently? Would those that work for us agree or disagree with that above list regarding our style? If there seems to be a struggle in your ministry in the personnel arena, perhaps an open discussion about these points might prove insightful.

If we would prefer to have the look and feel of an effective environment, try this list:

- Atmosphere is comfortable, somewhat relaxed
- Mission of the team is well understood AND accepted
- Members really listen to each other
- Open disagreement is permitted at a healthy, constructive level
- Some decisions are reached by consensus, almost always after some input
- People feel free to express ideas and feelings
- Team is self-conscious about its own operations
- They keep each other and the leader out of trouble
- They do what is required to make the team reach its goal, not just what the leader asks them to do.
- They approach tasks with a sense of energy and enthusiasm.

We do not arrive at either of these lists by accident. Each day we make decisions which will point us in a direction. We are always working on the relationship aspects of our staff even if we are unaware of it. The successful employers purposefully aim at the second list to improve the motivation of their staff.

There are many ways to examine employee motivation expectations, and the specifics could take entire books to explore. In general terms, employees typically desire:

- A level playing field where the ground rules do not fluctuate or are enforced unequally
- Consistency of purpose and vision
- Appropriate leadership not domination
- Honesty and integrity; say what you mean and mean what you say – always follow through on our word
- Clear, obtainable, measurable goals
- Clear, open, trustworthy communications
- Celebration of the victories when appropriate and appreciation of them with rewards and recognition

Employees and people in general, want to be known as individuals that have personal worth. In addition, people like to be understood and to have understanding of how they fit into the greater plan and vision. People like to know that what they do matters. People also like to be appreciated and given the appropriate recognition for their efforts and contribution.

A time proven system for success will include at least four procedures to head off future motivational issues:

- A well thought out ministry description
- The setting of clearly stated, obtainable and measureable goals
- Ongoing verbal feedback
- Timely reviews

We have covered creating a clear ministry description earlier, so let's spend a little time with the other three procedures, beginning with everyone's favorite topic — goal setting.

While it is difficult and labor intensive at times, it can be an effective tool to get staff on track and motivated on the "right stuff." Goals should be annualized, broken down into smaller tasks and followed up on a quarterly basis. A simple, short meeting can go a long way towards keeping folks on track. Effective goals should:

- Be clearly stated and understood by those who are to carry them out
- Be obtainable and realistic
- Include the resources needed for success
- Include a timeframe for completion
- Include measurement criteria to be used to measure success
- Include an accountability and communication plan
- Include expected results and outcomes for meeting the goals

After agreeing upon the goals, the next process of the system kicks in — maintaining ongoing verbal feedback. Verbal feedback may not always be possible, so phone calls, e-mail, text messaging, and other social media communication may have to work; however, nothing takes the place of face time if all at possible. Regardless of the vehicle used to communicate, give feedback!

People like to know how they are doing in completing the projects and tasks assigned to them, and specifically how their supervisor feels. Being proactive here will greatly enhance the employee's motivation and satisfaction. Consider these pointers regarding feedback:

- Give feedback early and often
- Utilize informal feedback for at least 80% of your total feedback
- Balance feedback between positive and constructive, with a heavier weight on positive
- Try to develop ways to remind yourself to "catch people doing something right each day"

- Be specific in your praise
- When giving constructive feedback be prepared with specific, direct and non-punishing comments
- Avoid generalizations such as "always" and "never"
- Give specific examples

Relationships take hard work. If we want those that work with us, and for us to remain motivated then we need to practice the Golden Rule — do unto others as we would have done to us. We do not like unspecific, vague, expectations but prefer truthful, timely comments and feedback. So do those that work for us.

Mentoring new employees also helps lead to long-term success. Connecting more experienced staff with new team members will help ease the transition and shorten the learning curve.

The Review Process

Many of us have had a bad experience with a review process in our work career. That is the single biggest reason people avoid the process — bad past experiences.

We can't allow previous failed processes of the past to keep us from using effective motivational tools in the future. That would be like saying, "I heard a bad sermon on Sunday, so no more sermons!"

With review systems, one size does not fit all. Some folks lean more toward task-oriented review systems, others lean toward a more relational approach, and some are in between. There is a learning curve involved in using reviews, so don't give up. As you grow in your ability and knowledge of each person, you will find a style, or more likely, a mixture of several styles that will work.

There are basically two main styles of reviews - Task/Quantitative and Relational, however most of us will end up using some sort of combination of the two.

The Task/Quantitative Style system is more systematic in nature. It attempts to directly tie the review process to the job description and goals and objectives. It is an excellent and precise process that can be an effective communications tool.

Advantages
- Clearly communicates in detail
- Measures specific progress in each area
- Helps build an improvement plan
- Leaves little room for miscommunication

Disadvantages
- Time consuming
- Somewhat quantitative
- Can be overwhelming for staff at first

They key to this system is to determine the appropriate areas that need to be evaluated in order for this person to be effective in this organization and at this specific position. It's not a list of personal pet peeves; it's about being effective in the job.

The Relational Style system is less quantitative and of course tends to focus on the relational aspects of the job. This system allows for feedback in both directions, the employee "self" evaluation and the supervisor's evaluation.

Advantages
- Less time consuming
- More user-friendly
- Less quantitative, therefore more personal feeling
- Creates a forum to discern gaps in performance perception between employee and employer

Disadvantages
- Less specific
- Less quantitative — can seem vague, harder to measure
- May allow for specific problems or deficiencies to continue to go unaddressed

Perhaps a combination of the first two options is what is best for your organization. Take bits and pieces of each system and design your own! Remember, one size does not fit all. You have to be comfortable with the process, and you will develop skills as you use the review process. Perhaps start small and work your way up the ladder of detail and/or complexity, but make sure you implement some sort of review process to assure good communication.

We have primarily focused on paid staff, and we will specifically deal with volunteers in chapter seventeen. For now, consider some of these volunteer specific motivation thoughts:

- Have a specific written ministry description
- Have a starting and ending time for their service
- Use appreciative verbiage when "recruiting," for example, "Will you be on this committee?" is not as appreciative as, "I know you're really gifted in this area, and it seems to fit with what we need. Are you willing to help with this need?"
- Have work available when they arrive, they don't like to waste time
- Don't make up busy work; volunteers hate that
- Make them feel a part of the organization
- Regularly and genuinely appreciate them, and their work!
- Appoint a good, organized leader to each "committee" to avoid frustration
- They are motivated for a reason, find out what it is and make sure their needs are being met
- Recognize volunteers publicly when appropriate
- Have an annual or semi-annual recognition time, lunch, dinner or just a social mixer
- Send occasional thank you notes

When It Is Time to Release Staff

Firing staff is one of the most difficult and challenging aspects of ministry. Every situation seems like a failure and personal loss. There are a multitude of reasons for termination ranging from fraud, sexual sin, disloyalty, or a failure or inability to perform the required tasks. Staff leaving due to termination will almost always result in a grieving process. Grieving typically involves a cycle of denial, anger, acceptance, and recovery. In short, firing a staff person is traumatic.

While not enjoyable, when it becomes necessary, termination, or releasing the staff person must be accomplished, for the underlying issue will not resolve itself and will only fester and quite possibly infect others.

While dealing with sin issues is easier to grasp emotionally, the confronting and eventual termination process still involves certain steps that we will outline later on in the process. For now, let's consider an employee that is underperforming.

Many people are hired to perform a task for which they are not qualified or trained to do. This will lead to frustration on both sides of the desk. Before termination perhaps some other options could be explored such as:

- Additional professional training
- One-on-one mentoring
- Peer-to-peer mentoring
- Update work tools, IT hardware/software
- Create an on-going learning environment

Each employee is different, and perhaps more discussion would help. If the issue is not sin related, then spending some additional time attempting to redeem the employee may be an acceptable solution.

If you have exhausted your options, and it is still apparent that the staff member needs to be released, then following these steps will assist you.

Given the litigation-saturated nature of our times, it is important to make sure you have a plan regarding dismissing an employee. Keep good records, for they may be needed later on to justify your actions.

Begin the process with direct, specific communication. This includes reminding the employee of other times the issue(s) have been discussed with little or no improvement. Explain to the person that you are giving him or her a verbal warning, because the issue has not improved. Tell them this is not a documented conversation, but if things do not improve, future conversations about the issue(s) will be documented, and future steps may/will include probation and/or termination.

If the situation does not improve as a result of the verbal warning, then a written warning is in order. If someone is getting close to needing to be on probation, explain to them as part of ongoing feedback that if their performance doesn't improve, probation is the next step, and it can result in termination. Tell them that your conversation is being documented.

Here is a sample conversation to consider some possible techniques to use:

"Sally, we've talked before about the way you're answering the phone. When you answer, your tone of voice and choice of words is resulting in a perception that you are too busy and don't want to be bothered. The result is that members are calling me instead of you to get basic information, and this is unacceptable. In addition, outsiders may feel unwelcome at our organization. Please think about this and pray about it, then let me know tomorrow your plan to make this better, starting tomorrow."

At this point, depending on how your organization is set up, you may want to notify the personnel committee or governing board of the situation. This would include the goals you have set up for the employee to correct the situation, the employee's progress toward those goals, and the consequences you have communicated.

Make sure your employee documentation is kept current with names, dates, circumstances, action requested and taken, evaluations and necessary facts relevant to the discussion. It would be wise to have both parties sign the documentation.

While these actions may feel like you are "case building," without the proper documentation, the organization is open to many legal issues. In addition, some employees respond better to the seriousness of the event once it is written down. While they may ignore the verbal warnings, there is something more real-feeling to writing and signing a document. If the problem persists, then probation will be the next step.

When implementing probation, remind the employee how they arrived at this point. Their behavior and the impact of it, needs to be explained clearly. For example:

> We've talked 3 times about this situation, and the last conversation, as you know, was documented because your actions had not yet improved to the level at which you are expected to be. Because of the way you are answering the phone, members are feeling as though they shouldn't bother you with questions, and outsiders are not feeling welcomed.

The purpose of the probation is to provide a redemptive path, and if that fails, it will help smooth the termination process. During this meeting, very clear goals should be set, and very clear consequences should be explained if they are not met, including termination. For example, we might tell Sally the following:

> The expectation is that you must answer the phone in a courteous, respectful and polite manner every time you answer the phone. You must demonstrate increased teamwork during the next 30 days, as assessed by your peers and your supervisor.
>
> Failure to meet the expectations laid out in this document in the timeframe specified may OR will result in termination of your employment. Failure to show immediate and sustained improvement in the areas laid out in this document may OR will result in termination of your employment.

Sally, at this point, has been given every opportunity to improve. She has had multiple conversations about her job performance and should clearly understand what is expected from her in order to continue working on the staff.

During the probation time at least one conversation is necessary to follow up on the timing and job performance, and to provide feedback. If there is no change, the employee will certainly have an expectation of termination.

After the probation period is expired and it is apparent that the required changes have not occurred, then set a day and time for the dismissal meeting. Sooner is better for all involved. While no two situations will be the same in a termination, some general guidelines will prove helpful.

- Have at least two other people present.
- Make the conversation quick and to the point. A definitive statement such as,"While both sides have done their best to make this relationship work, it is not working out, so we are ending your employment effective today."
- Arguing will not produce anything of value at this point. Move the conversation to release options.
- Be compassionate, offer guidance if appropriate such as a reference or severance package.
- Provide them with exact, written steps of what is expected now. Clean out the desk, how to tie up loose ends, etc. Help them with every stage of the process with compassion, for the employee has just lost their job.
- Make sure that the necessary security steps are taken regarding passwords, data security, property protection etc.

After the painful reality sinks in that the job cannot be saved, most employees will turn their attention to a severance package and their personal reputation.

There are a variety of tools that can be used to create a meaningful severance package:

- severance pay
- benefits extension (e.g., health insurance)
- extended vacations
- leaves of absences

A general rule of thumb in industry is to provide one week of severance for each year served. That is not required, but generally the organization will fare better by erring on the side of being generous. Be sure to spell out vacation pay, sick pay, regular pay, severance pay and so forth, so it is clear as to what is being received.

Understand that while severance packages are important, most employees are *more* concerned about their reputation and the stigma and embarrassment that go along with the ending of employment. Try to create options that will help them save face. You will be surprised how impacting that will be.

We are serving the King, and we are attempting to handle His business in the best possible manner. Terminating an employee is a messy, painful event. We must strive for the best possible solution, demonstrating the fruits of the Spirit in the process. In the business world there are terms used that we should use, such as creating a "win/win" situation. How can we achieve the desired result in the best possible manner? This means the separation is good for the staff member *and* good for the organization. Be creative. Ask them for feedback and ideas. Find out what is important to them and try to work out a good solution.

Here are five different strategies that are much better than the termination approach:

- **Voluntary resignation** – they decide on their own to voluntarily resign from their position
- **Involuntary resignation** – they have been given the option of resigning or being terminated and they chose to resign under pressure
- **Voluntary retirement** – they are close enough to retirement that they decide this is the best option for all concerned
- **Involuntary retirement** – they are close enough to retirement and they are forced to retire
- **Mutual agreement separation** – there is sufficient agreement by both sides that it is mutually agreeable to dissolve the employee/employer relationship

You may want to decide in advance which release option you want to steer them toward. In steering them toward the best option for the organization, you can present the options like this:

> "On ___ (date) you were placed on probation, because you were not meeting position expectations. Because you have not demonstrated immediate and sustained improvement in your performance, we need to take the next step. We feel it is in the best interests of all involved if you were to voluntarily resign from your position. With that, we would offer you the following package to close out your relationship here. If you decide you do not want to resign, then we will be left with termination and this is the package . . . ."

While not all employees will accept your leading, or even leave graciously, we need to make every attempt to side with mercy and compassion.

Termination of a staff member not only impacts you and the employee, but affects many others as well. Effective communication is important to help with the transition.

For the remaining staff, to the extent possible, gather all staff as soon as possible and share the decision that has been made. Share with them the current transition plan and what is expected of them. Explain the implications for the future with regard to covering responsibilities and so forth. Those who remain are often fearful for their positions and may have been negatively impacted by the terminated employee. Clear, kind, effective communication will help during this transition time.

The larger organization may need some general communication as well. News spreads fast, and bad news even quicker. A letter of explanation, a bulletin announcement, or a brief announcement from the pulpit is usually a good choice, depending on the visibility of the person leaving. You want to be as clear as possible regarding the nature of the separation and as sensitive as you can be considering the previous employee, their family and friends. The truth is that whatever is said, it will be too much for some, and too little for others. Wisdom is needed on how much to share and when always striving to be redemptive and proactive.

Depending on the person's visibility to the general public, the circumstances regarding the departure, and the need, use good judgment in dispensing the details to the general public. Those that need to know need to know and the rest will be fine with less information.

Finally, learning how to hire, evaluate, review, motivate, and terminate employees is less than an exact science. Expect trial and error and plenty of growth opportunities as you navigate these waters. Strive for consistency, and always add a great deal of prayer.

Questions to Ponder

1. Would those who work for me say that I care for them as people? Why or why not?

2. In thinking about the work environment of the staff, what words would I use to describe it?

3. How is the communication between myself and the staff? What would they say if asked?

4. How could I improve the motivation, review process, and relationship aspects of our team?

5. If I am in the process of terminating an employee or have had to fire someone before, how am I doing based on this chapter? What would those around me say?

9 The Bounty:
How to Handle Incoming Funds with Integrity and Accountability

Never count the offering after using glue or eating honey.

Every ministry expects to receive donations, and if they hope to survive long term, they will derive policies to make sure the money is handled with integrity. When someone writes a check, drops cash into the offering plate or box, or makes an electronic transfer to our ministry, an unspoken agreement is triggered. The donor expects us to handle the money properly and to use it for the purposes intended, and we who received the donation understand that we will give an account to God for its usage.

Paul, the apostle, wrote these challenging words long ago, yet regarding the way we handle the money entrusted to us, they still apply:

> **Prove all things; hold fast that which is good. Abstain from all appearance of evil. (1 Thessalonians 5:21-22 KJV)**

In order to not violate the trust given to us by the donor, we need to establish and follow appropriate guidelines. Given the all-too-often headlines regarding fraud and financial mismanagement appearing in our news outlets, this is even more important in the church today.

There are many ways that people can give money (even non-cash gifts that we will cover later in the chapter) to our ministries and all of the gifts need to be handled with integrity. We also need to keep in mind protecting the reputation of the church as well as those counting the money.

Here is one overriding principle:

Money should never be collected or handled by only one person.

By doing so, they are open to all manner of accusation without any viable protection. At least two people should always be involved, and three is better. This provides ample protection for those dealing with the funds and helps limit the temptation to commit fraud.

The Offering

The primary way money will be given to the church is through the offering box or the passing of the plate during the worship service, so we will address this first.

If an offering box, sometimes referred to as a retiring offering is used, they should be locked and only opened by two people. These boxes are typically located near exits and usually contain a slot on the top for the cash or check and an opening on the bottom for the money to be easily removed. They can also be located in the wall and function as a drop safe, which is highly recommended if this method is used to receive the primary offering.

If the traditional method of "passing the plate" is used, then the money should be in plain sight at all times, and never counted alone. Whoever collects the money should never place the money in their pockets or take the money out of the room alone. By doing so, the person who has the money opens themselves to accusation (and temptation) with no one to defend them. We are to avoid even the appearance of evil.

The Bounty

If the money is not counted immediately, it should be placed in a locked safe, locked file drawer, or some other place that is safe, and *dual control* procedures should be followed. Dual control primarily means that at least two people are always present, and no one is ever alone with the money. Did we say that people should not be alone with the money yet?

In addition to the offering received during the services, money can arrive from a variety of sources. Dual control should be used regardless of where the money came from or how it ends up in the offering.

If the potential to receive cash donations through the mail exists, then mail should be opened by at least two persons so that immediate dual control can be established.

Pastors and church staff should resist taking offerings directly from members and instead direct them to the offering boxes or wherever the offering collection is located.

Money collected for special events (dinners, youth/mission trips, etc.) should be received by two persons and counted and verified by both of them. The money should be placed in a sealed envelope with the total amount and the General Ledger code, (or at least what it is for), include the signatures of both people written on the outside of it, and either placed in a safe place or immediately given to the person in charge of counting the money.

After the offering and any donations or funds received in the mail or through other sources are ready to be counted, then the actual offering count can be performed. The actual count can happen immediately after the service or if necessary, the next day. If the money has to be held overnight, make sure it is locked somewhere and can only be accessed by those responsible to count it.

Care should be administered when choosing people to count the money. In many ways, they need to be the most spiritual, mature people you can possibly find. They will be seeing information that may dramatically impact them. Those who count the money need to be trustworthy and able to keep what they observe to themselves. James, the apostle, had some pretty harsh words about showing favoritism to the rich, and those that count the money will soon learn who gives what, and how much. Unless they are mature believers, this information can impact them adversely. Those who count the money will learn who the large donors are as well as those who do not give. Choose wisely.

We recommend utilizing a written counting ministry job description form and offering counting team confidentially agreement. Please see the resource section in the back of this book for examples, and make sure you use these forms before assigning members to the counting teams.

Every church will use some sort of system to keep track of the checks and cash given and to record these amounts for the donor. We have provided sample count sheets and recording forms that are also available for download to help with this critical task, so see the resource section for these.

Depending on if you use an outside accounting service, a computer program, or a manual system, the detail requirements for the count and deposit will vary, but utilizing the following pointers will greatly assist you.

You have funds to count, offering counters screened and ready to go, so now what? Here is a list of factors to consider:

- At least two people should always be present when counting offerings – no exceptions. (Three is preferable.) Why three? Bathroom breaks, interruptions, and sickness happen. Ideally the count team should consist of enough people to establish a rotation so that no one is counting every week.

- Detailed, written instructions are highly recommended so that all counters understand the procedures. Individuals involved in the count should be able to perform all of the processes, not just their piece. We recommend rotating tasks so that all counters have experience with all the processes.

- Carefully consider the location used to count the offering. It should be private yet not secretive, contain all supplies needed, so no one has to leave the room, be free of all clutter (completely clear table or desk), and have the ability for all counters to see each other while the count is being performed.

- Loose or unidentified cash should be separated and counted first. A double blind count should be utilized – one person counts the money and records their total unbeknownst to the other person. The second person then counts and calls out their total. If the two agree, the count stands. If there is a discrepancy, the first person simply says "No," and the count is performed again until both totals match.

- If envelopes are used, counters should verify the contents against what is written on the envelope. For balancing purposes, the counter should write "cash" or "ck" and the amounts received in the upper corner of the envelope.

- Depending on your accounting system, the offering should be broken into the General Ledger accounts, such as "General Offering," "Missions," and "Building Fund." The balance of the split of accounts must equal the total deposit.

- Maintain the integrity of the deposit. Do not "switch out" money so someone can get cash or make change or move money around so separate deposits can be made. If someone needs change or cash, the offering is not the place to get it. Do not pay expenses out of the offering.

- Nothing should be thrown into the trash during offering counting without two people verifying that no valuables are contained in the contents.

- Checks should be immediately endorsed with a restrictive stamp, "For deposit only," and the bank account number.

- The documentation for offerings and deposits and contribution recordkeeping should be clear to those NOT involved in the process. Anyone looking at the documentation should be readily able to figure out what happened. No secret codes or shorthand should be used.

- All counters should sign their full names to each document retained from the count.

- Check the floor before leaving, to ensure nothing was dropped.

- Each counter should understand that they are responsible for the entire deposit, not just their part.

Two deposit slips should be created for each offering counted. One of the deposit slips will be attached to the count sheet and given to the accountant or person in charge of recording, and the other one will go with the money to the bank. This step provides an additional deterrent to fraud and helps secure the integrity of the deposit.

After the deposit is made, the two deposit slips should match the count sheet and then be attached to the count sheet, thus confirming that nothing has changed in the deposit after it was counted.

Balancing the bank deposits to the general ledger and the contribution system each month has proven to be the single biggest key to reducing fraud connected with the offering. This three-way check will catch any alterations made.

There are sample forms that you can download for free from the ICM resource website. In addition, you can find a sample of detailed instructions for counting in the resource section of this book so you don't have to reinvent the process. Please feel free to use any or all of the forms to assist you in this important task of counting the offering.

Recording Contributions

To meet the requirements for the IRS, any contribution record or acknowledgement should include this wording:

"No goods or services were provided, other than intangible religious benefits, in exchange for these donations."

In addition to cash, checks, and electronic transfers, stocks and other assets may be donated to the church and may be an extremely beneficial transaction to both the church and the donor.

It would be beneficial for each church to establish in writing a gift acceptance policy and assure that the staff are familiar with what the church will and will not accept as donations. If the church will accept old computers, for example, that should be noted, but if not, a policy will make everyone's life easier when someone wants to donate outdated items.

Gifts of publicly traded stock can be beneficial to donors when the value of the stock has increased from the original purchase price. Rather than selling the stock and making a cash donation to a charity, the donor may realize greater tax benefits by transferring the stock to the charity. That is, the fair market value of the stock may be taken as a charitable contribution while avoiding capital gains tax on the sale of the appreciated stock. Church Treasurers should be careful to correctly receipt stock donations, as well as advise potential donors of their substantiation requirements.

After someone gives a gift of stock, then provide an acknowledgement of the gift. This document/letter should include the following:

- Name and address of the church

- Name of the donor

- Date the stock was donated

- Detailed description of the stock including the number of shares received

- Remember, do NOT provide a value for donated stock

- If no goods or services were provided to the donor, then include a statement indicating that the only goods or services provided are intangible religious benefits. If any goods or services *were* provided to the donor in exchange for the contribution, a statement must be included, indicating the value of those goods and services.

The donor will be responsible to provide for their tax records the following:

- Obtaining written acknowledgement by the Church as detailed above before filing a tax return claiming a deduction for the contribution

- Documentation of the fair market value of the stock at the time of the contribution, as well as the cost basis of the stock

- If the stock donation is valued at $500 or more, complete and attach to tax return: Section A, Part 1, of IRS Form 8283

A church may receive non-cash contributions beyond stocks from donors in furtherance of their exempt purpose/mission. In order for the gift to be tax deductible to the donor, a written acknowledgement must be received from the church for property valued at $250 or more. Depending on the value and type of property donated, additional reporting and substantiation requirements may exist as outlined below. Items donated for a fundraiser auction may be exempt from reporting requirements. Follow these instructions for other type gifts:

- Written acknowledgment of the gift that includes the name and address of the church, name of the donor, date the property was donated, detailed description of the property (not value), and a statement indicating whether any goods or services were provided in exchange for the contribution

- For donations valued at more than $5,000 the church must fill out Part 4 of IRS Form 8283 "Donee Acknowledgement" (not an acknowledgement of the value)

- Additionally, if a church receives a non-cash contribution valued at more than $5,000 and within three years of the date of contribution sells, exchanges, consumes, or disposes of the donated property the church must file Form 8282 with the IRS and provide a copy to the donor. This does not apply to gifts of publicly traded stock.

Like stock contributions, there are responsibilities on the donor side in order to receive the full benefit for their tax deduction.

- The donor must obtain written acknowledgement from the charity as detailed above before filing a tax return claiming a deduction for the contribution

- For donations valued between $500 - $5,000, the donor must also complete Section A, Part 1 of IRS Form 8283 and enclose it with the tax return on which the charitable contribution is claimed.

- For donations valued more than $5,000 the donor must obtain a qualified appraisal of the donated property and complete all parts of Section B on IRS Form 8283.

Special reporting requirements exist for vehicle (car, boats and planes) donations. The church is required to report information about the donation to the IRS on Form 1098-C. Form 1098-C must also be provided to the donor within 30 days of the donation date if the church keeps the vehicle, or within 30 days of the sale date if it is sold.

When a *donor* receives goods or services in exchange for a cash gift or gift of property, the charity is required to provide additional disclosures on the written receipt or acknowledgement that is provided to the donor including:

- A good faith estimate of the value of goods or services received

- A statement informing the donor that the amount of the tax deductible contribution is limited to the difference in the value of the cash or property contributed and the value of the goods or services provided by the organization

Exclusion to this requirement includes the receipt of token goods or services that are insubstantial in value, such as key chains, bookmarks, and calendars. The general threshold for an item to qualify as a token gift is the smaller of $95 or 2% of the amount of the contribution.

Two other issues almost always arise when discussing contributions — the gift of time and service and designated gifts for mission trips. Let's tackle the easy one first.

There is NO tax deduction allowed for contributions of services to a charity.

However, volunteers may deduct unreimbursed expenses that occur from the result of their donated services. Examples include transportation costs, postage stamps, stationery, or other materials. Any costs claimed as a tax deduction should be substantiated with cancelled checks, receipts, and mileage logs. If expenses total $250 or more for the calendar year, written acknowledgement (following other non-cash donation receipting rules) from the charity needs to be obtained before filing the income tax return.

Mission Trips

Many churches sponsor mission trips across the country or around the world. Individuals given an opportunity to participate in a missions experience are often required to raise a specific amount of funds to offset the trip cost. Are contributions raised by these individuals tax deductible? Can a person make a tax deductible gift to cover their own mission trip costs? Keep reading for the answers!

The IRS expects a church to use all tax deductible gifts in a manner consistent with the church's tax exempt/ministry purpose. This means tax deductible gifts made to a church to help individuals participate in a mission trip must be used for ministry. If any portion of the mission trip covered by donated funds is not significantly ministry-related, it would not be consistent with the church's tax exempt purpose, and it's possible that at least a percentage of the contributions given would not be tax deductible.

For example, if a church sponsors a pleasure trip (e.g., cruise, Holy Land trip, etc.), none of the amounts paid would be tax deductible since the purpose of those trips is not ministry related. *Ministry related* means trip participants must be involved in active ministry (activities normally associated with evangelism, discipleship, or any of the typical benevolent functions of a church), not simply observing or enjoying ministry.

In order for a contribution to be considered tax deductable, two primary principles must be followed. First, the gift must be given *to the church* and not the individual, and second, the church must *maintain control* over it. In addition to these two principles, the church must maintain a no refund policy.

It is rarely appropriate for a church to refund a contribution. Doing so typically sends a message to the donor and to the IRS that the gift was not controlled by the church to begin with and should not have been tax deductible. Sometimes a potential mission trip participant does not raise enough money to cover his/her cost of the trip. If an individual raises funds for a mission trip and then cannot participate for any reason, the funds raised by the individual should not be returned to donors. In these circumstances, the funds are often used to defray the cost of the trip at large, another participant's cost, or some other missions-related purpose of the church.

To meet the IRS requirements, a church can show its control over tax deductible gifts by printing the following statement on fundraising letters and contributions receipts:

"Contributions are solicited and received with the understanding that ABC Church has complete discretion and control over the use of all donated funds."

This communicates to donors that their gift can be used for any ministry-related purpose of the church if a potential mission trip participant cannot, for any reason, participate in the trip. This policy should be communicated to all trip participants prior to raising funds, and communicated to prospective donors when a gift is requested.

There are other ways a church can exhibit control over tax deductible contributions for mission trips including:

- Have the church or partnering agency be responsible for disbursing all mission trip-related expenses.

- Ensure that all trip participants are under the complete direction and supervision of the church throughout the entire mission experience. Allowing someone to go out on their own could indicate a personal activity rather than ministry.

- Give participants appropriate training and tools needed to conduct active ministry.

As long as the principles noted above are followed, the IRS allows an individual to give tax deductible gifts to cover the funding requirements of their own or family member mission trip costs.

The Bounty

Chapter Summary

We have discussed receiving money and how to properly count it. We addressed the absolute necessity of having at least two people count the money so temptations are limited, and reputations are protected. We covered receiving and documenting non-cash donations, and how they could benefit the ministry. We also referenced how to deal with mission trips and the often asked questions regarding donated service.

All of these issues and their solutions are critical to ensure that we are doing Kingdom work in a way that avoids the appearance of evil. The Church should be the standard bearer of excellence in how She takes care of the money entrusted to Her.

After the ministry receives donations, the next logical step is the spending of them. We will cover that topic in the next chapter, but before we move into how to deal with expenditures, let's pause a few minutes and reflect.

Questions to Ponder

1. If someone followed us around all day, would our lives, specifically how we deal with money, be beyond approach and completely avoiding the appearance of evil?

2. Are there any changes that you need to make to the way you count the offering? If so, what are they and when will you do so?

3. What is the reputation of your church in your community regarding finances? What should it be?

4. What changes could be made to help strengthen your church's testimony regarding handling money?

5. What one new insight did you learn from this chapter?

10 Sailing with the Right Provisions:
How to Handle Expenditures

You Can Only Spend Money Once, Choose Wisely.

After we have received donations, taken the proper steps to count them, record them, and safeguard them, the next logical step to consider is how to spend them!

Some areas are fairly straight forward and do not require a great deal of understanding on how to accomplish the task. If there is a rent payment due, you pay it. Utilities must be paid for on time or they will be shut off. Employees like to receive a paycheck and so do vendors.

We will address some of the finer points on these type payments when we discuss reporting in the next chapter. Each of the above situations will need to be categorized and recorded somewhere, and most likely, someone will need to know what was spent. In addition to the reporting aspects of the disbursements, most churches will operate on some sort of a budget, but we will defer that discussion for now.

Since most pastors are not accountants, let's begin by defining a term or two. "Accounts payable" means people you owe money to, like office supply vendors, the bank if you owe money on your facility, and your insurance company. Most churches will not have accounts receivable, but in case you have rental property or sell books and such, this is money that is owed to the church.

In this chapter we will be primarily dealing with accounts payable. Every ministry will probably have expenses associated with a meeting place, staff of some sort, insurance, and outside vendors. How we pay these people or companies triggers a great deal of paperwork and is the subject of many legal discussions and laws.

Most pastors do not need to be experts in these issues, but ignorance of their importance can end up triggering lawsuits, IRS fines, and a real headache.

First, most accounts payable activities will take place via check signing. We typically pay our bills with a check or through an internet bill paying system. Regardless of how a bill is paid, the following pointers should be kept in mind. These will protect the ministry, and those involved in spending the money. Just like we discussed in the previous chapter, we want to handle the money with integrity, protect those involved, limit temptation and avoid the appearance of evil.

When paying by check:

- Require two signatures on every check – no exceptions, because exceptions become the rule.

- Ensure clear backup documentation for every check attached to check *prior to signing*.

- Eliminate the use of "emergency" manual checks if on a computerized accounting system.

- Ensure that the person(s) creating accounts payable checks does not sign them.

- Check signers should not be related to each other, should not be two staff members and should probably not be the Senior Pastor. As often as possible, have at least one check signer to sign most of the checks so they can check for trends and other issues.

- Never, ever, sign blank checks in advance.

- Do not allow use of debit cards to access church funds. There is typically little protection from the bank in the event of theft, they are easily abused, and it is difficult to accurately track cash balances when using them in a ministry setting.

- Voided checks should be kept on file.

With the rise of online paying of bills from our computers and even our phones, some groups may not use that many checks. EFT's (Electronic Fund Transfers) still need good controls and most of the above pointers are still valid but will take a bit more work. Before a bill is paid online, make sure that two people are aware of it, and someone with the authority to do so has approved it. E-mail works well for this process, but it is easier to forge, which is a risk. Print out a hard copy of both the invoice paid and the approval to avoid any future problems and to leave a clear trail for anyone who needs to see the transaction at a later date.

We will discuss large expenditures such as capital improvements in a latter chapter. For now, it is wise to make sure that large disbursements are properly documented and approved by the governing body, and this is especially true in tight cash situations.

Payroll

After paying for a place to meet, the utilities to keep it comfortable, and the necessary supplies to keep it running, payroll is often the next big issue. Since most pastors are the first employees hired, let's look at how to pay them properly.

Ordained or licensed clergy are often misunderstood employment classifications. This section is intended to help clarify the unique nature of clergy employment status and give practical advice on the handling of payroll taxes. In addition, there are several articles in the Treasure Chest section discussing these issues that will provide additional insights.

By IRS mandate, legally ordained and/or licensed clergy (hereafter referred to as "clergy") are required to be "dual" status tax filers. This means that clergy are treated as employees for benefit purposes (health insurance, retirement plans, etc) and self-employed for taxation purposes.

The pastor's compensation package will typically consist of a base salary, a designated housing allowance, (regardless of whether the pastor owns or rents their home, or is provided a parsonage) and a combination of benefits. These may include medical insurance, auto allowance, conference and book allowances, a retirement plan, and perhaps some other allowances like phone, entertainment and travel.

Wise planning on how to classify the parts of the salary package can make a significant difference when it is time to pay income taxes. Consulting a tax advisor is a smart step; just make sure the advisor is familiar with the specifics of clergy taxation.

Housing Allowance

The housing allowance is a wonderful, often underused tax shelter for pastors. Clergy are currently eligible to have their expenses related to their living quarters separated from their salary, and if justified with actual receipts, they are allowed to reduce their taxable wages for federal and state income tax calculations.

It is important that receipts are kept and only items that are related to the upkeep of the home are included. However, a great deal of deductions is lost every year due to poor recordkeeping. A good habit to develop is assuring that all qualified housing receipts are immediately marked after the purchase and kept together for easy access when tax time rolls around.

Remember that any expenses related to the house are included in this exemption. Some are obvious, like the house payment, utilities, furnishings, and such, but others are often overlooked such as maintenance, repairs, insurance, cleaning supplies, lawn care, closing costs, and even refinancing expenses. A little bit of extra work during the year in receipt keeping can yield excellent deductions during the tax season. (See the Resource Section for a sample housing allowance worksheet.)

The amount designated as housing allowance must be declared no later than December 31 of the year *prior* to the year for which it is being declared and must be confirmed, accepted, and otherwise legally approved by the church or its governing board and must appear in the minutes of an official meeting. Once declared, the housing allowance cannot be adjusted unless:

- A new job with a different qualifying organization is accepted

- Actual monthly expenses change significantly (i.e., new house with a larger payment). At that point, only the difference of the new and old housing monthly expenses can be claimed for the remaining months. No other makeup amounts may be included in the change.

Pastoral Payroll Taxes

Another confusing pastoral payroll topic involves the FICA tax. Since pastors are considered self employed, the rules are different than a typical employee.

During the first two years of employment as a clergy (by the filing of their second tax return where they earned at least $400 of ministry income) they have the right to "opt out" of the Social Security System if they can morally sign an agreement that they have "religious beliefs that prevent you from accepting government benefits from taxes paid into a government system from compensation received from a church." Most people attempt to make this decision based on the investment worthiness of the Social Security System. In reality, it has nothing to do with rate of returns or benefits, but rather must be driven by a religious objection.

If a pastor has chosen to opt out of the Social Security System, then they will not be responsible for paying in the self-employment

FICA payments equal to 15.3% of the salary and housing allowance. (Current rates subject to change) Clergy must also understand that unless they have worked enough to qualify for Social Security coverage, (generally estimated to be the equivalent of 4 calendar quarters earning a minimum of approximately $1,120 per "credit" or $4,480 to get the maximum 4 credits/year for ten years) they and their family will not receive retirement, disability or supplemental death payments. (If a spouse has earned enough credits, then they and the children may be eligible to receive benefits from any change in their health or life status.)

If they choose to stay in the social security system, then they will be responsible for paying 15.3% of their combined salary and housing allowance.

The IRS requires quarterly payments (that do not match the calendar quarters) or clergy have the option of taking out extra federal withholding tax from their paychecks to compensate for the amount owed for social security.

The self-employed social security tax is broken down into two parts OASDI — Old Age Survivors Disability Insurance and Medicare. Current rates are 12.4% for OASDI and 2.9% for Medicare.

In addition, OASDI is no longer deducted after you reach the annual limit; see IRS website for current level. Medicare has no limits.

The IRS does not require that federal income tax withholding be deducted from clergy's paychecks, and this can come as a shock to many pastors. Clergy are still responsible for paying federal income tax on their base salary, but actual liability will depend on marital status, total household income, deductions for interest payments on their home if they own it, the number of dependent children, and other tax deductions and tax credits allowed by federal income tax laws.

There are two options for paying in estimated federal withholding income tax; however, the church and pastor may agree to withhold tax from their paycheck, or the pastor may pay into the government quarterly in the same manner as they pay the FICA tax. In fact, both the federal tax and FICA will be added together to determine the actual tax owed by the pastor as they work their way through the 1040 tax form.

Just a word of caution here about taxes. Most tax preparers are not familiar with the details regarding pastoral income tax. When considering hiring someone to assist in the preparation of your tax return, make sure they understand the tax laws that are specific to pastors. Failure to do so can result in unnecessary fines and shortchange yourself in deductions.

State income tax withholding is also based on salary. Actual liability owed is computed in a similar manner as federal income tax, just at a lesser rate. Check with your state website for up-to-date information and payment requirements, as they differ from state to state. Like the federal tax, payment can be made through the regular payroll check withholding or through quarterly payments.

Before We Move On

One issue that often arises regarding a pastor's compensation packages and the payment of FICA tax (Social Security) is fairness. The following is an attempt to clarify the decision-making criteria that churches may want to consider when formulating pastor's compensation packages.

The standard we recommend when formulating the pastor's compensation is to be certain that there is a level playing field among all church staff. When paying custodians, secretaries, and other non-ordained staff, the church treats those people as "regular" employees. FICA tax of 7.65% is deducted from their paychecks, and the church is then required to match 7.65% and pay that in to the federal government with what was deducted from the employee's check. (We will discuss non-clergy payroll issues shortly.)

Ordained pastors are considered "dual status" employees. They are employees for benefits purposes and self-employed for taxation purposes. We believe that the special status should not alter the amount of compensation. We further believe pastors, regardless of what they choose to do with their retirement or benefits, should be compensated on an equal basis, just like all other employees.

Although the church is not permitted to directly pay in matching FICA funds for pastors, they should be given the matching amount, just as all other employees are receiving through the mandatory matching FICA that the church pays on behalf of the employee. This would equate to a pastor receiving 7.65% of their salary and housing, as added compensation to his/her paycheck. It will be considered taxable income, but it should not be considered a part of their wage package unless the employer FICA contribution is considered a part of a Secretary's or Custodians' compensation package. The church is simply giving matching FICA tax directly to the pastor instead of to the government. At this point, all staff would be treated equally. If the church opts to do this, giving these amounts around the same time the quarterly payment is due works very well for the pastor.

Another commonly held opinion is that if a pastor elects, for religious objection reasons, to opt out of the Social Security system, then why should the church have to give them the 7.65%?

Again, we believe that what a pastor chooses to do with their personal finances is not related to the decision of treating employees equally. The pastor, after receiving equal compensation, is then responsible for providing benefits and retirement income for his/her family. If they choose, for religious reasons, not to participate in the Social Security system, then it is still their responsibility to find and implement benefits and retirement income for themselves and/or their family. This decision should not impact how the church compensates them.

Other Employee's Payroll

After the pastor(s) is (are) hired, a church will often begin to expand the staff with support people. While pastors are subject to a unique tax situation, non-clergy are not.

For non-clergy these questions regularly arise — "Are not-for-profits required to pay over-time?" "Can we make all employees salaried?" or "Are we subject to the Federal wage and hour laws?

Federal wage and hour guidelines govern and enforce wage and hour laws. While some may argue that in order to be governed by the federal wage and hour laws you must be "involved in interstate commerce," we contend that every organization is bound by these laws because every organization has at some point made a long distance phone call, made a purchase on the internet, or traveled across state lines to attend a conference.

We recommend that organizations review all payroll and personnel procedures to ensure compliance with Federal Wage and hour regulations as listed below. There are two categories of employees — exempt and non-exempt, and the primary issues involve how to administrate overtime pay and compensatory time off.

Exempt from Overtime Employees

These employees must pass three tests to be considered exempt from overtime pay:

- Salary level test – employee must be paid at least $23,600 per year (this is not required for doctors, lawyers, or school teachers)

- Salary basis test – employee must be paid a guaranteed minimum amount in any work week in which any work is performed

- Duties test – based on actual job tasks rather than just job title

The duties test can be broken down three ways:

- Executive job duties: regularly supervises at least 2 FTE (full time equivalent employees), management is the primary duty of the position

- Professional job duties: learned professions that generally require an advanced degree such as doctors, architects, clergy, teachers, nurses, accountants, etc.

- Administrative job duties: high level office & non-manual positions that are directly related to management or general business operations, the primary component of which involves high-level decision making (policy maker). Secretaries, clerks, or administrative assistants do not qualify.

If the employee passes these tests, then they are exempt and generally do not receive overtime pay unless the employer opts to pay overtime.

Regarding compensatory time for exempt staff, this can be administered at the discretion of management. There are no regulations governing the schedules of exempt employees. However, documentation is always a good idea so that the employee and the Organization can be prepared for any questions that may arise in regard to this issue.

Non-Exempt from Overtime Employees

Employees are automatically classified as non-exempt unless they meet the above criteria.

Regulations require that non-exempt employees be paid 1.5 times their regular hourly rate for any hours worked over 40 in the standard work week. The overtime only applies to actual hours worked. If a sick day, holiday, or vacation day is taken in the week, then all hours worked under 40 will still be paid on a straight time basis. For example, an employee is scheduled to work 8 hours per day, Monday through Friday. A paid holiday falls on Monday, and he works 10 hours Tuesday, and 8 hours Wednesday, Thursday, and Friday. Although the employee worked an additional 2 hours on Tuesday, the total hours worked during the week is only 34. He would receive 8 hours holiday pay (if applicable) and 34 hours of regular pay.

Compensatory time for non-exempt staff is legal only if it is taken within the same work week. All other forms of bonuses, extra time off, or any other arrangements or plans in lieu of overtime pay, documented or undocumented, are illegal for non-exempt employees.

We also recommend the following in regard to Federal Wage and Hour regulations:

- Document the regulations in your human resource policies in general, and specifically reflect the current wage and hour regulations regarding exempt and non-exempt personnel.

- Train the staff on the implications of conforming to the laws.

- Implement two levels of record keeping:

  - Exempt semi-monthly exception time sheet: This is a very simple form that allows exempt personnel to record any exceptions they had in their work schedule on a semimonthly basis. It would include space to record sick time, vacations, funeral leave, and holidays. It would also provide a place to accurately record additions and subtractions from comp-time. This adds accountability without oppressive controls.

  - Non-exempt weekly time sheet: This simple form allows non-exempt staff members to accurately record their actual work hours for the week. It also allows them to write in vacation, sick time, funeral leave, and holidays for accurate payroll processing.

Reimbursement Plans

We have looked at some of the issues surrounding payroll, the uniqueness of pastor's pay packages, and overtime pay. Most ministries will also provide a reimbursement plan for their clergy and support staff, and the IRS has some requirements that you need to know.

Accountable reimbursement plans are a means by which an organization can legally reimburse employees for business related expenses while eliminating any IRS reporting or employee taxation.

Per IRS guidelines, an accountable reimbursement plan must meet the following requirements:

- There must be a business purpose for the expenses.

- There must be a proper substantiation of expenses to the employer.

- There must be a proper handling return of any unused, excess reimbursements.

If these guidelines are not strictly followed, reimbursements are to be counted as income to the reimbursed person. (See the sample reimbursement plan in the resource section.)

In addition to the above conditions, these points must be taken into consideration:

- The church must budget funds for the accountable reimbursement plan. The budgeted funds cannot come from or be included in an employee's salary package. Funds should be budgeted just like any other church expense, such as utilities or maintenance expenditures.

- The plan should be written and must be church-approved, but the plan does not have to be voted on by the church. If the church's governance empowers the finance committee or executive staff to make the determination of budgeted funds for the accountable reimbursement plan, then this is acceptable to the IRS.

- The accountable reimbursement plan is a "use it or lose it" process. If the employee does not use the entire budget line item designated for reimbursement, he cannot receive the overage.

- The substantiation of expenses and the return of excess reimbursements must be handled within a reasonable time as defined below:
    1) An advance can be made within 30 days of when an expense is paid or incurred.
    2) The employee must provide the church with a receipt and written explanation within 60 days of incurring the expense.
    3) Any excess amount is to be returned to the church within 120 days after the expense is paid or incurred.

- Original receipts are required for all expenditures over $75. If a receipt is not provided, the reimbursement becomes taxable income.

- The receipt plus written explanation should document the amount, date, place (for transportation, travel, and entertainment expenses), business purpose and, for entertainment expenses, the business relationship of the person(s) entertained. For business mileage reimbursements, this means an itemized log that details the above for each separate trip.

- The committee or staff overseeing the plan has the right to determine if a receipt presented for reimbursement is an acceptable church-related business expense for reimbursement.

- The church should not report any expenses reimbursed properly under an accountable reimbursement plan as taxable income on the employee's W-2. However, all advances and/or reimbursements without timely or adequate documentation should be added to the employee's W-2 as wages in box 1. We recommend allowing this only on an infrequent basis as allowing for reimbursement outside of the plan requirements may cause all other reimbursements to be considered unaccountable by the IRS as well.

What Can Be Reimbursed?

The church can agree to reimburse reasonable church-related business expenses such as the following:

- Conventions, conferences, seminars, and other workshop fees or costs. If the continuing education event furthers the employee's learning for their current position, and the educational event does not qualify the employee for a new position, then the church can reimburse the employee for associated costs.

- Church-related business travel. The IRS allows the church to reimburse its employees the IRS standard mileage rate plus parking fees and tolls for business miles driven for church-related purposes. The IRS does not allow a church to reimburse for commuting miles from home to the church no matter how many times the employee goes back and forth each day. Also, the church can reimburse meals its staff incurs if the required travel takes the employee away from the church field during meal times. Individual meals are heavily scrutinized by the IRS and should be infrequent in occurrence.

- Costs associated with church-related, business, overnight trips. The church can reimburse its employees for lodging, meals, and other costs associated with overnight church-related business travel.

- Subscriptions, books, tapes, CDs, DVDs, equipment, and other similar tools. Sermon resources and other educational materials can be reimbursed by the church if the resource has a church-related business connection. Likewise, the church can pay for church-related business equipment like PDAs and computers. Any equipment purchased is the property of the church and should be retained by the church if the employee leaves or is terminated.

- Hospitality expenses required by the church to entertain others. The church can reimburse its employee's expenses associated with providing a business meal for individuals like prospects or church members if the meal had a clearly identified church-related purpose.

Automobiles for Clergy

Many churches grapple with providing transportation for their pastor(s). The following is an attempt to clarify the basic tax laws regarding three potential methods for handling the use and/or lease of automobiles.

Option 1: Mileage Reimbursement (Recommended)

For the year 2014, the IRS has issued the mileage reimbursement rate of 56 cents per mile. This means that if the church establishes a mileage reimbursement policy for when church staff use their personal vehicles for church business, the maximum reimbursement rate is 56 cents per mile. While many churches choose to reimburse at a lesser rate, it would appear to be prudent to use the government standard, so as to avoid issues of people feeling used and/or abused for Kingdom service or, in extreme cases, encouraging people to inflate their actual mileage to compensate for lower reimbursement rates.

The IRS requires that a mileage record be kept of all reimbursed miles. The record must be kept for audit purposes for at least five years either by the church or by the individual. We recommend that the church retain the mileage records for backup to the reimbursement check issued. The mileage record should include the destination location, date of travel, purpose for the travel, and actual miles driven. The IRS further stipulates that mileage between home and the church is not reimbursable. They consider that mileage a part of the normal employment process.

If a person leaves from home to go to a church function or appointment, then drives to the church office following the appointment, only the difference in total mileage of the trip minus the mileage going from home to the church is reimbursable. Example: Normal distance from home to the church is 10 miles. You leave from home to go to the hospital and then on to the church, for a total of 15 miles. Only the difference (15 miles minus the normal 10), or 5 miles is reimbursable.

In addition, all documented mileage reimbursements that are at or below the IRS issued rate are not taxable. They are not reported on 1099 or W-2 documents.

This method is the cleanest and most accountable manner in which to handle mileage, and it protects the church in case of an IRS audit.

Option 2: Auto Allowance

The church can provide an auto allowance that can be used for a lease and/or a purchase of an automobile, and/or the pastor can use their own personal vehicle and use the funds for direct reimbursement of fuel, maintenance, and/or insurance. Exact records must be kept.

The auto allowance can be justified by keeping the same mileage log as referred to in option 1. If the total miles times the current government rate is equal to, or exceeds, the auto allowance, then the allowance is considered justified and is considered non-taxable. If however the mileage method is used and the amount of allowance is greater than the actual miles driven, then the excess portion of the allowance must be counted as taxable income.

Because the IRS guards against "non-taxable" compensation, the record keeping is extensive for the allowance approach. Basically, all the direct expenses for the automobile must equal or exceed the auto allowance, or the residual automatically becomes reportable, taxable wages. In addition, whatever percentage of mileage that is driven for personal use must be recorded and deducted from the expenses that offset the allowance. If audited, without impeccable record keeping, the IRS will review other vehicles owned, total miles driven, lifestyle, etc., and rule on what percentage of personal miles they believe is reasonable.

While the idea of an auto allowance sounds appealing, we do not recommend this approach because of the complexity of laws and record keeping required.

Option 3: Automobiles Provided by the Church

The church can purchase and/or give a donated automobile to a staff member if they wish. In either case, if the title of the auto transfers to the staff member, the fair market value of the auto becomes taxable wages for that individual in the year the title is transferred. At that point, the auto is owned and operated by the staff member as if they had purchased the auto themselves.

The church can lease an auto for a staff member, make the lease payments, and cover the cost of insurance and fuel if they wish. Records must then be kept of what percentage of the miles driven is for personal use. Whatever the percentage of personal use amounts to, it must then be used to calculate taxable wages. Example: If the total of the lease payments, fuel, and insurance is $5,000.00 in a year and the records indicate 20% personal mileage, then $1,000.00 of taxable wages must be added to the staff member's 1099 or W-2.

If the church allows a staff member to use a church owned automobile, then policies and corresponding record keeping will need to be established governing the use of the auto and who pays for what. Once again, the IRS will be looking for taxable wages to be calculated for any personal mileage used.

A good accountable system of recordkeeping should be in place to satisfy IRS regulations and to reduce the chances of abusing the auto policy for personal usage.

While this is a viable option, we believe this option has too many complexities and risks and would highly recommend using option one.

1099 Issues

The final issue we will address in this chapter is how to properly deal with 1099's. A great deal of confusion circles around the usage of these forms, and this section will help bring clarity.

Many churches like to classify people as independent contractors to avoid paying the employer side of social security tax, reduce payroll processing expenses, or save the church money on worker's compensation insurance. The IRS has stringent requirements for classifying workers as independent contractors. Many positions that churches often misclassify as independent contractors include custodians, nursery workers, sound technicians, musicians, and substitute workers. The following is an attempt to clarify the issues.

In order for a person to work at a church legally as an independent contractor, we believe it is prudent to consider the following guidelines:

- The church cannot substantially direct the person's duties; the church can only give them overall tasks to complete.

- The church cannot control or set their hours that they work.

- Since their "company" provides the service, they can send anyone to do the job.

- They cannot have an office at the church that is their primary office.

- It cannot be their only source of income.

- The church needs to have a written contract in place including cost, delivery of Services, duration (i.e. six months, one year, etc.) and a termination clause.

- They cannot participate in any employee benefits plans (insurance, retirement plans, etc).

- The contractor must provide annual proof of worker's comp and liability insurance naming the church as additionally insured or the church could be held liable in the event of a claim.

- The church must issue a 1099 at the end of the year for all contract wages paid if the total amount for the year exceeds $600.00 to one contractor. We strongly recommend that no payments are made until an accurate and fully completed W-9 is completed by the contractor and on file at the church.

Given these requirements, many workers such as those in the nursery, kitchens, and other service areas are not 1099 contractors, but employees.

Regarding interim pastors, there is disagreement over whether they should receive a W-2 or 1099. Factors such as length of service, who supervises them, and whether they are a contractor, come into play in the decision on how to report their salary. For the best practice we recommend always using the W-2 to report salaries, but seeking tax and legal counsel would be wise to avoid any future IRS issues.

While there are advantages to the church to pay independent contractors who regularly work for the church such as avoiding the need to pay the employer's part of the FICA tax and the ease of terminating their services, we would recommend against their regular use.

We recommend against the use of independent contractors (that regularly work at the church) because we believe it can create the following problems for the church:

- Less control over the position

- Leaves the church open to an IRS challenge, which the church only has a 50/50 chance of defending, not to mention the cost and hassle of litigation

- In the event of insurance claims, the church may encounter issues with worker's compensation coverage or liability insurance coverage such as sexual misconduct, etc.

- The church is open to contract disputes with the independent contractor

- Based on how the individual/company is filing their taxes, it could bring an unwanted tax audit to the church

Our conclusion is that we do not see enough cost-saving advantages for the church to move in this direction. It also creates unnecessary red flags for the IRS. The other looming question is, why is this such an important issue for such a small incremental (if any) tax break for the individual? Because the independent contractor will have to pay employer FICA, we don't see any large tax advantage for this shift. They can claim mileage and some home office expense (maybe), but it just does not amount to enough to place the church at risk.

Here are some detailed guidelines regarding the usage of 1099's and this information below is intended to provide general guidelines for the Form 1099-MISC.

The IRS has several versions of the Form 1099 depending on each form's individual purpose. The one most commonly used is the 1099-MISC. The IRS requires all businesses and non-profit organizations, including churches, to use this form to report specific kinds of taxable income paid to individuals and unincorporated entities.

The second most common 1099 form is Form 1099-INT, which is used primarily to report the payment of interest to unincorporated entities and individuals. The guidelines discussed here relate to the Form 1099-MISC.

An "unincorporated entity" typically includes sole proprietors, partnerships, and most limited liability companies. Often times, an incorporated entity will have "Inc." following the name of the company. Most corporations receiving payment for services are not required to receive a Form 1099-MISC.

Who Should Receive a 1099-MISC?

- Individuals and unincorporated entities who are not treated or hired as employees, but are paid to perform services ("services" include the performance of any action or labor that brings value or benefit to an individual or entity)

- Individuals and unincorporated entities paid $600 or more in a calendar year for their services

- Individuals and unincorporated entities receiving rent or lease payments – for the rental of real property and equipment.

In all cases, a valid name, address, and Social Security Number (SSN) or a Federal Employer Identification Number (FEIN) of the person or entity receiving payment is required for the completion of the Form 1099-MISC. Because of this, payments made for services or rent should not be made without first obtaining this information. The IRS recommends the use of the Form W-9 to obtain the required information of a person or unincorporated entity receiving payment for services and rent. The IRS requires back-up withholding of 28% on any payments if a W-9 is not collected before the payment is made.

Assuming the requirements for receiving a 1099-MISC are met, the circumstances in which a Form 1099-MISC may or may not be required include, but are not limited to the following:

Type of Payment	1099 Required?	Explanation
A *love gift* or offering paid to a person whether the funds originated from the members of a church or the church itself	Maybe	If a love gift or offering is collected and then given to a person already being paid as employee, the payment <u>must</u> be included in the employee's W-2 salary. If the recipient is not (or should not) be paid as an employee, a 1099-MISC must be issued to the recipient.
Gifts to missionaries	Maybe	If the gift is paid directly to the missionary in his/her name, then a 1099 is absolutely required. If the gift is funneled through a sponsoring organization and the check is made out to the sponsoring organization, then the sponsoring organization is responsible for IRS reporting.
Benevolent gifts	Maybe	Benevolent gifts to non-employees are not taxable and a recipient should not receive a 1099. If the recipient is an employee, the amount must be added to their W-2 salary regardless of whether services were performed or it was simply a benevolent gift.
Payments to U.S. citizens for services performed outside the U.S.	Yes	U.S. citizens receiving payment for non-employee services performed outside the U.S. must be given a 1099-MISC. These payments could also be subject to additional IRS

		regulations.
Payments to a limited liability company (LLC)	Yes	In most cases, LLC's are taxed as a partnership, which means they are required to receive a 1099 for payment of services. Because it can be difficult to know how an LLC is taxed, it is usually best to issue a 1099 to an LLC.
Rent or lease payments	Maybe	For real estate and personal property – unless it was a benevolent payment to a person in need, or on behalf of a person in need.
Prizes and Awards	Maybe	Prizes and Awards for $600.00 or more that are not for services performed. If it's a non-cash prize, the Fair Market Value must be reported. Prizes and Awards given to employees must be reported on a W-2.

Who Should Not Receive a 1099-MISC?

- Individuals paid as an employee should rarely, if ever, receive a 1099-MISC; these payments should be included in their W-2 salary
- Incorporated entities, unless the payment is for medical or healthcare services or attorney fees
- Recipients of less than $600 in a calendar year
- Recipients of payments for the purchase of products
- Non-employee recipients of a benevolence payment.

As long as accurate information is reported, it is rarely a problem to send a 1099 to a recipient even if it is not required.

There are often exceptions and gray areas to most IRS regulations. If there is a question about a specific situation not fully described above, please consult with a tax or accounting professional.

Summary

We do not expect you to grasp all the minute details of the tax code, payroll issues, or to become an expert in using 1099's, but you must be aware of the issues involved to avoid future problems.

Before we move into budgeting and reporting (everyone's favorite subjects) let's pause a moment and reflect on what we covered.

Questions to Ponder

1. After reading this chapter, how are you doing in the areas of check signing, document backup, approval systems, and spending controls? What could be improved?

2. Considering your pay package, would you now change anything? Are you keeping track of the receipts for the housing allowance and any reimbursable items?

3. Are you handling the employees of the church in the proper fashion? Overtime and compensation issues?

4. The 1099 requirements are complex, but are there any issues you need to deal with regarding their usage in your church? How about contractors? Any changes needed?

5. What procedures could be changed, enhanced, or strengthened to improve the financial integrity of your ministry?

11 Staying Accountable to the Owner:
How to Properly Budget and Report the Finances of the Church

Now, where did all that money go to?

As noted in the introduction, the pastor is the helmsman, not the Captain, nor does he own the ship. However, the church received donations and then spent them. Someone, somewhere, and probably several people will want to know how we spent the money. Regardless of your church leadership structure, reporting spending is critical to maintaining integrity. In addition, planning on how to spend the money, while not overly exciting, is a very necessary step.

Reporting and budgeting are not flashy, can seem tedious, and can feel like a waste of time. Most pastors would rather do anything than sit through another budget meeting. However, without a map, compass, and a frequent check on our direction, we can steer the ship into a mess or simply wander around aimlessly. It does not take much to get off course, and these two tools will assist us in accomplishing what we believe we should.

Budgeting is telling our money where to go instead of wondering where it went. Reporting gives us a snapshot at how we are doing in accomplishing our vision and goals. Both of these tools are critical to the success of the ministry, so let's start with budgeting. After grasping the basics of this process, we can then report to others how we spent what we planned to in our budget.

Budgeting

The word probably irritates you, and you are only reading this section because you have to. We hope to change your mind about budgeting in this section. Budgeting can be freeing, encouraging, uplifting, and even fun. Well, perhaps not overly fun, but after you are finished with this section, you may agree that budgeting is necessary and even helpful.

As we discussed in the vision chapter, budgeting should be used to enhance, filter, and guide your financial decisions. How we spend the money given to the church should have a direct tie into the vision God has given. If it doesn't, then perhaps the spending needs to be reevaluated. All budget processes should be bathed in prayer asking for the Lord's blessing, unity, and direction. One can never pray too much over the topic of money.

There are multiple ways to approach the topic of budgeting. Methods abound and so do acronyms. Let's just list a few with some of their advantages and disadvantages.

This first one is not really an acronym, but is very a common approach in many small to medium churches.

NADA – No Budget

Advantages
- Simple. No time investment, no accountability.
- Just spend money as it comes in.

Disadvantages
- Lacks a plan to measure results. Lacking in accountability and credibility.
- Does not focus resources toward meeting the vision of the organization/ministry.

LYPI – Last Year Plus Inflation

Advantages
- Low key, doesn't require a lot of thought, less political, less arguing, simple, quick and easy.

Disadvantages
- Lacks leadership, does not address the changing needs of the ministry, does not strategically seek to enhance the vision/mission/goals and objectives of the organization/ministry, and does not address dying or dead branches of ministry, thereby allowing them to continue indefinitely.

ETAEC – Everyone Takes An Equal Cut

Advantages
- Low key, doesn't require a lot of thought, less political, less arguing, simple, quick and easy.
- Touts of being "fair" to everyone and treating everyone equally. As if "equally" = "fair".

Disadvantages
- Lacks leadership, does not address the changing needs of the ministry, does not strategically seek to enhance the vision/mission/goals and objectives of the organization/ministry, does not address dying or dead branches of ministry, allowing them to continue indefinitely.

- It also does not reward those who have been good stewards, nor does it bring correction to those who have been poor stewards.

WYASLYP – What You Actually Spent Last Year Plus

Advantages
- Easy, simple, less time consuming than other approaches, and is based on actual expenditures, the only real manner to judge "real" needs.

Disadvantages
- Lacks leadership, does not address the changing needs of the ministry, does not strategically seek to enhance the vision/mission/goals and objectives of the organization/ministry, and does not address dying or dead branches of ministry, allowing them to continue indefinitely.
- It also does not reward those who have been good stewards, nor does it bring correction to those who have been poor stewards.

As you can see, there are multiple ways to plan a budget and many of these are used in the Church. While they may get you to where you want to go, we believe that there is a better way — a more team building, vision-enhancing, goal-accomplishing, and effective way.

It is an undeniable fact, that where we place our time and money is a direct reflection of where our heart is. While this may cause some to disagree, simply check your personal day timer and your checkbook, and see if it does not clearly define what you value the most!

Organization/ministries are no different. We make claims to be about this or that, but what do our budget and programs tell us? If we say our organization/ministry is about evangelism, and the annual budget for evangelism is $100.00, and we hear one sermon a year on witnessing, it appears we are not being totally honest with ourselves.

But how do we wrestle this difficult, sometimes political, territorial process of budgeting into a process of aligning and mobilizing financial resources to meet the vision, mission, goals, and objectives of the organization/ministry? Glad you asked.

SOAR - Strategic Organizational Alignment of Resources

Advantages

- The entire process focuses on strategically aligning resources with the vision of the organization/ministry. It further focuses and allocates resources based on needs related to meeting the specific goals and objectives which are in direct support of the vision of the organization/ministry. It can be less political in that the focus is on vision, not individuals or territories.

- It annually adapts to the changing needs of the ministry. It is flexible and growth oriented. It can also measure the effectiveness of those requesting budget funds in that they will be held accountable for meeting the goals they purport with the funds they have requested. Accountability through alignment.

Disadvantages

- It takes more time than any other model. It forces people to examine their respective goals and budgets and can damage egos in the process.

Before implementing a budget, every church must grasp its vision and mission, and it should have a set of goals in place to achieve what God has called it to do. Budgets provided the blueprint to help accomplish the vision.

Pastoral Helmsmanship

The pastor, leadership team, volunteers, and the people in the seats need to understand what the vision is for the church. "Where are we going?" type questions must be answered. If there is no vision and end goal in mind, how will anyone know if you are making progress towards its completion? More importantly, how will people be able to help or buy into the vision if there isn't one?

We need to understand that God is the source of the vision of our organization/ministry. God may choose to use us to lead and/or communicate that vision, but it must be God's vision. Too often our own vain imaginations and personal desires cloud the skies above us and hinder us from seeing God's heavenly vision.

While exact methods vary from organization/ministry to organization/ministry, finding and discerning the vision is usually a long-term *(3-12 months)* process that includes:

- Extensive individual prayer and quiet time for leader or leaders
- Regular corporate prayer time
- Broad spectrum of leadership and congregational input
- A self-examination process by which the organization/ministry comes to grips with the resources God has blessed them with and what God has not blessed them with.

After gaining insight into the vision, the leader, along with the rest of the leadership, must communicate the vision to those who follow. How do we do that?

- Say it early and say it often
- Create the vision in an easy to remember format
- Adjust the verbiage as necessary for clarification and impact
- Use as many forms of media as possible: written, video, spoken, posters, banners, bulletin boards, testimonies, pins, coffee mugs, pens, etc.

- Use creative redundancy, *(saying the same thing again only in a different manner* ☺*)*

A significant part of the SOAR (Strategic Organizational Alignment of Resources) budgeting method involves goal setting to accomplish the vision. Having a vision and mission statement is good, but not enough. Involving leadership and communicating to those in the church is necessary, but that is still not enough. A critical component of accomplishing the vision through the leadership and church members is goal setting.

Goals

One acronym that is common when discussing goals is the SMART one. Simply put, if we are to have effective goals, we need to incorporate the following into them regardless of their time frame:

- **Specific:** Goals should be clear and understandable by those who are charged with the responsibilities of carrying them out. (This usually means that they are in written form.)
- **Measurable:** When met, those involved should easily know and understand they have achieved success.
- **Attainable:** Goals should be realistically within the reach of those who are attempting to reach them.
- **Relevant:** Ensure that ALL goals support the Vision/Mission of the ministry.
- **Time-Bound:** Effective goals have realistic and specific timetables attached to them.

SMART goals are typically broken down into three groupings based on a time horizon. These are presented not as a law, but as a guideline.

Pastoral Helmsmanship

Near-Term Goals – *(6-12 months) or the coming year*

These goals are the ones that most like to focus on. The gratification of completion can be seen and felt. The departmental or ministry leaders are normally responsible for generating, managing and implementing short term goals in a larger church, and the pastor with other lay leadership in a smaller church. These type goals could include:

- Attending a conference
- Increasing attendance in Sunday School
- Teaching through a book of the Bible
- Expanding ministry through lay leadership

Intermediate Term Goals – *(1-3 years)*

These type goals could include:

- Additional staff being hired
- Expansion of city-wide ministry
- Missions/evangelism programs being implemented
- Financial goals
- Beginning a small group ministry

Long Range Goals – *(3-7 years)*

Long Range goals are good for those folks that are compelled to dream deep into the future. They also help provide a sense of long-term direction for the ministry. These goals might include:

- Future ministry expansion
- New programs
- New facilities
- New location

When goals are reached, they should be communicated and celebrated appropriately!

- To affirm/appreciate those who worked to achieve them
- To set up future goals for success

The goal setting process is just that, a process. It will probably not work perfectly the first time it is implemented. However, over several years of training, implementing and refining, the system can produce some amazing results.

After making sure the vision is in place and well communicated, the leadership is all on board and the membership understands where you are heading, once the goals have been established and prayerfully considered, it becomes time to fund it! Enter the budget.

Putting Numbers on the Page

Depending on the size of the church, those involved in the actual creation of the budget will vary. In a small church, the pastor, bookkeeper, perhaps the treasurer and some board members might participate. In larger, more department-oriented churches, each department head might submit a budget proposal.

Regardless of who is involved in the process of creating the budget under the SOAR model, it should reflect the overall vision of the church. Each church should have a vision and purpose for existing, and the budget must reflect them to properly use the resources for the most Kingdom benefit. This is not the time to push personal peeves or pet projects. This is the time to actually allocate the funds necessary to accomplish the God-given goals of the church. This is spiritual business!

There is always a limited amount of money chasing an unlimited amount of vision or goals. As those charged with being stewards of God's resources and specifically the money given to the ministry, seeking His will regarding the spending of those dollars is critical to the process.

Seeing the entire ministry through the prism of SOAR will help to assure that the money spent is well spent. Every department head, volunteer, and board member should desire that the budget reflects the individual church's vision and goals. The question to ask is:

How will these expenditures further the work of the Kingdom through our church?

The issue is not so much about the dollar amount as it is about accomplishing the goals and furthering the vision of the church. As each goal is evaluated through this perspective, the merit rests on the goal, and how they tie into the vision, not the dollar amount.

We have not talked about the approval process because this will vary from church to church. In a larger church, there may be committees involved, and in the smaller ones, perhaps only a couple of people. Some churches vote for adopting the annual budget, and in others, the leadership board does.

Regardless of how the final approval happens, the process of SOAR will greatly assist in making sure that the dollars spent are actually going towards accomplishing the vision.

In a larger church setting, appointing a SOAR leader is very helpful. This individual will meet with department heads, and other parties involved, reviewing and helping to assure that the budgets submitted are in line with the vision.

As the individual components of the budgets are submitted, goals can be reviewed. Questions can then be asked as to how these expenditures fit into the overarching vision of the church. If an objective is submitted that has nothing to do with the ministry-wide goals that have been communicated, then these can be reevaluated as to their appropriateness.

As the individual parts are considered, they can be placed into the bigger picture of the funds that are actually available. Leadership will ultimately determine what will be approved, but the SOAR process provides an excellent refining tool to assure that every budget reflects the overall goals.

Staying Accountable to the Owner

Every church has limited funds to spend. As projections are considered for the future, we all know these can change rapidly. Budgets are tools which provide guides to help keep us heading in the right direction. We prayerfully plan on how to spend the projected resources in the best possible way. Along the way, we realize that change may have to happen.

Finally, how do we even figure out how much money we are going to have to budget? The answer is, it depends. If you have history to take into consideration, then you probably have some idea of what has taken place in the past. Trends are available to get a general idea of what may happen in the future. For example, if over the last five years, the income has been around $350,000 per year, then unless something dramatic happens, it is probably safe to use that number again in your projections.

If trends point upward or downward, then the appropriate adjustments must be taken into account. Wishful thinking is not planning. Until there is some history, then it will be more difficult to project. Micromanagement may be required in the very early stages of ministry until some patterns become obvious.

Known factors must be considered and planned for. Expansions, staff additions or subtractions, and ministry enlargement or shrinking, all may have a major impact.

Known external factors should be processed in our thinking as well. A college town or a city with severe financial hardships might limit the growth potential. Conversely, a church in a high growth area might expect a steady increase in its membership.

Budgeting is an inexact science and therefore will never be perfect. However, not having a plan will almost certainly guarantee poorer stewardship than having one. Not aligning your resources with your vision, mission, and goals will certainly not help you be effective in completing them, but doing so will.

Don't forget that there are many SOAR forms available for you to use from the ICM website listed in the Resource Section of this book.

Reporting

We have collected money and planned on how we will spend it through the budgeting process; now we need to think about how to communicate this spending.

Opinions vary regarding who should know the ins and outs of the finances of a church. Some groups have regular business meetings that are open to everyone. Others have closed meetings where the budget and expenditures are discussed. There are, of course, pros and cons to both methods.

In open meetings, questions can be asked by those that donate, or in some cases, by those who do not give but still want to know. Providing open financial statements to the general congregation may be a good practice, or it may simply open up a major can of worms. Some churches have addressed this issue in their founding documents. Other churches need to decide who will see what, with how much detail, and when.

Given recent trends that many donors are not giving as much or as quickly to the church due to fraud, mismanagement of funds, and a general lack of trust toward the church, open financial records should be considered. Wisdom needs to be used in the formatting of any open documents. The details needed by the finance board or department head probably do not need to be seen by every member of the church. For example, it might be better to group salaries than list individual ones. However, each church will have to make that decision.

Regardless of who ultimately views the reports, there are standards that should be observed to assure financial accountability and proper oversight.

The money received will most likely be held in a bank and therefore, generate bank statements. In most churches there is no need for multiple bank accounts. A proper accounting system will allow whatever recording flexibility and fund segregation that is required.

Most banks and other financial institutions are insured for up to $250,000. If warranted, additional bank accounts may be needed for savings, money market accounts, and perhaps a building fund. The church should work diligently to consolidate all small bank accounts that are under the church's purview. Deacon's funds, Sunday school class funds, men's ministry, women's ministry, special missions etc. should all be under the church's accountable accounting system and not handled by individual persons or factions. This can become confusing very quickly and also allow a greater chance for fraud.

Each bank account will generate a monthly statement, and it should be reconciled promptly. This should be performed by someone not involved with the preparation or signing of the checks nor by the person making the deposits. By adding this step, if there are any alterations to the deposit made after it was counted or if there are any unusual checks paid, they can be caught quickly.

Account balances for all bank accounts and investment accounts should be reconciled monthly and match the financial statements.

There are two main methods used in accounting – Accrual and Cash Basis. In addition most churches will usually end up following a third method called Modified Cash Basis. While pastors do not need to become highly trained in these accounting procedures, some familiarity is helpful. It is important that the pastor and the leadership understand which method is being used.

ACCRUAL BASIS – income is reported in the fiscal period it is earned, regardless of when it is received, and expenses are deducted in the fiscal period they are incurred, whether they are paid or not.

CASH BASIS – revenues are recorded when cash is actually received and expenses are recorded when they are actually paid, no matter when they are invoiced.

MODIFIED CASH BASIS -This allows accounting transactions that actually happen during the calendar month be posted to that month, both income and expenses. However, modifications that make sense are made; for instance, fixed assets are recorded on the Statement of Financial Position, payroll withholding tax is shown as a liability even before it is paid, and credit card expenses incurred during the last month of the year can be shown in the current year's budget by posting the expenses to a payable account.

In order to help keep track of where the money is being spent, most churches will utilize some recordkeeping system. There are several available that operate on the computer, some are still manual, though these are tedious at best, and even some that are cloud based (on the internet.) In addition, an outside accounting service can be hired, thus providing professional oversight and even additional integrity to the accounting procedures.

Any system will need a general ledger that consists of account names and numbers. A chart of accounts that is specific to your ministry is usually developed, and then every expense is assigned a number so it can be easily tracked. (See the resource section for an example.)

The two primary documents that are viewed monthly, or should be, are the Statement of Financial Condition (also commonly known as the Balance Sheet) and the Statement of Financial Activities (also known as the Income Statement, Profit and Loss, P&L, or Budget Comparison)

To be of any real value, accurate, balanced financial statements should be prepared and distributed to those responsible to review them no later than the 15th-20th of the next month. The finance team, financial board, and/or church leadership team should review these statements monthly.

This snapshot of the church's current financial condition will provide useful information and prompt questions such as:

- How much cash is on hand?
- Are there any unusual expenses?
- How do the actual expenses compare to the projected ones in the budget?
- Are there trends we need to be made aware of?

The purpose of reports is to help provide meaningful data in a timely fashion. The object is not to be overwhelming with details or information. Design the reports, which are based on your chart of account breakdowns, to be meaningful to you and your leaders. Too much data is almost as bad as too little.

The financial statements are tools that are used to see how the church is doing in implementing the vision and goals. If the reports are not helping, change them to where they do provide the information needed.

Finally, no matter the size of the church, an independent review of financial reporting, policies, and procedures should be done annually by a qualified person or committee. Invest the necessary funds for a qualified accounting or bookkeeping firm or outside CPA firm that specializes in working with churches and/or ministries. If funds are not available, consider swapping services with another church.

Spending the money donated to the Church is both a privilege and responsibility. Multiple people have entrusted their giving into your hands in order to help you fulfill the God-given vision that you communicated to them. Maintaining integrity is essential, for once that trust is violated, it is extremely difficult to reacquire. For medium to large churches, membership in the ECFA (Evangelical Council for Financial Accountability) might well be worth the investment to secure.

By doing the tedious work of budgeting and preparing financial records, that trust you worked so hard to receive can be kept. Budgets help to assure that spending of the money is being planned carefully according to the vision of the church and that the reports confirm it.

Questions to Ponder

1. What do we need to do differently with our budgets after reading this chapter?

2. How would you implement the SOAR method of planning in your church?

3. How can you assure that your current expenditures are reflecting your vision? What changes do you need to make?

4. How could the financially oriented meetings you have be more helpful and productive?

5. How could the reports you currently use be more helpful towards accomplishing the mission of your church?

12 Barnacles, Sails, and Swabbing the Deck:
Facilities Management

If we fail to maintain the ship, she will not sail true.

During the first two centuries, the church was generally nomadic, meeting in homes, synagogues, and outdoor gatherings. The first buildings purposefully built for Christian worship likely date back to the third century. Although the word church, as used in Scripture, means "the called-out one," the word is commonly used to describe the building used for worship.

In many congregations, 80% of the budget goes to buildings and personnel. This leaves very little for missions and ministry. A building project that brings great joy and pride to a congregation in one generation may cause encumbrance and grief to the next generation.

Facilities management might better be understood as ministerial stewardship. The majority of pastors inherit the facility used by the church. Some pastors will lead their church to build new facilities, sometimes even relocating the church in the process. A growing minority of pastors utilize rented facilities, and an even smaller number meet in homes.

Saddleback Church in Southern California averaged over 10,000 in

Pastoral Helmsmanship

attendance before they built their first permanent facility. Prior to that time, the church met in four different high schools, numerous elementary schools, bank buildings, recreation centers, theaters, community centers, restaurants, large homes, professional office buildings, and stadiums. Their first building was a 2,300 seat tent. Pastor Rick Warren often said, "You can come if you can find us."[6] Building is both expensive and risky. Many communities are filled with religious edifices that are outdated, unsafe, uninviting, and empty.

This chapter will address principles for new construction as well as insights for pastors who have inherited facilities that seem to offer up more challenges than opportunities.

Building Principles

The Vision should drive building programs, not the other way around. If you are unclear of the purpose and vision, the building will probably end up being a distraction.

One of the all-too-common pastoral dysfunctions is to make a building program the vision. These types of pastors are often great salesmen, and they use the honeymoon phase of their ministry to promote a building program. Rather than seeking alternatives to building to sustain growth, these pastors promote a building program, elevating the program to the level of vision. Vision brings excitement and unity—even false vision—and the church comes together to see the vision through. Plans are drawn, loans are approved, and excitement builds. Attendance grows as the new building progresses. Attendance peaks around the time the building is dedicated. The pastor is a hero, and his visionary success is recognized by other congregations. Soon the pastor is "called" to another, usually larger church, leaving the congregation with a large debt and no vision. The next pastor is hindered by a massive debt, declining membership (for where there is no vision, the people find another parish) and people with little motivation to give.

---

[6] Rick Warren, The Purpose Driven Church, 45-46, Zondervan, 1995.

Perhaps it would be better to at least consider the alternatives to building a new facility. While a nice fresh building is often high on a pastor's bucket list of dreams, building programs that are not supported by sustainable growth will put the church into bondage both financially and in terms of mobility.

The Eighty Percent Rule

The 80% rule states when a facility nears 80% capacity, additional growth will be limited and additional service times (or a new auditorium) should be developed. Although some would point to sell-out concerts and full-to-the-brim restaurants as proof the 80% rule does not exist, time and practice shows that the American church-going public tend to avoid churches that violate the 80% rule. Sadly, many pastors focus only upon the worship space when considering this phenomenon; however, the 80% rule applies to parking lots, small group space, fellowship space, and bathrooms.

A church in Kansas was plagued with a growth cycle that plateaued at 80, and then plunged to 50 despite the new auditorium and excellent location. Two problems existed. The first was the parking lot, which was at 90% capacity when the church had 80 persons in attendance. When spotters were posted in the parking lot, they observed people driving in and then leaving, unable to find a good place to park. After developing 8 new parking spots, the church grew to over 90 people for the first time.

The second 80% violation was in the small group room use. The couples' class was by far the most successful, running 16-18 persons. However, the room, which was certified by the fire department for 20 people, was full. At the same time, a senior women's class with 5 participants was occupying a room certified for 32 occupants. The 80% rule was keeping the successful class from growing, while the large, empty feel of the senior women's class was counterproductive as well. Making the change required finesse, as neither class wanted to move, but the results were growth in both classes.

Rented Facilities

Many churches can rent office and administrative space, thus providing additional small group rooms and a reduction on major utility costs. Rented facilities can also include those rented just on weekends or special dates, such as community centers, schools, and theaters. Rented facilities however, often involve annual contracts, liability coverage, and other contractual obligations.

Shared Facilities

This option utilizes nearby businesses or community organizations that will allow the church to "share space." An example of this was a church in Lenexa, Kansas which used a nearby Pizza parlor for Sunday School space for three years. The church had three classes meeting in the restaurant from 9:30-10:30 am. The restaurant opened at 11:00 am, by which time the small groups were gone. This option has endless possibilities, including parking, small group space, and special event areas.

Homes

Since the first century, countless churches have started in homes. The intentional use of homes for small groups and special events is grounded in Scripture and practical. The use of homes can expand the geographical footprint of a congregation while providing the benefits of small, intimate group experiences for attendees. Many churches are discovering the benefit of a "both/and" approach to small groups by providing on-campus and in-home small group options. Leaders who desire to encourage home groups as an alternative or supplement to on-campus groups will do well to ensure the homes and hosts are prepared, and that the strategy is thought through properly. Some churches have experienced home groups becoming cliquish, so consider ways to minimize this and other liabilities. It is often wise to seek out other pastors who are using home groups successfully and glean from them the best practices.

Third Places

Third place locations are simply where people want to hang out. For most people, first place is home, second place is work, and third place is where one wants to be. For many, coffee houses are third place locations that can also be used for small groups. In the 1990s, we started a weekly group for pastors that met at a local book store with a coffee shop. Two decades later, this group still meets weekly to provide members with encouragement, support and prayer.

The key to successful third place meetings is to "not stand out." Over the years, we have seen church group after church group come and go in this coffee shop. Some were asked to leave, as they were disruptive to the other customers or simply insensitive to the management. For example, we had to rebuke one member of our group who would come with a 24 oz. coffee from a gas station because it was cheaper than what the coffee shop charged. When using a third place, remember you are not paying rent, so be a great witness by being committed to being a blessing to your host. Consider tipping well and cleaning up after your group before dismissing.

Multiple Services

Moving from a single Sunday morning service to multiple services generally requires far more planning than anticipated. Once again, the purpose for the change should be clearly connected to the vision, mission, and the need of the church. Many congregations have sought to use multiple services as a means to bring peace to the worship wars, using one service for a contemporary service and the other as a traditional service. Although this has worked for some congregations, generally the outcome is less than desired.

When going to a multi-service, one must keep in mind issues such as parking, ingress, egress, and impact upon small groups such as Sunday School and nursery. In addition, some will feel isolated from those in the other services, so prayerful consideration should be given to beginning a second service.

Multisite Services

"One Church, Many Places" is the solution for growing churches today. The multisite church is an approach going back to the first-century, when the church met from house to house. Just as the first-century house church was driven by practical and missional considerations, today's multisite churches are also driven by practical considerations and mission. David Ferguson notes that using this approach provides a healthy congregation the opportunity to promote their "Good Name" while at the same time providing that "New" enthusiasm and excitement a new church generates.[7] The challenges should also be well researched, as multisite churches tend to reproduce the positive and negative aspects of the main campus. Homogeneity, poor orthodoxy or the liabilities of super-star status preachers are characteristics that are often reproduced in the extended locations.

General Rules for Worship, Education, Fellowship, Administration, and Parking

When new construction is necessary, securing sound advice regarding state and local regulations is imperative. The pastor will do well to have a general understanding of the potential cost and space needs. Often called "rules of thumb" for planning, the following provide the pastor with a general idea of what is needed for the construction to propel the vision of the church forward.

---

[7]Dave Ferguson, "Multisite Churches," a paper given at the American Society for Church Growth, Fuller Theological Seminary, Pasadena, CA., November 4, 2004.

Facilities Management

General Rules for Building

Most churches will need 1 acre for every 100-125 in attendance. This does not include the 80% rule, so in practice, use the lower number.

Outdoor recreation requires an additional 1-4 acres. A softball field requires 1 acre, volleyball about .7 acres, and soccer about 2 acres. Playground spaces are normally planned at 75 square feet per child.

Parking

For planning, you will want 1 space per 2 persons in attendance, 100 spaces per acre. The Americans with Disabilities Act (ADA) guidelines for Handicap Accessible parking are:

- 1 handicapped space minimum, plus 1 additional for each 25 spaces.
- Over 100 spaces, 2% of parking must be handicapped accessible.
- Standard parking spots should be 9 feet by 18 feet; Handicapped are 8 feet by 18 feet with 5 foot access aisle and van accessible are 8 feet by 18 feet with 8 foot access aisle.
- The 80% rule generally applies to parking, so plan accordingly.

General Auditorium Size

- Up to 300 capacity: 15-20 square feet per person.
- Above 300 capacity: 17-20 square feet per person.

Congregational Seating

Pews – Fire Code allocates 18" per person in a pew; however reality dictates a more conservative 21" to 24" per person. Spacing between rows of pews is 36" from the cap rail of one pew to the cap rail of the next pew.

Pew length – 14 or 15 people maximum per pew. This rule is based on how quickly a pew can be evacuated in an emergency. Based on life safety codes, no more than 8 people from the middle of a pew or 15 people total.

Seating Cost

When purchasing sanctuary seating, cost should not be the most important consideration. Since your seating decision will be something you'll be living with for at least a generation, purchase the best seats available. Choose the type of seating that works best for your worship style – whether traditional pews, flexible church chairs or theater seats, it is a very wise investment to purchase the best.

Handicapped seating

Requirements will vary by local code. The following from the Americans with Disabilities Act (ADA) may be used as guidelines for worship centers with fixed seating.

Capacity of Seating in Assembly Area Number of Required Wheelchair Locations
- 4 to 25 (1)
- 26 to 50 (2)
- 51 to 300 (4)
- 301 to 500 (6)
- Over 500 (6), plus 1 additional space for each total seating capacity increase of 100

Balcony
- Capacity: Less than 50 percent of main floor seating
- Rise depth: 3 feet 6 inches for first row, 3 feet 4 inches for the back row, 3 feet 2 inches for other rows
- Cross aisles: 4 feet minimum

Facilities Management

Other aisles: Same as aisle width on main floor

A Kansas church found themselves in a pinch when the pastor, insisting a seating capacity of 3000 in the new auditorium, accomplished his goal by using 18" theater seating. However, to accommodate larger members, a special section of 22" seating was provided at the back of the auditorium. Even prior to dedicating the new building, this section had become known as the "fat people section." The word-of-mouth and media storm resulted in negative growth. The church also was soon without a pastor.

Educational Facilities

- General Education: 40-50 square feet per person
    - Preschool: 35 square feet per child
    - Birth-24 months: 7-10 square feet per room maximum
    - 2 year olds: 9-12 square feet per room maximum
    - 3-5 years old: 12-16 square feet per room maximum
    - Children: 25 square feet per child (floor) 40 square feet (desks), 30 children per room, maximum
    - Youth and Adults: 12 square feet per person

Minimum Room Size (all ages): 200 square feet minimum, with no walls less than 12 feet long.

Administration

- Pastors Office: 140-250 square feet
- Staff Offices: 120-200 square feet
- Reception/Secretarial: 200 square feet (main)
- Support Staff 120 square feet
- Conference or Meeting room: 15-25 square feet per person
- Media Library: 1-2 square feet per person
- Many churches fail to include sufficient storage for decorations, floral arrangements, and closets in general.

Asking those who actually use the space might provide insight often overlooked.

Fellowship

- Dining capacity: table seating, 12 square feet per person. 15 square feet per person for round tables. Generally plan to accommodate ½ the worship center capacity.
- Kitchen: 25-33% of the dining area.
- Many churches fail to adequately plan for sufficient space for wedding receptions and other gatherings that would not need to use the sanctuary.

Music & Worship

- Rehearsal Room: 15-25 square feet per person (approx 10% of total worship center area)
- Music library: 1-2 square feet per choir member
- Practice Rooms: 80 square feet minimum
- Robing Rooms: 5 square feet per person
- Chancel Platform: Recommend Depth 8'0" to 12'0". Height - This varies greatly but on average 24" to 36"
- Praise Band / Orchestra Area, allow 20-25 square feet per instrument
- Video Projection Screen(s): Allow no more than 10 times the distance to the farthest seat in the congregation. If the farthest seat is 70' away, the screen should be 7' tall.
- Choir Platforms are generally constructed so that each platform is 3' 4" which gives the choir member room to stand in front of their seat. The height of each choir riser should be a minimum of 6" and a maximum of 8"

The choir area should have an acoustically reflective floor – not carpeting –use hardwood, stone, vinyl, or other material.

Restrooms

- Commodes: 1 per 15 women
- Commodes: 1 per 30 men
- Urinals: 1 per 30 men
- Sinks: 1 per commode

Other Issues

- Doors: Minimum 36"
- Hallways: Minimum 5' 6"
- Custodial closets: One per 15,000 square feet required
- Debt: Maximum of 2.5 times the church annual income the previous year
- The most efficient plan for your church will be in the shape of a rectangle – other shapes will require more square footage per person as well as be more expensive to construct.

Final Thoughts

When evaluating a new building or purchasing an existing one, involve the people in the decision making process who will actually be using the facility. For example, is there sufficient closet space for janitorial supplies and equipment, church decorations, wedding and communion supplies, etc? Effectively cleaning and decorating an owned facility takes a great deal more storage space than anticipated. Inviting the people who know into the discussion ahead of time will save many potentially hurtful discussions after the move.

The building should serve the mission of the church, not the other way around. Generally, new construction should be the final course of action after other options have been explored or implemented. Meeting with pastors and leaders who have recently completed a building program will often provide regional and practical insights that will inform you and your congregation.

Questions to Ponder

1. Why do we need a building and is there some other way to accomplish this need?

2. Where is our church in relation to the 80% rule — seating and parking?

3. Are we properly using the space we have? Are there any changes that need to be considered?

4. Who is responsible to assure that we are following the laws and guidelines, and to properly evaluate our facility needs?

5. Have we thought through the building process in light of the vision, finances, and personnel within the church? Explain.

13 Icebergs, Hurricanes and Torpedoes:
Risk Mitigation

The Titanic did not have insurance; I wonder if they regretted it?

Wherever two or three are gathered a risk will soon follow. Tripping over a tear in the carpet, slipping on a wet floor, fire, theft, fraud, sexual harassment or abuse, etc. can wreak havoc with church budgets and reputations. Risk management is a term used to describe the process of dealing with these types of issues, and the pastor is the one ultimately responsible. Thankfully, through a combination of insurance, budgets, internal controls, and common sense, many risks can be limited or avoided.

Shoveling the snow and throwing down some ice melt will help keep people safe as will making sure there are no tripping hazards in our gathering places. Having fire inspections and installing some financial internal controls can also help reduce our risk. Doing background checks and planning will help prevent major heartaches. Some accidents and disasters are unavoidable, but many can be attributed to poor planning and a lack of common sense. As pastors we have a responsibility to protect the members of our church as well as feed and lead them.

In reference to fire, property, liability, health, and other common exposures, purchasing insurance allows the church to share the risks with an insurance company. For a negotiated fee based on actuarial data, an insurance company will agree to shoulder the burden of many risks that would be very difficult for most churches to self-insure. Most churches will need insurance to cover such exposures as:

- Buildings and personal property
- Vehicles
- Personal and professional liability
- Counseling and officer/directors coverage
- Employee dishonesty and theft protection
- Social media exposure
- Medical, dental and other health coverage
- Disability insurance
- Workman's compensation

Most pastors do not need to become experts in the inner workings of the insurance business, but they do need a general understanding of the risks involved. Listed in the resource section of this book are several church-centric insurance companies that we recommend. Please contact them to speak to a local agent for your specific needs. Ask questions and compare between companies to receive the best value. In addition, ask other pastors which company they use and why.

If you have an agent in your church, please be careful with expectations. Just because they sell insurance does not mean that they will necessarily have the best interests of the church in their mind or even be an expert in the church insurance field. If they are willing to read policies, shop around for you, and explain what the church needs, they can be an excellent resource, however.

Insurance needs, prices, and trends change often. Someone in your church should be shopping the market on a regular basis to assure that you have current coverage at the best price possible. Wisdom dictates doing this before the need arises, and good stewardship demands doing it regularly.

Risk Mitigation

Other Risks

In addition to insurance needs, there are other risks associated with ministry. We discussed pastoral immorality and its devastating effect on the church, but what about sexual misconduct elsewhere? Staff and board members, children and nursery workers, youth pastors, and anyone else representing the church should be insured against a potential risk in this arena.

Standards of behavior need to be implemented to assist in this growing threat. While your liability insurance may handle the legal claims associated with sexual misconduct of someone connected to your ministry, the destruction to the ministry's integrity and good name will potentially suffer great harm in the event of this type of conduct.

Those associated with the church, if they are going to have any contact with children, should receive a thorough background check. The church's expectations regarding sexual behavioral boundaries should be included in the job description and philosophy statements of the ministry. These important issues should be discussed in the hiring process for staff, and during the interview process for volunteers. Topics such as:

- What are the grounds for dismissal regarding sexual behavior?
- What is acceptable in the humor realm?
- How about a dress code?
- What about personal conduct outside of the church?
- What about social media usage?
- What about pornography and the consequences of using it?

These, and many other issues, must be considered and discussed prior to serving in the ministry. Procedures must be in place to handle violations of the policies. Who will handle it? Who will talk to the media if necessary? What about the families involved? What about confidentiality?

For the pastor these issues can be overwhelming. Where do I begin? Who do I talk to? How do I know that I am covering what needs to be discussed? Fear not! You do not have to create these documents and policies from scratch, please turn to the Resource Section at the end of this book and check out the abundant free resources for sample job descriptions, confidentiality agreements, and dozens of other sample forms. It is not necessary to become a human resource guru, just make sure you know one that offers free forms! When in doubt, seek professional help sooner than later.

Fraud

A group of leaders walked into the bank to sign the final papers for their new building loan. Finally, after years of fundraising, the down payment had been raised. As the loan officer pushed the document across the table towards the president of the counsel, soft sobs could be heard from the back of the group. A shaky voice said, "Don't sign it." Everyone turned and stared at the source of the voice, the church treasurer. "Why on earth would you say such a thing?" he was asked. His reply, "There isn't any money, I spent it all. I have a girlfriend..."

Pastors being led away in handcuffs, church staff being fired for stealing, and administrators sneaking out of town due to financial mismanagement happen. In fact, these things happen more than we might suspect. The news outlets gleefully share the stories. The enemies of Christ rejoice when Christian fraud is exposed, while the church or ministry suffer and many times slowly dies.

Shocking? Overdramatized? We could only wish it was. Based on research from Miller Management Systems, LLC (Glenn's company), a Church accounting and management firm based in Kansas City and Springfield Missouri, only about 20% of churches operate in what is known as the "fireproof" condition of ministry. 80% are a "fire hazard," financially speaking.

Fireproof and fire hazard are not referring to the amount of old storage boxes around the furnaces, but to the financial accounting and money management procedures a ministry uses. While we would not

Risk Mitigation

be comfortable with attending a worship service in a facility that was labeled a, "fire hazard," we seem perfectly content to attend the same place where the finances are at risk.

The fact that so many Christian ministries are at risk is indeed bad news. The good news, however, is that with some inexpensive changes, most ministries can move from being a fire hazard to nearly fireproof. Does it cost huge amounts of money to make these changes? It costs no more than moving the boxes away from the open flame of the furnace. There might be some inconvenience and a small amount of resistance to implementing change, but isn't it worth it to limit the risk?

It has been said that "no system is perfect or can prevent fraud 100%." While there are elements of truth in that statement, we can certainly learn the basics behind the behaviors and circumstances that can lead to fraud, and then work to prevent those circumstances.

In the 1940's, Donald Cressey of Indiana University did an extensive study of fraudulent behavior. Nearly 70 years later, his hypothesis is still considered to be the best model explaining occupational fraud via the Fraud Triangle.

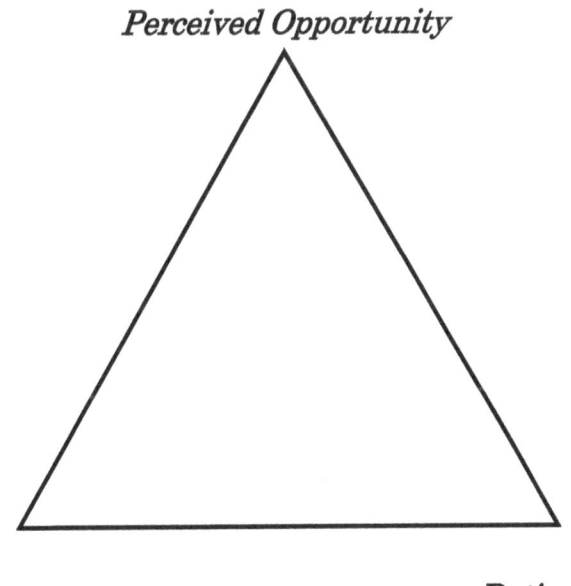

Pastoral Helmsmanship

Pressure

While the church cannot be held directly responsible for people's outside pressures like: gambling habits, shopping addictions, loss of spouse's income, medical bills, bankruptcy, living beyond means, and so forth, we should always be on guard to help people in need and guide them to solutions that do not involve fraud. We must provide an atmosphere where those under external pressures can express their needs and find help.

As pastors we need to be aware of the spiritual condition of those under our care. Relationships are needed, and communication is necessary to provide insights into pressures that someone may be facing but unwilling to share freely. Asking questions and allowing the freedom to share difficulties may just help prevent someone from falling into fraud. We cannot prevent people from sinning or cheating, but we should be able to assist those that really want to avoid it.

Rationalization

Again, while the church is not responsible for the rationalizations people use to allow them to commit fraud, we should be teaching, preaching, and discipling people toward godly behaviors. God spoke to Cain before he murdered his brother and said, "Sin is crouching at the door, and its desire is to master you, but you must master it." All sin begins in the mind, and fraud is no exception. The human mind is exceptional at rationalization. We can excuse almost any behavior in our lives through the power of reason and justification of ourselves. All fraud has at its base some form of rationalization. For example:

- The government doesn't spend my money correctly; therefore, I cheat on my taxes.
- The church does not reimburse me properly; therefore, I pad my expense account.
- The church does not pay me enough, therefore; I deserve this or that.

- My spouse does not meet my needs; therefore, I deserve to cheat on him or her.

Christian people lie, cheat, steal, and then defend their behaviors with the power of rationalization. We must be on guard to listen for and take action upon such sentiments when we hear them.

Perceived Opportunity

The third aspect of fraud is the real or perceived opportunity to complete the theft successfully. Every ministry is responsible for reducing, removing, or eliminating the real or perceived opportunity to get away with fraud. While we may not be responsible for outside pressures or rationalizations of individuals, we must create strong policies, procedures, and enforcement that keep honest people honest.

Let's look at some of the procedures that can be implemented that will help move any ministry from the danger zone to the safe one. We have covered some of these before and will address others later, but for now let's look at what we can do to help limit fraud.

Whenever fraud takes place, it is at least partially due to the presence of opportunities. Logic would dictate that if we could limit the opportunity, we will limit the instances of fraud. While many of these are or should be obvious, most groups are not implementing them, so they bear repeating.

Cash Receipts

Every ministry receives money. Who handles it, who counts it, and how it is deposited and reported will help determine how safe the ministry is. Here are some guidelines that cost nothing to implement.

- Money should always be counted by at least two people. Three is better.
- Checks received in the mail should be opened in the presence of two people.
- Both counters should sign off on the final count sheet.

- Cash should be counted by both counters independently.
- Money counters should rotate to limit the possibility of collusion.
- Counters should not be related.
- All checks should be immediately endorsed with a deposit stamp.
- A duplicate deposit slip should be made out at the time of counting, one copy is deposited, and the other is given to the bookkeeper/accountant. These two deposit slips should never be together until after the deposit is made, thus limiting the opportunity for changing the original deposit.
- The bookkeeper/accountant matches the deposit slip processed by the bank, to the contribution database and the General Ledger each month.
- Written instructions are provided explaining exactly what is expected.

If any ministry does all of those steps above, opportunities for fraud will be limited. The actual out-of-pocket expense for the ministry so far is zero.

Cash Disbursements

If a ministry receives any donations, they will eventually spend them. A great deal of fraud takes place during this process, but it can be prevented with good controls.

- Every check, with no exception, requires supporting documentation and two signatures. A signature stamp does not count and will not limit fraud.
- Check signers are not related and not in a direct supervisor/subordinate relationship if at all possible.
- Blank checks are never signed — Ever.

- The same person who generates the check does not sign the check. At least one of the check signers signs all the checks to look for reoccurring patterns.
- Employee reimbursements are made only *after* receiving proper documentation. Petty cash funds should be avoided.
- If credit cards are used, documentation is required for every purchase and is examined by someone other than the user of the credit card. Debit cards should be avoided.
- Voided checks are clearly marked "void," and the signature section is cut off. They are stored in a secure location, never thrown out.
- Bank statements are reviewed by someone other than the one who writes or signs the checks. Even better is to have the bank statement mailed to someone else's location outside of the organization for review.

If any ministry will follow these steps for spending within the organization, the opportunities for fraud will be severely limited. The actual out-of-pocket expense for the ministry so far remains at zero.

Payroll

Since most ministries will hire employees, it is essential to follow wise and legal procedures. As recent headlines have shown, the IRS is not overly friendly towards Christian groups, so great care is needed.

- All compensation changes need to be approved by someone other than the employee and must include appropriate documentation.
- All compensation must be processed through the approved payroll system, including love offerings, special gifts, and bonuses.
- A current W-4 and I-9 is on file for every employee.
- The correct usage of W-2 vs. 1099's is critical.
- Housing allowances, for those that qualify, are approved by the appropriate people before the current year begins.

- All applicable wage and hour guidelines, employee classification, and overtime laws are followed.
- All payroll taxes and the required reports are filed in a timely fashion according to the current laws.

The IRS does not play nice, and many ministries have been audited and fined for failure to follow the above procedures. While there may be a cost to begin to obey the law, this cost is minimal compared to the fines and bad press received if the ministry fails to do so.

Bank/Investment Accounts and Financial Statements

Unless the ministry keeps its funds strictly in cash, financial institutions will be involved. Each of these banks and investment firms issue statements to their customers. The following procedures will provide an additional layer of protection to the ministry.

- A minimum number of bank accounts are used and are balanced to the penny monthly.
- These balances must tie into the General Ledger and the contribution statements.
- Someone other than the person creating the checks should review and balance the statements.
- Strict, generally accepted accounting procedures should be used to reconcile and report to the appropriate committees responsible for the funds.
- Financial statements should be timely and complete and again follow generally acceptable accounting procedures.

All of the above procedures have an extremely low cost to the ministry. Compared to the expense and devastation caused by fraud, the cost is non-existent. Any ministry can implement these guidelines and should. We as Christians should hold to the highest standards in our handling of money and never settle for anything less.

Risk Mitigation

In addition to the above steps, there are a few other issues to be considered in our desire to move to being a fireproof ministry in our finances:

- The consideration of an annual audit from an accounting firm that specializes in Christian ministries. Prices vary depending on frequency and the exact type of review wanted. For example: a simple Compilation typically will range around a few thousand dollars depending on the size of the company. A Review will double that with a full Audit being four times more expensive. Shopping for the best price is mandatory, and make sure you understand your goals and reasons for the services hired.

- If at all possible, try to have a wise, experienced, competent financial officer or treasurer on your board. Someone who understands accounting is very helpful.

- Consider hiring an outside firm to assist with accounting, payroll, and human resources to assure accuracy, add a measure of separation of duties, and a buffer from lawsuits. Also consider an annual fraud risk assessment by an outside group.

- Approve an anti-fraud policy for the church and make sure all employees know of it. Include an "intent to prosecute" clause to communicate the seriousness of the issue.

Even with all of the above, we can never eliminate every chance of theft or fraud, but we can certainly take these steps to help limit the opportunities and temptations. We can leave our front door open when we go on vacation and just hope all is well, or we can install a deadbolt. We can remove the paint cans and boxes from the open flame by our furnace, or just pray they do not explode. As in so many other areas of our life, the choice is ours. Choose wisely!

Social Media

Technology has changed the lives of almost every person in ministry. Smart phones, tablets, computers, and presentation devices are common place in the church. Every pastor that wishes to reach the younger generation will need to become somewhat proficient with these tools.

While wonderful in speed, power, and the ability to enhance our messages, there is a dark side. Time wasters, distractions, and personal relationship substitutes are problem issues, and some even wonder about the electrical bombardment of our brains.

Many studies are pointing to the negative impact of social media on marriages, families, and addictions. "Smart phone withdrawal," "Facebook deprivation," and "Textclaw and iPosture" are now entering counselors' and physicians' terminology for diseases.

These drawbacks do not mean we should not use the new technologies, but we must use wisdom when doing so. In fact, social media in all its aspects has opened evangelism and discipleship possibilities unheard of before our generation. Christians from all over the globe can connect in an instant. Isolated pastors can find many support groups and shut-ins have access to unlimited teaching and worship events.

The pastor will need to address this growing issue sooner than later. What is acceptable for the staff regarding personal usage and time invested during work hours or is it only while off duty? And a host of other questions will arise. What about the liability risks? What about a staff person (paid or volunteer) representing the church in the social media world? Are there limits to photos being posted? What about violating someone's personal preferences or privacy in cyberspace? The list of questions is growing and seems endless.

Cyber Liability Insurance is a new policy trend with many insurance companies and is worth looking into. If the church or pastor maintains a blog, website, or shares their worship services on the internet, there is liability potential.

While it is impossible to control all aspects of what someone does in cyberspace, the issues are not going to go away; they are simply going

Risk Mitigation

to become more pronounced. Incorporating a social media policy would seem prudent. (See the Resource Section for a sample one.)

In addition, discussing expectations with staff and those representing the church is becoming very important as our churches reach beyond brick and mortar into cyberspace. Social Media is a great tool if used properly; however, like any other tool, if wielded improperly, pain, damage, and lawsuits can follow.

Questions to Ponder

1. What steps have you implemented to prevent risks in your facility, and who is responsible to do so?

2. When was the last time your church had a complete insurance review by a competent agent?

3. In considering the Fraud Triangle, how is your ministry doing in limiting opportunities for failure to occur?

4. What would an auditor find if they reviewed your procedures right now?

5. What changes will you make in light of the information provided in this chapter?

14 Navigating the Legal Waters of Ministry

When the Coast Guard fires a shot, it would be wise to stop.

While churches are recognized as exempt from Federal and most State taxes, that does not mean they are free from all the laws of the land. Churches are granted freedom in many arenas to operate unimpeded, but the following areas must conform to the laws of the land.

- Employment/Wage Practices
- Tax Law — Clergy, Exempt/Non-Exempt Employees
- Americans with Disability
- Child Protection/Endangerment
- Sexual Abuse Issues
- Land/Facility Use
- Political Issues

Laws vary from state to state and Federal law is often updated and reviewed, so please make sure you research these topics with qualified professionals. Our goal in this chapter is to provide you a guideline to prompt you to recognize potential legal battles before encountered.

We discussed in detail the laws regarding employment and wage practices in chapter ten, we won't revisit them here. Remember that churches are required to follow most of the common laws regarding hiring, firing, wages, benefits, etc. in employment law. If in doubt, consult a professional for clarity. Lawsuits are expensive, damage the reputation of the ministry, and often ruin relationships. Learn the laws and follow them.

Americans with Disability Act

Churches and religious organizations are exempt from the rigors of the ADA; however, a church is not exempt from the moral obligation to provide equal access for all. In addition, churches may be subject to the Rehabilitation Act of 1973 which states that if the facility receives any federal funding, the church cannot discriminate on the basis of disability.

Here is the basis for the ADA exemption for churches:

> The equal access exemption for religious institutions has been upheld by courts on the basis that requiring religious entities to comply with the ADA and allowing the government to initiate enforcement proceedings against religious entities would amount to an impermissible government interference with religion. As explained by the federal court in Chipkevich v. University of Scranton, exempting religious entities from the ADA's equal access provisions allows them "to design their facilities and perform their services in accordance with their religious tenets."[8]

The moral issue, however, still needs to be addressed by the leadership of the church. Should every person have access to the worship service and programs offered by the church? Is it okay to overlook those who are less able due to a physical disability? Is the

---

[8] http://www.ehow.com/about_6385337_ada-regulations-churches.html

cost to provide access to seating, moving freely around the facility, the use of restrooms etc. really the issue here?

Each leadership group will have to address these concerns, but the answer seems clear to the authors. Every church should provide as much access as possible for every member. God will provide the funds, and our places of worship should be readily accessible for all. While churches are not subjected to the legal requirement according the letter of the law, it seems like the Spirit of the law would speak to loving and doing whatever is possible to assist those in need.

Child Protection Laws

Richard Hammar is well known as a tax and legal expert regarding church matters. Here is a sample that he provides on his website regarding this all too common problem of child abuse. Every pastor would be wise to research their local laws and consult competent legal counsel in this area.

> ***Key point 4-08.*** *Every state has a child abuse reporting law that requires persons designated as mandatory reporters to report known or reasonably suspected incidents of child abuse. Ministers are mandatory reporters in many states. Some states exempt ministers from reporting child abuse if they learned of the abuse in the course of a conversation protected by the clergy-penitent privilege. Ministers may face criminal and civil liability for failing to report child abuse.*

Sadly, it is all too common for ministers to learn that a minor is being abused. This can occur in a number of ways, including a confession by the perpetrator in counseling or a disclosure by a friend or relative of the victim or abuser. Often, ministers want to resolve such matters internally through counseling with the victim or the alleged offender without contacting civil authorities. Such a response can have serious legal consequences, including the following:

- Ministers, who are mandatory reporters under state law, face possible criminal prosecution for failing to comply with their state's child abuse reporting law;
- Some state legislatures have enacted laws permitting child abuse victims to sue ministers for failing to report child abuse
- Some courts have permitted child abuse victims to sue ministers for failing to report child abuse.

As a result, it is imperative for ministers to be able to answer the following questions:

(1) What is the definition of reportable "child abuse" under my state child abuse reporting law?
(2) Am I a mandatory reporter of child abuse?
(3) What if I learn of child abuse in the course of a conversation that is protected by the clergy-penitent privilege? Am I still required to report?
(4) How do I report child abuse?

Each of these questions is answered in the table that accompanies this article, based on the current child abuse reporting laws in all 50 states and the District of Columbia.[9]

Sexual Abuse Issues

We discussed some of the issues regarding sexual failure in the chapters dealing with occupational hazards and risk management. Pastors, elders, and directors are in a position of authority in the church and therefore have a responsibility to protect those under their care, not abuse them.

During the course of routine counseling, sooner or later the pastor will be faced with dealing with an abuse situation. If it involves a child or minor, please see the previous section and take whatever

---

[9] http://www.churchlawandtax.com/cltr/2013/july-august/2013-child-abuse-reporting-laws-for-churches.html

action is dictated by your governing board and state laws. The situation gets a bit cloudy when it involves spouses.

While the reporting laws are vague, every situation where this issue arises should be considered serious. Domestic violence is one of the hardest and saddest problems to deal with in counseling. Embarrassment, shame and fear dominate those involved.

The safety of children and the victim should be paramount. Differing Biblical views over divorce and separation abound, but protecting the victim should not be argued. Whether to call in legal authorities is not an easy choice. Often victims believe they have caused the abuse and are resistant to freeing themselves from it. Some would rather endure than flee or see the one causing the abuse arrested.

Unless the pastor/counselor is specifically trained in this field, referring to a professional counselor would probably be a wise step. It would be helpful for pastors to understand and know what the legal requirements are for the state regarding abuse before encountering it. Ask a qualified legal expert in your state for advice and an understanding of what the law requires.

Those living under abuse will require a significant amount of pastoral help as they adjust to living without it. A great deal of support and care will be needed to help repair the damage caused. Those causing the abuse are often unable to understand the seriousness and long term consequences of their actions.

Pastors and counselors should read books covering the topic and if possible attend training sessions to at least learn some of the basic signs of abuse and how to help with the healing process.

Land and Facility Use

Many local governing boards began placing obstacles on churches for new construction a few years back. This action prompted the Federal government to establish RLUIPA - Religious Land Use and Institutionalized Persons Act in 2000.[10]

---

[10] http://www.justice.gov/crt/about/hce/housing_rluipa2.php

These laws prohibit zoning and landmarking laws that substantially burden the religious exercise of churches or other religious assemblies. They also ensure equal treatment between religious and nonreligious groups. It is not too big of a stretch to see why local governments would prefer tax-paying occupants against tax-free ones. Churches tend to create a big footprint with buildings, parking, and other use buildings, all free from taxation. This law assures that churches can acquire permits to build without interference from local governments.

The intent of the law is clear — it is to protect church facilities and property. Home churches are not protected by this law and any attempt to gain tax-exempt status for a personal dwelling based on this law will most likely fail.

Political Issues

Recently, many churches have recoiled against the apparent blind eye turned to liberal churches and punishment of conservative ones endorsing political candidates. A national movement began a few years ago daring the IRS to take churches to court over this issue.

The current law does prohibit churches from endorsing or condemning particular political candidates or parties. That does not mean that churches cannot address moral issues, host debates, be a polling place, or have town meetings. Churches may distribute voters' guides as long as they assume a neutral position and refrain from endorsements or condemnations.

Jay Sekulow writes the following on his website regarding the topic and it sums it up nicely:

> In sum, churches have clear First Amendment rights to speak out on the moral issues of the day, and to develop, prepare and distribute information on issues of public policy. These rights include the distribution of voter guides which are neutral and unbiased in the presentation of a candidate's position on a broad range of issues. Also, voter guides cannot endorse candidates, or urge individuals to vote for or against

candidates. Churches also have the right to engage in a limited amount of lobbying activity, as long as such activity does not constitute a "substantial" part of the churches' total activities. Moreover, non-church exempt organizations may engage in lobbying activity so long as they do not exceed the expenditure limitations specified in § 501(h).[11]

Politics, as with all these issues, should be viewed through Kingdom eyes. What is best for Jesus and the furthering of His Kingdom? What role should the church leaders play? We are to be wise as serpents and gentle as doves. We must not lose sight of our primary ministry in our perceived fight against Caesar.

Questions to Ponder

1. When was the last time you reviewed the current employee tax laws to ensure that you are in compliance?

2. Do you agree that the Church has a moral responsibility to guarantee access to their facilities by those who are physically challenged? Why or why not?

3. What programs or systems do you have in place to assure that the children under your care are protected?

4. What training do you have in place to assure that those who counsel others are aware of the current laws regarding physical or sexual abuse?

5. What do you believe and practice regarding political practices within your church? Why?

---

[11] http://aclj.org/churches-organizations-/political-speech-non-profit-tax-issues

Section Two Review

In Section Two we presented multiple practical matters that most pastors must deal with regarding administration — hiring and firing staff, budgeting, financial integrity, reporting, facilities management, and how to navigate the risks and legal icebergs that try to destroy every church.

In Section Three we will continue our journey into administration but with an emphasis shifting to how to work alongside those in ministry. We will learn how to understand and work with differing personalities and how to solve the inevitable conflicts that will arise. In addition, we will address how to work with volunteers, lead a ministry through change, and even how to conduct meetings that are enjoyable and not burdensome. We will round out this section with some final thoughts from what we have learned about ministry that we trust will be both challenging and encouraging to you.

Section Three
The Pastor as Helmsman

15 Understanding Yourself and the Crew:
None of Us Work Alone

I'd be a great pastor if it wasn't for all these people.

One common truth about all churches everywhere is that they all contain people. Another truth is that there are no two people exactly alike. Every pastor will sooner than later find this reality to be absolutely true.

A friend one time said, "If two or three of you can agree on anything, I myself will show up to see if it is true." This of course is a play off of Jesus' promise to be in our midst if two or three agree on anything. My friend had been a pastor for many years.

We can spend our lives fighting with others in the vain attempt to change them into our image, or we can embrace the truth that their Creator made them in His image. Every person is a unique expression of our creative God. If two people are identical in all aspects, one of them is not needed.

The goal of this chapter is to help us realize that personality differences are normal, healthy, and can greatly benefit the ministry, if we will learn how to embrace them instead of fighting them.

One common tool to help discover these differences is the DiSC Behavioral Profile assessment tool. There are free versions that are available online or you can hire a company to administer them. No test is perfect, but these type evaluations help shed light on underlying personality differences.

Since we are unique creations in Christ, each of us bring to the team different viewpoints, traits, strengths, and weaknesses. Many relationship problems can be solved and even avoided by simply understanding why people say and do what they do.

Whether you are a solo pastor or part of a large staff, we will interact with many people. There are leaders, deacons, elders, volunteers, and those within our family and friendship spheres. Every one of the people has a basic personality that helps to shape their viewpoint, words, actions and reactions.

A pastor does not need a degree in psychology to benefit from understanding these differences. Simple assessments, such as the DiSC Behavioral Profile tool, will give enough insight into some of the differences to greatly enhance your working relationships and help reduce unnecessary conflicts.

Understanding why people respond the way they do will help us learn to relate to the God-given team we build around us.

DiSC Basics

The initial DiSC model comes from Dr. William Marston, a professor at Columbia University in the 1920s. This model has been used by over 40 million people to help discover basic personality traits. Over the years the model has been enhanced and is currently the most used personality evaluation model in the world.

There are many variations of how this profile tool is administered. For example, on this website - *https://www.discprofile.com/what-is-disc/overview/*, participants fill out a questionnaire which consists of questions that attempt to force you to pick or grade on a sliding scale, a preference between two choices. For example, how would you respond to these two statements?

Understanding Yourself and the Crew

- "I would rather work on a team than work independently".

- "I think achieving results is more important than being comfortable".

Depending on which version of the DiSC test you are using, you will state I agree or disagree, or use a sliding scale such as: Strongly agree, strongly disagree, neutral, etc. Based on your answers you will usually end up in one of four possible quadrants in the DISC circle. There are no right or wrong answers, for this is simply a self-evaluation process. We feel, believe, and act in certain way because of our underlying personality traits.

DiSC is an acronym which explains some of the underlying tendencies that each of us possesses:

- **Dominance** – direct, strong-willed and forceful
- **Influence** – sociable, talkative and lively
- **Steadiness** – gentle, accommodating and soft-hearted
- **Conscientiousness** – private, analytical and logical

This profile test measures your personality and behavioral style, not intelligence, aptitude, or your value system. The questions attempt to describe how a person will behave in a specific situation. For example, how someone will respond to challenges, pressures, how they will work with others, and how they will work with rules and boundaries.

DiSC may seem a bit professional and sterile, so let's use a different analogy that Glenn has copywrited — Canoeing. Picture your staff, your leadership team, or whoever else you work with going on a canoe trip. You might very well hear some of these comments from the various people along the ride, and they would be insightful to consider.

First, we need to convert the DiSC profile into canoeing names. To find these we could ask the question,

Pastoral Helmsmanship

"What type of canoer are you?"

After reviewing the answers we discovered that there are four types of canoers. Here then would be the breakdown with some typical statements from each personality type:

"THE MAD PADDLER" - "D" on the DiSC Profile
This canoer might be found saying things like:

- "Let's go! We've wasted enough time talking, get in the canoe!"
- "Come on, stroke, stroke, stroke, we can beat the other canoes there!"
- "We can take those rapids! Hang on!"
- "Yes, we lost one small child and a dog, but we were the first ones back to base camp!"

"THE SPLASHER" – "i" on the DiSC Profile
This canoer might be found saying things like:

- "Can we stop here and play in the water a while?"
- "Hey look, a place to sit and talk!"
- "Don't you just love the scenery, the beauty, the leisure of it all?"
- "Just being here with you all makes the snakes, bugs and canned Spam all worth it!"

"THE MAPPER" – "C" on the DiSC Profile
This canoer might be found saying things like:

- "Ok, I just want to review our inventory of supplies one last time before we leave."
- "According to my calculations, we should pass a large oak tree with an eagle's nest 24 feet, 3 inches up from the first Y branch left of the large granite rock just around the next bend in approximately 4.32 minutes.......... this is so exciting!

- "Ok, there are exactly 1.8 cans of soda for everyone on the trip, so enjoy!"
- "If we were all rowing with our paddles at the same depth like the manual called for, we could use approximately 16% less energy and arrive at our destination 12.2% early!"

"The Life Preserver" – **"S"** on the DiSC Profile.
This canoer might be found saying things like:

- "Would everyone be happier if we stopped and ate lunch together?"
- "Would anyone like my .8 portion of a soda?"
- "Straying off course for a small adventure? Ummmm, I'd prefer to keep to the plan, if that is alright with everyone else."
- "I know this is a long and difficult journey, I feel your pain, literally!"

It does not take any advanced education to see how a group of people who are very different in their personalities will make life and working together — interesting. Most of us tend to think that everyone is somewhat off, or at least not as right as they should be if they thought just like us. We may not say those words, but we often act like it. Realizing that others do not think like us, process like us, or respond like us, and that they are still okay, is eye opening.

Why do people react like they do? Let's continue looking at our fellow canoers to glean some more truth. We use the word "environment" to refer to the workplace. These truths are insightful at home as well, but in our discussion, we are referring to those we work alongside.

"D" The Mad Paddler

When the environment is perceived as unfavorable, and the person feels more powerful than the environment, he or she will act to change, fix or control the situation.

Pastoral Helmsmanship

"i" The Splasher

When the environment is perceived as favorable, and the person feels more powerful than the environment, they will act to persuade others to their point of view.

"C" The Mapper

When the environment is perceived as unfavorable, and the person feels less powerful than the environment, they will respond by setting clear rules within the situation and work hard to follow them.

"S" The Life Preserver

When the environment is perceived as favorable, and the person feels less powerful than the environment, they will work to support the situation as it is and support others as well.

    Every person is different, and most are a mixture of differing personalities. Age, experience, and spiritual growth all play into the relational temperament as well. However, assessment, such as the DiSC Profile one demonstrates that most people will clearly land in one preferred style. Grasping these differences will assist in learning how to work as a team.

    Realizing what someone's underlying personality style is will help when forming teams and assigning tasks. This knowledge can also help to limit frustrations by realizing why a person speaks and responds the way they do.

    As we become more aware of the strengths and weaknesses associated with each personality category, we will realize how to maximize the benefit for the entire team.

    We should grow in our respect and appreciation for the differences instead of attempting to convert everyone into our preferred style. Differing views when considering a task or problem should help, not hinder the process, if we learn to embrace the diversity. In fact, this is not really a new science but an old piece of wisdom.

> For the body does not consist of one member but of many. If the foot should say, "Because I am not a hand, I do not belong to the body," that would not make it any less a part of the body. And if the ear should say, "Because I am not an eye, I do not belong to the body," that would not make it any less a part of the body. If the whole body were an eye, where would be the sense of hearing? If the whole body were an ear, where would be the sense of smell? But as it is, God arranged the members in the body, each one of them, as he chose. If all were a single member, where would the body be? As it is, there are many parts, yet one body. The eye cannot say to the hand, "I have no need of you," nor again the head to the feet, "I have no need of you." (1 Corinthians 12: 14- 21 RSV)

We are different but that does not mean we do not have value. Each member of the team will bring strengths and weaknesses, and if utilized successfully, the team will be stronger because of these differences.

Other Models

The DiSC personality model is not the only one that can help us figure out why others think and act the way they do. If you have interacted with people in even a small fashion, it does not take long to realize that we are all different. Husbands, wives, children, co-workers, bosses — everyone approaches problems and relationships a bit differently.

Some people see the world in black and white, and others gray. There are those that are sticklers on the details and those that prefer to not let the details get in way of a good story. Those who tend towards the black and white view often have trouble with those others "who play loosely with the truth." The story tellers view the sticklers as legalistic and smothering.

Pastoral Helmsmanship

It is probably safe to say that most congregations, staffs, boards, and ministry teams are comprised of a mixture of personalities. This can be a tremendous strength or a constant source of frustration.

In the Christian realm, this understanding of differing personalities has been broken down by referring to "spiritual gifts." These can include administration, teaching, serving, leading, etc.

Part of the leader's task is to recognize the gift and make sure that the person is encouraged to use this gift to its fullest. Servants love to serve and not necessarily administrate. Forcing someone into an arena in which they struggle is not the best use of their gifting, and it may enhance relationship struggles.

Another way of viewing these differences in people is labeled "Spiritual Motivations." These four breakdowns included the terms: Prophet, Mercy, Exhorter, and Organizer. To understand this type of breakdown of personalities, let's change our example from canoeing to someone walking through a door and dropping a plate full of dishes — how would each personality type respond?

Prophet - "Well, you know, if you would have been more careful that would not have happened. If you would simply look around and pay more attention, you would not have tripped. I hope you have learned a valuable lesson from this mishap."

Mercy - "Oh, I am so very sorry. Are you okay? Please don't feel badly about this, I have done it many times in the past. It will be fine; let me help you clean up this mess."

Exhorter - "Now, the reason this happened is because there is a hole in the carpet. If we patched that hole this could be avoided next time. In addition, the plates were improperly balanced on the tray. We need to write up some policies in order to assure that this event is not repeated."

Organizer - "Someone get a rag, broom and mop. We need to clean up this mess quickly. Make sure you check for any broken bones. You are going to have quite a bruise there, so be sure to put ice on. In fact, someone get that ice right now. Schedule a carpet repair man to fix that hole ASAP."

There are, of course, other ways that people could respond, but these four are fairly typical. What else is normal is that within our boards, groups, and staffs, all of these personalities will be represented. More importantly, if we fail to recognize these differences, there will be needless conflict.

The prophet type person will be upset with the mercy one and vice versa. The organizer will be frustrated with the person always explaining everything but never doing it. Finding out what the underlying personality traits are is very important, and then helping each other learn to appreciate them, is even more so.

A wise pastor will lead his staff and leadership team through an evaluation process to discover these underlying traits. The vehicle used is not as important as the truth uncovered. Using DiSC or any other tool will provide insightful information as to why someone thinks, speaks, and acts the way they do.

Spiritual maturity demands that we learn to use our personality traits in a redemptive way. Just because we may be in the "Dominance" category using DiSC, or we may see the world in black and white, or function in a prophet type viewpoint, does not give us license to be rude, harsh, insensitive, or judgmental of others. What we discover through testing are our underlying personality traits. These God-given traits still need to be brought under the control of the Holy Spirit and sanctified for His usage.

The same principals hold true with those we serve. A staff or board member armed with his or her personality information can and should be instructed on how to bring this knowledge under the Lordship of Christ. We all need to learn how to embrace the difference in others instead of demanding that people think and act like us.

Summary

We need to understand those around us and to understand ourselves as well. What is our primary personality bent? When we approach a problem or relationship, where do we fit in the DiSC model, or the Spiritual Gifting one? We should learn how our style impacts others. How do we relate to those other people who are different than us? Do we appreciate their viewpoints and strengths, or do we waste it because we are trying to convert them to our preferred style? Can we grow to learn how to respect and appreciate the various God-given personality traits as gifts, and not something to be endured? We must if we are to succeed in leading others.

As leaders, we need to surround ourselves with people who are not the same as we are if we want a broader view. We will make better decisions if all the points of view are considered. Yes, it takes relational work to mesh together all those different canoers, but how boring would the journey be if we were all the same?

If the goal of our ministry is to further the work of the Kingdom, then we will recruit, train, enjoy, and endure those who are different than we are. We will help those around us do the same thing. In our staff and board meetings, we can learn how to appreciate each other, we must if we are to fulfill the second greatest commandment — love your neighbor as yourself.

Every pastor will be involved with conflict, it is unavoidable. The next chapter will help you become prepared for the inevitable, but before moving along, please stop and consider the following questions.

Questions to Ponder

1. Thinking over the last relational conflict endured, what could you have done differently after reading this chapter?

2. Think about your board or leadership team through the canoeing illustration presented in this chapter. Who would fit where?

3. After placing each person in one of the personality types, what could you do to enhance your relationship with them now?

4. How could you use this information to help your current relationships within your leadership structure?

5. How could you reorganize, reprioritize, and help those around you see the truth in this chapter and then maximize effectiveness because of it?

16 When Mutiny is in the Air:
Conflict Resolution

Why can't we all just get along?

All pastors will have a few people in their lives that simply drive them crazy. Sister Sandpaper and Brother Long Tongue are in every church. You know who they are in your group. They are the people who make the air in the room get warmer and stuffier when you see them. The room seems a bit smaller and you find yourself looking for somewhere to wander off to. Are they in our midst by some cosmic accident or by divine plan? What are we supposed to do with them? How, as a shepherd, do we treat them?

In addition to having people in our lives that scratch the irritation nerve, we will be drawn into conflict, so how do we deal with the inevitable relational issues that will arise in our midst? We will suggest some ways to help with those difficult people towards the end of the chapter, but first, let's learn how to navigate the choppy waters of conflict.

Pastoral Helmsmanship

Here is a shocking truth — there is always going to be conflict in the church. "Wow, that sure is negative," no, just a factual reality. The early church struggled, and so will we. Paul broke fellowship with Barnabas in Acts 15:39 (BTW - How do you not get along with a guy named, the son of encouragement?) and then later on pleaded with two sisters to learn how to get along. (Philippians 4:2) The Jewish-Gentile conflict dominates most of the early Church, and the disciples always seemed to be bickering. Conflict is simply a part of ministry.

Since we cannot avoid it, we better learn how to navigate through it and if possible, redeem it. In every conflict there are at least four wills involved. God has a will, so do our enemy the devil, and the two parties involved in the disagreement also have wills. How do we walk through this maze of wills? Purposefully, prayerfully, and keeping in mind that God's will is the one that should really matter the most.

When we fail to effectively deal with conflict, the following dysfunctions can happen in our ministries:

- Relationships suffer
- Low motivation/morale
- Lack of unity
- Wasted time
- Poorer decision making
- Loss of valued staff
- Sabotage, damage, theft
- Increased health claims
- Physical violence
- Litigation
- Perspectives are not broadened, resulting in a lack of personal growth

Psalm 133 is a beautiful picture of unity:

> **Behold, how good and pleasant it is when brothers dwell in unity! It is like the precious oil on the head, running down on the beard, on the beard of Aaron, running down on the collar of**

his robes! It is like the dew of Hermon, which falls on the mountains of Zion! For there the LORD has commanded the blessing, life forevermore. (RSV)

What a contrast between "life forevermore" and the list of dysfunctions. Hurt feelings, damaged relationships, territorial battles instead of teamwork, loss of health, and even lawsuits are all an indictment of improper conflict management.

The calling card to the lost is our love one for another (John 13:35), yet the organized Church is known more for division and strife rather than love. We can and must change this perception. Sometimes we actually structure our ministries that empower conflict.

Before we jump to solutions, consider some of the highpoints from Paul's exhortation to the Roman believers in Romans 12:9-18: God actually expects His people to know and practice this list; for He would not have written them to tease us!

- Love must be sincere. Hate what is evil; cling to what is good.
- Be devoted to one another in brotherly love.
- Honor one another above yourselves.
- Never be lacking in zeal, but keep your spiritual fervor, serving the Lord.
- Be joyful in hope, patient in affliction, faithful in prayer.
- Share with God's people who are in need. Practice hospitality.
- Bless those who persecute you; bless and do not curse.
- Rejoice with those who rejoice; mourn with those who mourn.
- Live in harmony with one another. Do not be proud, but be willing to associate with people of low position.
- Do not repay anyone evil for evil.
- Be careful to do what is right in the eyes of everybody.
- If it is possible, as far as it depends on you, live at peace with everyone.

The Five D's of Resolving Conflict

We are going to share with you a proven method of helping to resolve conflict within the Church. There is no perfect system because the process involves imperfect people. However, if we ever hope to change, we must begin. Some people will never come into agreement, but the majority of people will if we follow these steps.

I. Discern

There are four steps necessary to properly discern the conflict. Each of these is necessary to make sure that we understand the conflict *before* we attempt to move to solution.

Step One: Stop and take the time to properly discern the situation. Is it simply a difference or a real conflict?

Difference

- A difference of opinion or point of view
- A difference in style or preference (personality, problem solving, conflict handling style)
- A different method or process (different from yours!)
- A different interpretation (than yours!)
- A communications breakdown creates differences that are not really present, just perceived

If it is a difference, handle the difference with maturity and with the fruit of the Spirit!

- Patience
- Peace
- Love
- Understanding

At the right time and place, talk it through, ask questions, and try to gain perspective and understanding. People will generally respond very well to open ended, thoughtful questions that are designed to gain understanding and perspective. This method can usually go a long way toward resolving "differences." We estimate that well over 50% of conflicts are simply differences and should be treated as such.

Conflict

- An offense has been taken
- A person feels threatened physically, emotionally, or spiritually
- A person(s) feels emotionally injured or hurt
- Strong feelings of anger and/or frustration are present for a prolonged period of time
- Unforgiveness is present
- A person perceives they have been treated unjustly

Usually conflict is driven by something. Defining the conflict driver can assist you in developing the best response or approach to the conflict. We need to determine if these issues are present:

- Facts or Data – when two parties simply have different information – is there a third party antagonist involved?
- Processes or Methods – when there is a difference of opinion over how things should be done
- Goals or Purpose – when two parties cannot agree on a common goal, or perhaps a power grab or unrevealed anger
- Values – when the parties disagree about basic meanings

We also need to consider if the conflict is a task-oriented conflict or if it is relationship-oriented. Some people do not work well with others and some simply do not have the skills or aptitude to get along with others. Discerning this difference will also assist in helping to resolve conflict.

Step Two: Are the 3 key ingredients necessary for dysfunctional conflict present?

Interdependency - The first ingredient generally needed to cause real conflict is when co-workers or co-laborers have to depend on each other to accomplish their work or to be successful in their ministry, paid or volunteer.

The higher the dependency, the more impacting the conflict can become. Conversely, the less impact a co-worker's or co-laborer's behavior or work has on an individual, the less chance for conflict.

Blame - Coworkers/co-laborers who routinely shift blame or refuse to accept responsibility for workload, issues of conflict, or problems in the workplace typically find themselves in more frequent conflict situations.

Anger - Anger is generally propagated by lingering feelings of injustice, unequal treatment, favoritism, unresolved offenses, feelings of abandonment or just not doing what they want you to do! They are emotionally upset, possibly sending destructive verbal and non-verbal signals to each other.

By understanding which of the factors are contributing to the conflict, you can better prescribe solutions for yourself and for others.

If one or more of the above ingredients are present, proceed to step three; if not, you may just have differences; see step one.

Step 3: Discern who is involved

You want to avoid involving folks who are not really involved nor need to be. Avoid the temptation to gossip, huddle, or otherwise validate your opinions with others who are not involved. Do not make the initial conflict a prayer request or sermon topic. Words spoken can never be taken back, and most of us have many regrets over that reality.

We must determine if the conflict is between two individuals, within a team, or perhaps between teams. Are there multiple individuals in conflict? If so, are they factions or groups within the team or department? Be certain you understand the dynamics of the conflict by who is and is not involved.

Is the nature of the conflict along departmental or ministry teams lines? Once again, be certain you understand the dynamics of the conflict by who is and is not involved. Also understand that groups behave differently from individuals! (They are often referred to as mobs or mutineers!)

Step 4: Discern what type of contest this really is.

There are normally three types of underlying conflicts, and discovering what type of contest this really is will shed needed light on how to bring an acceptable solution.

Is the conflict based in a *power contest*? Those in conflict use their resources (physical strength, threats, influence, corporate authority, allies, money, etc.) to coerce or intimidate opponents.

Is this conflict a *rights contest*? Those in conflict enlist a source of authority (parents, manager, judge, constitution, bylaws, etc.) to determine that their rights are more legitimate than their opponents' rights and therefore should prevail.

Is this conflict based in *position bargaining*? Those in conflict, with or without the involvement of a neutral third party, participate in non-adversarial dialogue with the intent to reconcile and preserve contradictory positions. This contest is normally won by those with superior debating skills.

Once the conflict is properly discerned, we understand who is involved and what type of contest we are dealing with, we can move on into the second "D."

II. Decompress

Whenever possible the old football strategy is appropriate, "the best offense is a good defense." If we can pre-empt conflict whenever possible, a great deal of time and relational damage can be avoided.

As we review our staff, boards, and volunteers, we should think over what are the potential conflicts that may arise. Which people are most likely to be involved and why? What events will trigger stress, or possible conflict? Can we provide enough up-front, before the conflict communication or clarification to help prevent it? We probably cannot all the time, but with better planning, perhaps some conflict could be avoided.

When conflict happens anyway, we need to follow these seven principles:

1. Calmly acknowledge dysfunctional conflict as it happens. Simply calling attention to it frequently prevents it from worsening.

2. Treat feelings as facts framing emotional acts and words as objective, factual information. It's easier to deal with "facts" than "feelings," and it honors human emotions.

3. Don't walk away thinking that it will disappear if you do! It most likely won't.

4. Don't power play by abusing your authority as a manager to render on-the-spot judgments. Reject the traditional management mentality of "don't bring your personal feelings to work!" People are people...they are emotional beings.

5. Use humor but be appropriate! Be careful not to insult or downplay someone's emotions by your humor.

6. Respond with serenity by developing emotional self-control. Don't give yourself permission to blow up, or people around you will

bottle up conflict to avoid your blow up, ultimately making the conflict worse! Use the conflict as a challenge to be overcome. Demonstrate self-control during high conflict situations.

7. Learn to listen well, thus demonstrating respect, kindness, and care. People need to know you actually hear what they say and are not simply trying to end the conflict.

After these initial steps have been taken, hopefully the situation has calmed down some. Emotions have been placed under control and now we can move on into attempting a godly solution to the conflict by thinking through step three.

III. Determine Approach

In the chapter on personality evaluation we referred to the DiSC tool to help discern our underlying traits. Another truth is that we all have a preferred method to handling conflict. Learning what we prefer as well as what method works best in each situation will help us move through the conflict.

The Thomas-Kilman Conflict Mode Instrument[12] is an excellent tool to gain further understanding into our preferred style of handling as well as understanding other's styles of handling conflict. According to this model, there are five basic personal styles of handling conflict:

- Competing
- Accommodating
- Avoiding
- Compromising
- Collaborating

---

[12] http://www.kilmanndiagnostics.com/catalog/thomas-kilmann-conflict-mode-instrument

Each of these styles has strengths and weaknesses. All of them are appropriate at given times. Let's briefly look at each one of the styles and give examples of when it may be necessary to implement it.

Competing Mode

- High assertiveness/Low cooperativeness
- The goal is to "win"
- Power oriented
- Ability to argue
- Standing up for your rights
- Defending a sacredly held position

When would it be necessary to operate in this conflict resolution mode?

- Quick, decisive action is vital
- When unpopular actions need to be implemented
- Issues vital to company welfare
- Protect yourself against people who exploit non-competitive behavior

Accommodating Mode

- Low assertiveness/High cooperativeness
- The goal is to "yield"
- Individual neglects own concerns to satisfy those of others
- Selfless generosity or charity
- Obeying orders when you don't want to
- Yielding to others' points of view

When would it be necessary to operate in this conflict resolution mode?

- When you know you're wrong

- When an issue is more important to others than to you
- When preserving harmony and avoiding disruption are critical
- To aid in associate development by allowing them to experiment and learn from mistakes

Avoiding Mode

- Low assertiveness/Low cooperativeness
- The goal is to "delay"
- Individual pursues neither their own concerns or those of others
- Diplomatically sidestepping issues
- Postponing issues until a better time
- Withdrawing from the situation

When would it be necessary to operate in this conflict resolution mode?

- When the issue is trivial
- When the potential damage of confronting the issue outweighs the benefits of resolution
- To let the situation cool down
- When others can resolve the conflict more effectively

Compromising Mode

- Moderate assertiveness/ Moderate cooperativeness
- The goal is to "find middle ground"
- Individual pursues solutions that partially satisfy everyone's concerns
- Splitting the difference
- Exchanging concessions

When would it be necessary to operate in this conflict resolution mode?

- When two sides with equal power are strongly committed to mutually exclusive goals (i.e. labor-management bargaining)
- To achieve temporary settlements to complex issues
- To arrive at expedient solutions under time pressure
- When resolution is moderately important, but not worth the effort or potential disruption of more assertive modes

Collaborating Mode

- High assertiveness/High cooperativeness
- The goal is to "win/win"
- Individual pursues solutions that completely satisfy all concerns
- Exploring disagreements
- Resolving conditions that create competition
- Confronting problems with creativity

When would it be necessary to operate in this conflict resolution mode?

- To find an integrative solution when both sets of concerns are too important to be compromised
- When your objective is to learn — to test your own assumptions
- To gain commitment and to integrate others' concerns into a truly consensual decision
- To work through hard feelings that have been interfering with an interpersonal relationship

Your ultimate success in handling conflict will not be determined by which style you are proficient at or most comfortable with; it will be determined by how effectively you utilize the various styles at the right place at the right time.

After we determine which mode we are the most comfortable with, the one we will usually operate in, and we think about which style may be necessary, we can move on to the second step in determining our approach:

What level of involvement is needed in order to effectively resolve the conflict?

One principle that is always important to remember is to attempt to deal with issues or allow them to be dealt with at the lowest level possible. Think carefully about your options before deciding how to intervene, if at all.

We have several options when we consider how to be involved in a conflict beginning with ignoring it. Sometimes the most effective method is to let the small issues work themselves out if at all possible. Use only when effective and not as an excuse for passivity!

Perhaps one of the parties involved in the conflict initiates steps to resolve the issues. If properly trained, and to the extent people involved see the value of this process, it can be a very successful model. If conditions are appropriate, do not be afraid to coach folks through this process. If the two people involved in the conflict can work this issue out without your intervention that is always preferred.

Perhaps the manager of the parties involved in the conflict initiates and facilitates steps to resolve the conflict and not bring you in. This process is utilized when the parties are unable or unwilling to resolve the conflict through self-mediation, or the time frame necessary for resolution is very short by necessitating circumstances.

Maybe there is a skilled neutral mediator — or a highly skilled member of one of the teams involved in the conflict, and they initiate and guide a structured process to seek resolution between the teams and or departments before bringing you in.

Whether the conflict is solved by the individuals involved, a manager, or team member, remember the goal is to handle the conflict at the lowest level possible.

If it becomes apparent that conflict resolution meetings are required then we move to step IV.

IV. Dialogue

If it is diagnosed that a meeting between individuals or teams is necessary, then use the following tools to be as effective as possible.

1. Invite each individual to the conflict mediation discussion

   - Ask each participant to attend a meeting to be facilitated by you
   - Meet face to face
   - Confirm in writing if necessary

2. Strategically choose a site for the meeting

   - Avoid "turf"
   - Ensure privacy
   - Avoid embarrassment

3. Allow for open-ended time commitment

   - The discussion should continue long enough to find a solution or clear next steps.
   - Don't artificially cut off the talk because the clock strikes "x."
   - Be sensitive to hour of day and day of week and energy levels of those involved
   - Also know when to stop, look for good progress/closure points

4. Hold preliminary meetings with each individual

   - Dispassionately describe what you know about the situation
   - Listen
   - Ask open ended questions
   - Clarify
   - Suspend judgment
   - Tell them a joint meeting is forthcoming

5. Define the problem

    - After hearing from all parties, define the problem specifically.
    - What is the "real" problem, issue or story behind the story?
    - Then define the problem to be resolved, but not HOW it will be resolved.

6. Describe success

    - To reach and document a balanced, behaviorally specific, mutually acceptable agreement that defines each person's future accountabilities.

7. Define the ministry implications

    - If this problem is not resolved, the ministry will be affected in the following ways...
    - No "threats" about their personal future, but if there are future implications, they must be presented in a factual manner

8. Manage the meeting

    - Pray not as a ritual, or out of routine, but genuinely spend time asking God for wisdom.
    - Insist on direct dialogue between/among the parties in conflict.
    - Set parameters to guide the discussion "by the rules," no walk-a-ways, no one-sided solutions, no power plays, no extraneous topics.

Here are some suggested rules that the leader should lay out in advance before the discussion begins:

- Be honest, and expect honesty from the other person

- Share emotions using "I" statements rather than "You" statements
- Agree that disagreeing is okay
- Avoid resolutions that are too quick; people need time to process their thoughts and emotions, to pray about it, and to process possible solutions
- Avoid name calling
- Avoid threatening behavior
- Avoid reacting to emotionally-charged comments made by the other person
- Avoid putting the other person's position or their character down. You can't expect someone to see eye to eye with you when you're looking down on them!

The temptation is for the discussion, to roam and range over a great deal of history because there have probably been some previous issues that have not been properly dealt with. Deal with one issue at a time and deal with the issue at hand.

As you walk through the discussion it is helpful to reflect on how you want to be viewed when the conflict is over! How you behave during this event will reflect and become part of your reputation.

As you begin the meeting:

- Open the meeting by re-stating the problem as you have defined it
- Review the implications of letting the situation persist
- Explain your role as mediator — a conversation facilitator
- Reiterate that the problem must be resolved by them, not by you
- Ask for someone to volunteer to begin the conversation. Then be quiet!

As you observe and go through the meeting watch for:

- Departures from the topic — no "dredging up" history or unrelated issues
- Changes in behavior that could mean further conflict (e.g., a talkative person becomes quiet, or a generally tactful person becomes tactless, etc.)
- Conciliatory gestures, including apologies, admissions of mistakes, and positive comments about the other person(s)
- Breakthrough moments · when there is a mutual exchange of conciliatory gestures, signaling an attitudinal shift from "me against you" to "us against the problem."

You will know it is time to seek resolution:

- When a spirit of conciliation has been attained, intervene to suggest a "resolution" might now be possible
- Describe what success looks like: balanced, mutually agreeable, behaviorally specific, and defines future accountabilities
- Act as scribe, tell them they will each get a clean copy, and hold a brief "signing ceremony" to reinforce the spirit of cooperation (if necessary)

V. Documentation

After the meeting and before everyone leaves, if the situation requires documentation based upon the serious of the conflict, the lingering nature, or the significance if unresolved, then provide a record of what happened.

In the document you could follow this format:

- Write what you as the leader of the discussion observed. Be concise but detailed enough to remember.
- Record where and when the meeting took place
- List what problems were created by the conflict
- List what Person "A" thought was a fair resolution
- List what Person "B" thought was a fair resolution

- List what was agreed upon for future action. Include specific instructions for who is to do what by when and for how long, etc.
- List what will happen if the agreement is honored
- List what will happen if the agreement is broken
- Have everyone sign and date the agreement.

By following these "5 D's," conflict can be successfully managed, reduced, or eliminated. Also by God's grace conflict can even be redemptive. People can see blind spots, grow in the Fruit of the Spirit, and sometimes even move on somewhere else. Paul and Barnabas split company and the Gospel spread even further, and new missionaries were engaged.

It is inevitable that conflict will happen, but conflict does not have to destroy the church, the pastor, or the parties involved. God still performs miracles, even bringing healing to wounded relationships.

Communication Pointers

At the root of many conflicts is poor communication. In our day of mass e-mails, quick snippets, and texting acronyms, miscommunication is escalating. Incorporating these helpful pointers will typically reduce the potential conflicts in your ministry.

When *sending* communication to others remember to:

1. Begin positively — try to begin most conversations with something positive. Be observant, look for the good in a situation or some portion of the project or process that you can give recognition for. In order to be effective, it must be genuine and specific.

2. Communicate cause and effect — state specifically what you have observed and the effect that it is having. Relate your observations to actions, not personality, intelligence or style; simply state the facts. Then, communicate and illustrate the corresponding result.

C – Circumstance or Situation
A – Action
R – Result
E – Evaluation

3. Create two-way dialog – make certain that the person you are communicating with feels comfortable in responding. Ask open-ended questions, encourage dialog, and ask for their observations of opinions.

4. Generate ideas and solutions together – point the conversation to generating solutions for improving the future. Examine multiple options. See if there is opportunity to agree on trying out a solution(s).

When *receiving* communication from others remember to:

1. Focus on the message, not the messenger – we may not always like or appreciate the person or the delivery style, but every piece of communication has something important embedded in it. It is our job to dig out the communication, and throw the wrapper away.

2. Listen calmly and attentively – show respect for the individual and what they are attempting to communicate. Often times, this will have a calming effect on the process for both sender and receiver. Don't prepare your response while acting as if you're listening! Wait three seconds before responding to anything the other person has said.

3. Clarify feedback without defending or over-explaining — restate what you have heard as clearly as possible by acknowledging their concerns in a recap format. Ask if you have understood what they were attempting to communicate. Ask for further concerns or details. This process extends value to the person and lets them know with certainty that you understand what they are communicating.

4. Ask for suggestions – after acknowledging the other person's concerns, ask for suggestions or ideas as to how to improve the situation. Dialogue about potential solutions and agree to what the next step in the process will be.

When addressing difficult issues with others, remember to:

1. Choose a good time – sometimes our timing can enhance the conflict resolution process. Poor timing can certainly hurt the process. It could be that you will need to exercise patience and wait for the best time to address an issue.

2. Make an appointment – ask for time to discuss an issue and give parameters of the discussion and approximately how much time you will need. Be courteous and respectful.

3. Go into the conversation with openness – yes, you have an issue or an agenda, but be open and receptive to the responses of the person with whom you're talking. You might learn something new that changes the situation.

4. Be a good listener – listen at least as much as you speak. Dialogue, don't have a one sided conversation.

5. Avoid blaming – look for solutions, not blame. Use "I," not "You," don't put the other person on the defensive.

6. Validate – at the appropriate times, summarize key points that you have heard and ask for additional insights.

7. Agree on the next step in the process, at the end of the conversation — don't leave a disagreement on the table, find a next step to agree on, even if it is only a decision to meet again to discuss the topic further.

We said we would give some pointers on working with difficult people. Here are a few for your consideration:

1. Discern their initial position – consider the other person's personality profile (DiSC) and how they might be viewing and approaching the situation.

2. Be consistent – consistency builds trust and respect. Difficult people do not like surprises; they view them as additional reasons for mistrust.

3. Refer mainly to your behavior – pointing fingers and blame shifting encourages negative responses.

4. Move forward – to achieve greater influence and success, you must forget the past and move forward looking for better behavior.

5. Be patient – don't look for instant recognition or a word of thanks. Bad behavior is a pattern that takes a long time to change. Even if people see the change and like it, egos might prevent thanking those responsible.

6. Reinforce good behavior – when you see progress, be diligent to reinforce the good behavior in public or in private, whichever is most appropriate.

We spend so much time dealing with, minimizing, and trying to avoid dysfunctional conflict we lose sight of the many benefits of **functional** conflict defined as:

> **"When a diversity of opinion and alternative ideas are regularly solicited, accepted, and embraced as an organizational norm, moving the ministry forward through continuous self evaluation, innovation, and improvement will take place."**

Most of us do not cherish conflict. Yet, God in His infinite wisdom surrounds us with people with whom it is easy to conflict. Was this on purpose or accidental? If it was an accident, then we just have to endure this purposeless frustration and make the best of it. If it was a divine choice, then we must learn how to grow from it, embrace it, and become part of the healing process to redeem it. As always, our frustrations can become God's opportunity to work in and through us.

In addition, we must never forget that there is a spiritual battle involved in the church. (See 2 Corinthians 10:4, Ephesians 6:10-18, 1 Peter 5:8, etc.) Forgetting we have an enemy that desires to destroy God's work and His people is a recipe for disaster. How much conflict is caused by the stirring of our adversary? How much could be resolved if we remembered this truth? We were given armor and weapons for a reason; perhaps if we used them wisely, a great deal of conflict could be avoided and removed.

Questions to Ponder

1. Why did God bring people together that irritate one another so easily?

2. If God places people around us that are difficult to relate to, what possible reasons could He have for doing so?

3. Thinking about a recent conflict in your ministry team, what could you have done differently to affect the outcome?

4. What benefits can you see from following the 5 "D's" presented in this chapter?

5. What style of conflict manager are you? Is this a good thing or not? Why?

17 The Belly of the Ship:
Delegation, Committees & Volunteers

*You never see a statue to a committee,
but we bet it took one to approve erecting it.*

The Body of Christ is made up of many members. Each of these members is different and is comprised of strengths and weaknesses, including the pastor. In order to further the work of the Kingdom, God decreed first that there should be committees — okay, probably not— but if we hope to be effective, we will learn how to delegate and empower others within our ministry.

We cannot do all the work alone; though in the small church, it may feel like it. One pastor describes his duties like this:

> "I have 35+ years experience — 4 churches in 2 states. Tenures of 7 yrs, 2 yrs, 6 yrs and at my current church for over 20 years. I knew I would preach, teach, preside over funerals & weddings, counsel, comfort & lead business meetings. What I did not know is I would also have to mow the lawn, shovel the snow (at 1 church I also had to plow the church parking lot), clean the church, plunge the toilets (on Sunday morning between services — in the ladies room), paint, do plumbing & repair work. Go up on the roof to remove the bees nests, service

the lawnmower, change light bulbs, put blacktop sealer on the parking lot, change the letters in the sign out in front of the church, plant flowers, weed the flower beds, order new flags for the flagpole outside, then change the flags, make, print & fold the bulletin etc. etc. etc."

In most job descriptions, this list would be referred to as, "Other duties as assigned." Most pastors like to preach and teach; it's all this other stuff that wears us out. However tedious these duties may seem, they need to be accomplished.

Most pastors also become acutely aware of their own limits pretty quickly. We soon realize at what we are good and with what we struggle. We would be wise to learn how to become skilled in the areas we are already gifted, and delegate those other duties to someone who would enjoy them. This may come as a shock to some of us, but there are people who actually enjoy doing what we despise. Delegation will make all parties involved in the process happier and more effective!

Committees (Teams)

Most churches have groups of people that gather together to help the ministry function. Decoration, building, maintenance, cleaning, food preparation, financial oversight, visitation, and a host of other opportunities await these groups. Most pastors will interact with these groups on some level. Learning some basic team building skills will greatly assist the pastor and the people involved in these service groups.

Wherever two or more gather together to accomplish a task, a team is established. This team may be in place for a short period of time, or for decades. Pastors can help organize these teams or they may spring up due to a need or simply a desire by like-minded people to accomplish something. Every church will have them, so let's learn to interact with them in order to be effective.

First, here are eight quick steps to easily kill your team before it even begins. For the record, we don't recommend you follow these:

- Be pessimistic

- Be hypercritical
- Fight change
- Find scapegoats
- Play your cards carefully
- Focus on self-interest
- Form a clique
- Withhold support

Our attitude really does impact how effective we are, and this is true with those we lead as well. If we allow any of these negative attributes to be active in our teams, they will struggle.

Teams are made up of individuals. As we have already seen, each person has a unique personality style, and no two people are exactly alike. So who do you pick for the teams? It depends. The particular tasks that the group will be accomplishing need to be considered when recruiting members. What is the required skill set for the members? While availability is important, if the person volunteering does not have the required skill set, the task will most likely not be performed well.

For example, assigning someone to the building maintenance support team who has no mechanical skills might not work well when the plumbing breaks. The same could be said about the finance committee. Just because a donor gives large amounts of cash, that does not mean they have an understanding of finances and should be part of planning the church's budget. Matching people's skill sets to the task is in everyone's best interest.

If the job needing accomplished requires urgency, find someone who possesses high initiative. If the task requires relating to people, find someone who is relational. Someone with detail skills should be doing work that requires accuracy, and if a specialized skill is required, don't put someone in place who is not trained. Matching skill sets to the task seems obvious, yet how many of us know people in positions of authority that have no business being there?

Most people will fit into one of four categories when they are placed on a team. Like the DiSC personality profile, these are general guidelines pointing out tendencies. Ignore at your own risk however.

Some people will be *task oriented*, some will *be goal directed*, some will be *process oriented* and some will *question* almost everything. Each of these personality types is helpful and needed. Each can also be annoying to other team members or the pastor. In spite of the annoyance, inclusion of all four types will assure that the group works better.

Communication is critical for the success of teams or committees. In every grouping, the following questions need to be understood by all involved:

- Who is the leader?
- Who are the other members?
- What role is each person expected to play?
- How long is the team to exist — just for a project or indefinitely?
- What authority does the team have?
- What deliverables (product, result, or service) are expected?
- What is the timing of the deliverables?
- To whom should the deliverables be given?
- What resources are available to the team?

Failure to address these questions will hinder the success of the team. In addition to the above, the team needs to clearly understand its purpose and how it fits into the overall vision of the church. Why do they exist? What are their goals? How do they know if they are accomplishing those goals?

Feedback is critical for success all along the journey. People want to know that what they do matters and that it is appreciated. Frequent verbal and written praise is very helpful. If the only time someone hears from you is when you are upset or disappointed, soon you will most likely be doing all the work alone.

This might be a good time to venture into a syndrome that most of us know, but are often afraid of facing. Let's call it, "Fear of not being viewed as the best syndrome," or perhaps, "Fear of someone else getting praise syndrome."

Are we really interested in furthering the work of the Kingdom, or is there a part of us that wants to further our own? Do we really care who gets the credit or praise when something goes well, or do we cringe just a bit if we do not? Are we insecure?

If we surround ourselves with gifted people we will accomplish a great deal more than we could by ourselves. This is risky to our ego, but excellent for the Kingdom. King David didn't have to go down into a pit and kill a lion on a snowy day, but he had a mighty man named Benaiah who did. Would we be okay with that?

What is wrong with having a church full of gifted teachers, musicians, evangelists, disciple makers, and others that far surpass our giftings again? If the goal is to expand the work of the Kingdom for the glory of Christ, we will not care who is ultimately used. If the water level rises, all boats rise as well.

We must not let fear or intimidation of gifted people stop us from enjoying the fruit of their service. Adding members to the worship team that are excellent musicians will only help the entire team. Embracing gifted volunteers who excel in something at which we are not very good will only help the church, not hurt it.

God gave and still gives gifts to the Church, and we must learn to lay down our egos for the advancement of the Kingdom. We learn how to maximize and release others into their calling and not fear them excelling. David's mighty men were still known as his men. We have nothing to fear if we are building God's Kingdom. After that brief pause for some personal introspection, let's get back to our discussion about teams.

Stages of Committees/Teams

Personal and corporate church experience has shown a strong correlation between groups that go through specific stages of development and their respective level of success.

While the length and intensity of each stage may vary, clear, empirical evidence points toward the necessity of working effectively to the degree necessary through all four stages to reach maximum effectiveness.

There are typically four stages a group passes through on their way to effectiveness:

Forming stage - This is the "get acquainted" stage where a newly formed team or new team members get to know each other. During this initial stage, members like to learn about who is in the group, how the group is going to work together, and what their roles and responsibilities might be. What is the purpose of the group? What are the boundaries of the group?

Storming stage - This is the stage that is often misunderstood and the stage that most managers attempt to circumvent. In this stage, the group has moved past the pleasantries, and is now getting serious about ideas, opinions, roles and responsibilities. As differences of opinion arise as to what the goal is and how the most effective manner to reach the goal is, conflict occurs.

Norming Stage - In this stage, the group is beginning to find itself. Its purpose is beginning to be clear as well as roles, responsibilities, and how the group will function together. The group is somewhat comfortable and is beginning to work together effectively.

Performing Stage - The group is now operating on "all cylinders." The group has reached a healthy level of interdependence and is performing their assigned tasks well. They know each other, they respect each other, and generally work well together. The most common misperception is that just because the group reaches this stage, it does not mean it will remain at this level without appropriate management.

Each stage of the life cycle involves the pastor to some degree or another. Here are some guidelines to consider as the stages become clear:

The Belly of the Ship

Forming Stage

- Understand the different team players' perspectives and address their specific needs early on in the process.
- Manage this stage with purpose. Invent processes to get the group immersed in the forming stage. Use ice breakers, causal gatherings, and social times to assist them in this process.
- Allow the proper amount of time for the group to work through this stage. You don't really want this stage to be too long or too short.
- Ask questions, allow for input, and get feedback on how the group is doing; then you will know when it is time to move them to the next stage.

Storming Stage

- First and foremost, don't avoid or circumvent this stage! If your goal is truly a high performing team, then allow a healthy level of storming.
- Set ground rules for healthy conflict. Monitor and maintain open communications and appropriate respect among team members.
- Evaluate how much storming is productive and be ready to move the group forward when appropriate.

Norming Stage

- When this stage arrives, communicate to team members what you see that is positive and what still needs to be improved.
- Allow enough time for a strong bond of norming to permeate the group. Don't rush them through this stage.
- Analyze when it is time to move them forward and coach them through the process.

Performing Stage

- When this stage is in progress, again let folks know the good behavior that you see. Don't be afraid to celebrate small, incremental victories so they get a feel for what accomplishment as a team feels like.
- As mentioned earlier, do not assume upon arrival at this stage that your work is done. The most difficult part of stage management is not getting to performing; it is maintaining it!
- Continue to invest time and energy in the group. Monitor the group periodically, ask questions, get feedback on a regular basis, and make adjustments accordingly.

Working with teams, committees, and volunteers is a learned skill. If you struggle at first, learn from the failure and try again. The Kingdom of Jesus is a group-oriented project and will not be accomplished by a solo performer.

We must learn how to work effectively with those in our midst. The vast majority of churches are comprised of a small paid staff and a huge non-paid one. Which one is more important? Learning how to recruit, train, work alongside of, and manage volunteers is a critical part of the pastor's skill set.

Here are some practical pointers when working with teams to help them achieve higher performance and success:

- **Establish a Clear Purpose** – A goal or series of goals must be established and regularly communicated to provide focus and consistency of purpose. This can come directly from leadership when necessary, but a more effective approach includes staff at all levels contributing to the process.
- **Promote Informality** – Rules, regulations, and formalities are usually a substitute for good management and leadership. When staff is not treated with value and respect, they seek protection in various forms, usually regulatory in nature. An

informal environment is more conducive to creativity, building trust, and promotes accountability vs. control.

- **Encourage Participation** – Effective teams have most, if not all members participating at some level in the goals and workload of the team. Consensus building is a lifestyle, not a politically correct process to labor through. If everyone has an oar in the water rowing in the same direction, it's hard to have time to complain.
- **Pursue communication** – Two-way, open communication enhances the ability of teams to reach new levels. If members can give and receive quality feedback, it will lead to a more productive team climate as well as higher levels of team productivity.
- **Practice Listening** – Effective teams are those in which the members have learned to genuinely listen to each other with respect. Team members attempt to understand input given, not justify the status quo or defend themselves. Civilized disagreement is promoted, and differing viewpoints are considered healthy.
- **Pursue Style Diversity** – Style diversity is more than race and gender; it speaks to the variety of differences that people bring to a team, including personality, education, skills, work experience, and a host of personal experiences that can add significantly to a group's outcomes. The more diverse a team is the more potential for optimal solutions.
- **Perform a Team Self Assessment** – Teams that regularly engage in healthy self assessments become more self aware leading to the ability to improve. Teams that seek out information both internally and externally to the group will formulate a more accurate assessment of their effectiveness, hopefully leading to self improvement. Once again, this is a lifestyle adjustment, not an event.
- **Form Appropriate Leadership** – Leadership who knows how and when to create interdependency by empowering, freeing up resources and serving others will build stronger teams.

- **Shared responsibility** – Establishing an environment in which all team members feel as responsible as the leader for the performance of the work unit is a good goal.
- **Future focused** – The team sees change as an opportunity for growth and embracing the future. It thinks in terms of the long term and makes decisions accordingly.
- **Promote Creativity** – Creativity is not only discussed, it is encouraged. The environment is open to new ideas, regardless of their source.
- **Respond Quickly** – The team is aware of the need to respond quickly to changes in the market or to take advantage of opportunities as they present themselves.

There are no perfect committees and neither are there people who serve or lead them. However, with practice, patience, and desire, we can all improve. Greater amounts of service and work will be accomplished by a team than by any one individual.

Here are some final thoughts to consider. Volunteers are not paid staff, and there is a temptation to make an unhealthy distinction. The Biblical truth is that every believer is in ministry; some of us are just blessed to receive a paycheck in ours. Volunteers are donating time and energy to the church because they care. We should strive to make them understand how much we appreciate their generosity.

The lifeblood of most churches is in its membership functioning together to further the cause of Christ. Whatever team or committee someone may serve on is reflective of their desire to help complete the vision and to serve Christ as well as the pastor. We must not take that gift for granted.

Yes, some people serve from completely wrong motives. Some serve to stroke their egos, build a false image, or fulfill something that is lacking in their personal life. When we happen to discover these insights, we gain an opportunity to pray for the person and perhaps be part of the redeeming process in their life.

Relationships are messy, and working with committees is messy also because they are always comprised of people. People take time, energy, are often exasperating, and can push us to the point of despair. People are also made in the image of God and are dearly loved by their Heavenly Father, and we demonstrate our love of God by how we treat them.

If we want to be effective in our calling, we will learn how to work with God's other children. In fact, without them, we would not even have a calling. The simple truth is that we will accomplish a great deal more learning how to release people into their gifting instead of trying to accomplish everything alone.

Questions to Ponder

1. How many committees/teams are there in my current church? How many people are involved? What percentage of my church is functioning on them?

2. Considering the eight negative attributes listed early in the chapter, which ones do I function in?

3. Rereading the nine questions that every team should understand, would the teams in my church be able to satisfactorily answer them?

4. Thinking of the stages of teams explained in this chapter, rank each committee you thought of in question 1.

5. Consider the twelve practical steps listed for working with your teams. Which steps would your teams state that you need to improve on?

18 The Calm after the Storm:
Leading through Change Management

Change comes to all, even those who resist it.

One constant we all face is change. How do we effectively navigate the waves of change that will hit our lives, families, and ministries? We have all probably been the victim of poor management of change, so what should we do differently? Change will come, and it can even be good.

As a young minister, (Rodney) my mentor suggested that ministry could be broken down into a simple equation:

$$\text{Prayer} = \text{Power}$$
$$\text{Obedience} = \text{Blessing}$$
$$\text{Growth} = \text{Change}$$

Over the years, I have frequently reflected on the truth and wisdom of his application of mathematics to the art of ministry. Growth will not occur unless change takes place. Sometimes, the changes are organic and take place unnoticed. At other times, change requires innovation, intentionality, and leadership resolve. This chapter is designed to provide a foundation for surviving change.

It is imperative to understand that not everyone responds positively to change. Sociologists tell us that 1 out of 20 people are innovators. Innovators are often called risk takers. They have the resources and desire to try new methods. Failure is not a setback for innovators. About 14% of the population are early adopters. These people are quick to see the benefit of change and adopt those that they believe are beneficial. An equal percentage of people are "early majority" and "late majority." These both take time to weigh the merits of a new idea. Early majority will embrace change when it is understood and fits with their perception of what is right for the church. Once the early majority are on board, the late majority will respond to the change for a variety of reasons, including a desire to show unity, peer pressure, economic necessity, or friendships. The final group, the laggards, makes up just 16% of the average community, but they are often quite vocal. These members base decisions on experience and often raise questions based on past failures.

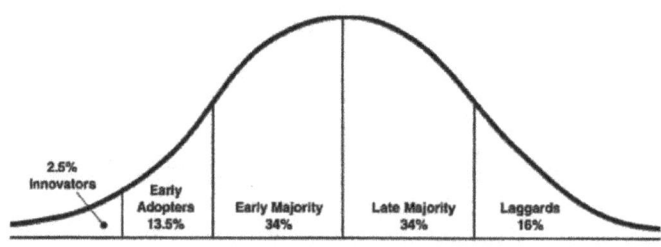

Bryce Ryan & Neal Gross, 1943

The first step in dealing with change is to properly understand the size and scope of it. We must answer questions like how many people are involved and how difficult will the change be to make. Depending on the answers, these changes can range from very minor to major to transformational in nature.

The Calm after the Storm

Minor changes include incremental or accommodative tweaks. Perhaps the system or process needs adjusting but not overhauling. *Major* changes can include new patterns and systems being installed with the old ones being discarded. *Transformational* change involves an entire organizational break from traditions, history, and previously held paradigms.

Before we explore how to walk through these changes, let's examine nine reasons why people and organizations seem to always resist change.

1. A small percentage of the population has a predisposed attitude against change of any kind under any circumstance. Researchers tell us that it can range upwards of 20% of the population. It is partly due to personality wiring and can also be due, in part, to prior negative experiences. There are also studies that indicate that birth order impacts our views regarding change.

2. Fear of the unknown – "what's going to happen to me?" Fear of the unknown is a powerful de-motivator when dealing with change. By nature, we do tend to look at things from our self-serving perspective first and the organization second. If the impact of change on our situation cannot be measured or determined in advance, that adds to the resistance we feel and act out.

3. Lack of trust – a lack of trust regarding potential changes can be fostered by a lack of trust in management or leadership and/or a prior bad experience in the current organization or at a previous organization. If a change "looks" or "feels" like a prior bad experience, it will naturally be resisted.

4. Fear of failure in the new environment is also a powerful de-motivator. If it cannot be discerned how the individual will fair in the new environment, resistance to change will increase.

5. Potential loss of status/job security/wages/benefits also creates resistance. While the fear of job loss and wages and benefits is completely understandable, surprisingly, loss of titles outranked a loss of income in research studies where job shifts have taken place. Don't underestimate the power of folks wanting to "save face."

6. Poor timing in conjunction with events outside of the organization is an often overlooked reason behind resistance to change. Often times, we propose a simple change of an office switch, and the staff member's response is disproportional to the actual change. This could be the proverbial "straw that broke the camel's back" syndrome.

7. Fear of losing relationships with staff, ministry constituents, and supervisor. This is also a powerful motivator of resistance. Studies have shown that a change in immediate supervisor is one of the most threatening issues relating to change that staff face (when they are happy with their current supervisor). Also changing those whom we relate with can also cause a high level of anxiety.

8. Lack of personal gain – unfortunately, because we are all people, if we don't see how changes will benefit us, we tend to resist it. Biblically, we ought to all be servant leaders, serve others before ourselves, place other's needs before our own, etc. But the reality is that sometimes, if not often, we place our own needs first.

9. Don't see the need for change – sometimes people don't understand the need because for them; the status quo is working just fine. Why put effort into making a change when, from their perspective, it isn't needed?

In addition to individuals that struggle with fears regarding change, so do ministries. Here are five typical reasons why:

The Calm after the Storm

1. They are comfortable where they are. They and their constituents are being served adequately, and therefore there is no compelling reason for change. Their needs are met, they are happy and they are satisfied.

2. Their corporate ego and pride prevent them from embracing necessary change. If they change or alter their path, someone might have to admit they were off track, or they needed to adjust, or that prior decisions were wrong. Most organizations have difficulty dealing with this.

3. They are unable or unwilling to see it. Sometimes, even a successful organization's vision becomes myopic. They are unwilling or unable to see what needs to change. This can be a spiritually based issue or a physical one.

4. Change is seen as an abandonment or criticism of previous leadership or previous success. It can even be seen as disrespectful and irreverent. Sometimes, even the most basic changes are resisted because it is not recognized that however successful those things were in the past, they are simply not working as well today.

5. They simply do not have the spiritual or intellectual gift needed to discern the need for change.

There will always be some resistance to change, so we should not be surprised when it occurs. It is a waste of time and energy to bemoan the resistance; we must learn to manage it.

Some resistance of change is helpful and healthy. In fact, it can be a good double-check of whether a change is needed and can cause us to further examine why we are making it.

If we want to help others in their acceptance of needed change, then we must first seek to look through their eyes and fully understand their reasons for resisting. After doing this, we need to determine the biggest underlying factors of the resistance and then devise a plan to address them.

Part of the process in leading someone or a group towards change is to highlight the potential impact of both accepting and resisting the change.

Potential impact of continuing to resist . . .

- Can lead to high stress levels and ensuing physical and emotional concerns
- Can keep an individual from reaching his/her potential
- Can create a negative, unproductive team climate
- Can prevent an organization from reaching its potential
- In extreme cases, can cause organizational failure

Potential impact of embracing change . . .

- Can reduce stress and stress-related problems
- Provides an opportunity for individuals to reach their potential
- Helps create a more positive team climate
- Fosters higher levels of personal and group creativity
- Enhances individual and group problem solving
- Helps organization to reach its God-given potential

If the change is determined as necessary in spite of the difficulties, then we will begin the process of implementing it. There is a process of accepting change, and it will more or less follow along these three paths — leaving the old path, finding our way, and starting on the new one. Each of these three paths will include a mixture of emotions.

Let's define these three paths:

- Leaving the old path refers to moving out of our comfort zone. Most people become used to a certain way of accomplishing a task, an order of service, or the routine of how things work.

- Finding your way is a manner of saying that while we are still a bit uncomfortable with leaving the known, perhaps the new will not be that bad after all. A comfort level of some sort is beginning to take place with the change.

- Starting on the new path is the time when the change has been accepted and the new begins to take on more of a familiar feeling.

Leaving, finding, and starting are the three common stages of accepting the change process. Below are some typical feelings, reactions, and thought processes under each category.

Leaving the Old Path

- Anger
- Denial
- Fear
- Sadness
- Loss of identity
- Loss of credibility
- Excitement
- Anticipation
- Hopefulness

Finding Your Way

- Low self-esteem
- Confusion
- Reduced morale
- Lower productivity
- Frustration
- Anxiety
- Helplessness
- Dependence

- Lack of comfort
- Creativity
- Anticipation

Starting on the New Path

- Relief
- Excitement
- Energy
- Confidence
- Feelings of nostalgia
- Sadness

Leaders need to be ready to recognize and assist their staff and congregation members through the different stages in an empathetic, coaching manner. Here are some tried and true steps to assist people in the journey:

1. Communicate

- Encourage people to share issues and concerns.
- Provide weekly updates as to what is known and not known.
- Allow time in staff meetings for appropriate venting.
- Validate fears as valid feelings.
- Then follow with "what's right."

2. Celebrate

- Don't be afraid to celebrate the past victories, people, and places.
- Allow grieving
- Acknowledge the good in the past, its value, and the fact that certain aspects will be missed. It's okay to grieve. Sometimes it's good to clean out the literal or metaphorical "old space" for closure.
- Consider allowing people to keep a token to help remember the old.

3. Be a coach

- Help people know what they should stop doing, what they should continue doing, what they need to start doing, and when to make those adjustments.

4. Be an example

- Support leadership decisions.
- Maintain a good, positive attitude.
- Lead by example. People will use your behavior for one of two things: a benchmark to reach for, or an excuse to sink to.

5. Get everyone involved

- Solicit ideas for how to do things.
- Re-recruit your good people.
- Acknowledge progress.
- Provide encouragement for what still needs to be done.

6. Set direction

- Set short-term and long-term goals that remind them of where they are headed.
- Reinforce the vision.
- Give them as much clarity of purpose as is possible.

7. Acknowledge concerns

- Empathize with their feelings of disorientation and confusion. This is normal in process. It's also okay, as long as they don't stay in that state indefinitely.

8. Focus on the future

- Talk about the new vision and how things are going to be.
- Discuss similarities and differences from the past.

9. Share impact

- Discuss how their work will impact the future goals and how that will impact the organization and themselves.

10. Continue to refine

- Position people to create an environment friendly to change.
- Continue to refine the changes made. Change involves transition, which is not a single destination; it is a journey/lifestyle.

Based on these ten steps or stages, it should become apparent that change takes time and intentionality to implement properly.

Change at the Committee Level

Did you know that individuals are different in behavior than groups? Did you know that groups respond differently than organizations? While it is true that individuals make up groups and groups make up organizations, when managing change, it is important to distinguish and work with the unique characteristics of all three.

Small groups are embedded in every ministry and at every level of ministry; from Sunday School classes to men's groups, from deacon boards to the quilting club, small groups are everywhere. They can either help bring about change or stop it in its tracks. Remember: If you cannot manage change at the group level, you will not be successful at the organization level.

When initiating groups through the process of change, it is important to understand the four distinct phases or "weather patterns" that groups go through.

- Denial
- Resistance
- Exploration
- Commitment

The Calm after the Storm

It is important to note that groups will go through these phases at some point prior to getting to commitment. It is not an exercise of how to avoid the different phases or rushing them through, but managing them through the phases effectively to get them to a high level of commitment.

Ever hear or, better yet, say of these sentences in your previous experiences dealing with change? If so, then you were probably in one of these four phases:

Denial — is a conscious or subconscious refusal to accept the organization's current or proposed future reality.

- "The sky is falling the sky is falling . . . yeah right!"
- "They've been threatening this for years — it will never happen."
- "They can change all they want — it won't affect me or what I do."
- "I was doing this before he came, and I'll still be after he is long gone."

Resistance - can be manifested by both overt and covert words and actions that impede organizational change. "Resisters" can persuade more open-minded colleagues that the change will be at best, worthless or at worst, harmful.

- "It's not fair! It's not right!"
- "They don't know what they're doing"
- "We tried that before and it failed"
- "We've never done it that way before!"
- "Over my dead body!"

Exploration — is an important transitional phase of the change process when previous "resisters" begin to discover value in the "new order" for themselves and for their functions. Although complete commitment to the change has not yet been achieved, the exploration phase is a critical time of guarded optimism and gathering momentum.

- "Hey, maybe this won't be so bad after all."
- "Well, maybe a variation of that plan would work."
- "Let's do a pilot program and see how it works."

Commitment — is just that — a thorough embracing of the change, a new covenant between the group and its members. Frequently, those who most resisted the change become the best advocates for the change after they have committed to it!

- "I saw this need a long time ago!"
- "I was on board from the very beginning!"
- "This rocks! It's about time we finally did this!"
- "This is going to be good!"

After understanding the natural stages that groups go through when processing change, the next step is to manage them through the stages effectively. Three distinct components necessary to help groups deal more effectively with each phase include:

1. Control — "Groups gone bad" are often referred to as "mobs," as in their ability to act like a mob in a very short period of time. A part of this group dynamic is the inherent need of the group to feel as though they have some control over their destiny.

The longer the group has been together, the stronger the "will" of the group or the feeling that as a unit, "they have rights." They can become territorial, and as a group, they will tend to do things as a group that as individuals they would not ordinarily do. This is a very powerful dynamic that must be managed.

2. Communication — Group communication requires creative redundancy (saying the same thing over and in different and unique ways!) Just because it is "in the minutes" or because it was said from the pulpit does not mean, as a group, they got the message. Groups tend to take in information, rehash it, and then come up with their own interpretation of the message. You cannot over-communicate to groups!

3. Commitment — Saying, thinking, or wishing you have group commitment doesn't make it so! Without true group-wide commitment, your group change process will fall short of the desired results. Regular and consistent work must be done to achieve and maintain group-wide commitment.

Here are some tools we have discovered that work in dealing with these three components: control, communication and commitment:

1. Control
Provide the team with some sense of control. Common control points are:
- Voting (sometimes open, sometimes secret ballot)
- Equal processing time, public and/or private
- Equal say or opportunity for input and/or venting
- A sense of being heard and understood
- Access to relevant or needed information (current and or historical)
- Understanding of process
- Understanding of time frame and/or next steps

Ensure that group members understand that:
- They are responsible for their behavior
- They are responsible to ask questions
- They are responsible for looking for ways to contribute
- They are responsible for using the change management tools available to them

Remind them that as a group member:
- They are cared about....not taken care of
- They have choices...not that they can be choosy
- They are supported.....not hand-held
- They are equipped...and have a source to go to for resources

2. Communications
- Be a good observer of behavior and learn when to use one-on-one discussions and when to address the group as a whole.
- Be open and honest telling the team what you can, what you can't, and what you don't know. Create an environment conducive to expressing and addressing group concerns openly.
- Be consistent by setting regular communication tools in place and stick to them, whether it is weekly meetings, a daily e-mail update, etc.
- Be accurate by being as factual as possible and represent all opinions fairly and honestly when communicating to the group.

3. Commitment
- Maintain a consistency of purpose by keeping the vision and objectives before the group at all times, thus helping to keep them focused.
- Provide appropriate leadership by learning where and when to assist the group. Provide the resources and training necessary for the change. Know when to help and when to back off.
- Provide a level playing field by not changing the rules every day. Treat people with equal value. Respect each person's contribution to the process. Praise in public, correct in private.
- Celebrate the victories because everyone wants to know and be known, understand and be understood, and celebrate and be celebrated. Don't underestimate the value of a personal thank-you, a card or note, or group recognition when appropriate. It doesn't always have to be a promotion, monetary incentive or a new office. Remember:

It's not the act of appreciation: it's the appreciation behind the act!

Our goal in helping others embrace change is to help create an environment that can incorporate and encourage people regardless of what stage of acceptance or rejection they are in.

We learn to realize that it takes longer for some to work through the various stages and that after coaching them, we allow them time to respond properly. People's first reaction is not always their final one.

Change at the Ministry Level

We have looked at how individuals embrace change, or not, and also how groups navigate through these waters. What about at the organizational level? Sometimes change happens at the vision, founding purpose, or other organization-wide goal level. These are major, ministry-altering decisions that demand prudence and skill in implementing if the ministry hopes to survive.

Whatever the underlying reason that is precipitating the change, there will most likely be resistance to making the change. Organizations are made up of individuals and groups, so all of what we shared previously must be taken into consideration if success is going to be achieved.

At this stage, there is something that is driving the strong desire for change. An issue, circumstance, or event that is significant in nature.

Perhaps the vision of the church is being seriously hindered, and the leadership needs to clearly define what changes need to be made to either redefine the vision or to make changes to assure that it can be implemented in the future.

Your leadership will be critical to communicate the vision, to help explain the reason for the necessary change or changes, to provide a listening ear to those concerned, and to overcome any resistance issues standing in the way.

It is important that communication increases, not decreases. That ample opportunity is given for information gathering, the exchanging of ideas and the broadening and inclusion of everyone involved. Having a clear communication plan for the change process helps assure proper communication at the appropriate levels takes place.

Plans will need to be established and these will need to include clearly stated, understandable goals. The resources will need to be provided to allow for any expenses associated with the implementation of the goals. There should be clear outcomes explained with benchmarks along the way to measure progress.

If the changes are taking a significant amount of time, then some pep talks will be in order to help keep everyone focused. Remind each person where the ministry is going and why. Explain how important their roles are in achieving these results. If everyone feels like they are part of the solution they are less likely to become part of any problem.

Change at this level will take time, prayer, careful planning, patience, and skill as a leader. If the change is birthed from obedience to the Lord, then we can rest in the fact that He will guide the process if we seek Him.

Summary

Change is a part of life. Change is a part of leadership. People come and go, and so do leaders. Visions expand, shrink, and change. Change is inevitable. The pain we experience in the process can be limited by how well we implement what was shared in this chapter.

Our purpose is to help others who are following our lead. God will almost always lead us to some sort of change sooner than later in our ministries. Those who follow us will learn from us how to navigate the sea of change.

Before we move into a chapter that we know will assist you in improving your many meetings, please stop for a little while and consider the following questions.

Questions to Ponder

1. Thinking back on a significant change you experienced in your life, what would you now do differently?

2. Considering the necessary changes in your current ministry, what steps could you take to better prepare the individuals involved?

3. Same question as #2 but think about the groups involved instead.

4. How important is communication to the process of change management? Explain.

5. What fears do you have about change? What can you do about them?

19 Mutiny Mitigation:
How to Lead an Effective Meeting

Could we please have yet another boring meeting?

Every pastor of every church regardless of size has meetings. Board meetings, training meetings, brainstorming and brain-draining meetings. With the inevitability of having to lead so many meetings, why is there so little insight given on how to conduct them? It seems that many church meetings are excessively long, not overly productive, and ineffective at communication.

Leaders of large ministries and organizations will spend 35-50% of their time in preparation for and in meetings. Pastors of smaller churches will spend less time, but still will likely need to spend 10-15% of their time in meetings.

While there are many ways to lead a successful meeting, we will present you with some proven methods to enhance your meeting times. If meetings are inevitable, then we had better learn how to use them to further the work of the Kingdom, rather than waste precious time.

Like a good meal, good meetings are composed of many good parts. Meetings, like meals, require planning and careful preparation. The following is an attempt to break down into component parts the various aspects of a good meeting. If the component parts of the meeting are communicated well and understood by participants, there is a greater likelihood of your meeting being successful.

Often overlooked, but very important is that every meeting will have a context and an environment. There is a location and a "feel" to each gathering. Will the meeting be formal or informal? In an office, conference room, restaurant, or outdoors? Each meeting will also be impacted by the people attending and their personalities. Preparing the room in advance can help the overall feel and flow of the meeting. For example, consider these factors:

- The room temperature, light and ambiance
- Seating and table arrangement — U-Shape, circle or more traditional classroom setup?
- The placement of refreshments, if appropriate, or materials
- Possible distractions and interruptions

Good meetings also start and end on time. Publish the expected starting and ending times and stay true to the time frame. Generally, any meeting over two hours becomes ineffective. If necessary, draw the meeting to a close and say, "we aren't finished, but we are going to end this meeting." Then set a time for another meeting to continue. You might be surprised at how fresh ideas arise when a new meeting to finish up takes place.

Often, the poorest decisions come late in meetings when everyone is exhausted and tired. Don't fall prey to this syndrome. Take the necessary time to do it right.

Before the meeting begins, think through the agenda, the direction you desire to go, and expected outcomes. Plan, plan, plan, and then be flexible as the need arises with your agenda. An agenda gives you, the leader, and participants the opportunity to focus, stay on task, and get more done. As you start the meeting, share these thoughts with those in the meeting. Most people like to know the plan and direction so they can be thinking about their possible input.

Good meetings (and most meals outside of perhaps some ancient Vikings) don't allow raw meat to be thrown on the table!

With the exception of an intentional brainstorming session, don't allow someone to bring up a topic that has not been "pre-cooked" or at least warmed up a bit. Items that are not on the agenda tend to be distracting and often times are meant to be disruptive, divisive, or harmful. If the topic is important enough to bring up at the meeting, then it is important enough to do your homework and get it on the agenda. Be firm but kind and ask the one bringing up the item to make sure it is placed on the next meeting's agenda.

After setting the agenda, give the content for the meeting. Illustrate the content if possible and give examples related to why you are gathering. Ask for questions or concerns to help focus the meeting.

When the meeting is winding down, summarize the meeting to assure the salient points are covered. If applicable, give specific direction for the future. Assign specific tasks to people with a follow-up plan. Ask for any final questions and thank those who attended.

Making sure that these components are considered and followed will help assure that the meeting is effective. If you want to dramatically improve the quality of your meetings — and who doesn't — try following this highly successful system we call:

The Four D's of a Quality Meeting

It is important for the meeting leader and the participants to have a clear understanding of what is taking place during this particular meeting. Explaining the purpose will help direct the meeting and bring a breath of fresh air to them.

Not every meeting will have all four of these parts, but the beauty of these "D's" is that once explained to the participants, clarity will follow. The goal of the leader is to help guide everyone through the process or purpose of the meeting. Understanding which "D" you are attempting to address in a particular meeting will assist those attending and take unnecessary pressure off of them as well as limit wandering conversations.

1. Data Collection — this is a meeting or a portion of a meeting where information is being shared, gathered, or discussed for understanding. Here, clarification questions can take place. It should be understood that this is not the time to debate the merits of the information or the potential decision at hand; we just need to understand the data and make sure we receive its full value.

The leader could begin this meeting by saying, "The purpose of this meeting (or section of a longer meeting) is to gather data and make sure we understand it. We do not have to make any decisions right now. We just want to make sure we are all on the same page regarding the issues or data."

2. Discussion — this is a meeting or a portion of a meeting where we discuss the various aspects of the data presented. What is the data telling us? Do we need more data? Do we need less data? If the information is true, what are the implications?

In this phase, participants only share their perspectives or views; they do not need to spend the time or the energy convincing others that their opinion is "right". It's not about right or wrong, it's about exploring and considering all possibilities so that the eventual decision made is an informed one. Everyone should be allowed to maintain their opinion as well as earnestly seek to understand other's opinion.

The leader could state, "Now that we have the data, what does it mean? Do we still need more or do we have enough? Is the information shared insightful? We still don't need to make any decisions; we are just analyzing and discussing the data presented to us."

3. Deciding — this is a meeting or a portion of a meeting where, after working through steps 1 and 2 properly, decisions can be made.

Keep in mind voting is acceptable and at times called for, but building a consensus is more valuable (and difficult). Also, not every decision discussed requires a group decision. Sometimes that falls to the leader.

The leader could say, "Now that we have looked at the data, discussed it, what do we do with it? This is the meeting where we make the decision."

4. Doing — this is a meeting or portion of a meeting where after working through the first three steps, it's time to assign roles and responsibilities. This is the step where people are assigned tasks and time lines, and the team moves into action mode. Regular and systemic accountability will need to be utilized to insure the agreed-upon items get done.

The leader now states, "We have looked at the data, discussed it and made the following decisions....now we will assign the tasks to complete what we agreed upon."

Using and communicating these steps through one meeting or a series of meetings will help participants navigate through difficult processes and hopefully lead to more productive meetings.

If performed properly, each meeting or section of a meeting is now more focused and the participants all knew exactly what was expected at the proper time. Rabbit trails can be avoided and everyone should buy into the conclusions made more easily.

No one begins as an expert facilitator, but with practice, the overall quality and effectiveness of the meetings can improve dramatically.

Since we are called to be leaders, let's explore some concepts of leadership that are often overlooked.

Leading and Serving at the Same Time

How do we who are called to lead serve at the same time? The truth is, with great difficulty sometimes. If you are in a position of leadership then you most likely are gifted in some way. Perhaps you are intellectually brilliant or extremely fast in speaking or thinking. Maybe you have a crystal clear vision of what should be accomplished.

Gifted people often struggle with those who are not as gifted. Leaders lead because they see something sooner or more clearly than others. If the other people saw it the same way you did, they would be leading and you would be following. Because of these giftings, we need to give extra grace in working with other people.

How then should we lead? Here are six thoughts for your consideration.

1. Allow for differences of opinions, be gracious to others, and really learn to listen to what they are saying. No one person has the sum total of all wisdom. Each of us has blind spots, and we need other perspectives no matter how strong we may be. Just because someone does not agree with us or see everything the same way does not mean they are incorrect, they may just see it differently than we do.

Many issues are not so much a matter of right and wrong, but right and left. Different may be better, and pride will blind us to seeing another's wisdom if left unchecked. We may miss a better way to accomplish a task if we refuse to be open to other ways of doing it. Humility is always in style for a wise leader.

In addition, each person has value and deserves our attention when speaking to us. Turn off the phone, put down the mail, and listen. We may marvel at our own ability to multitask, but it is often offensive to those who finally get to speak with us. I know we are busy, but if someone is speaking to us, we need to actually listen to them.

2. Always put the ministry first, asking the question, "What is the best for the ministry?" We lead from a position of service under the Ultimate Leader, Jesus. Jesus only sought what the Father wanted, and we should do the same. What is God's will should be primary.

The greater issue is about furthering the Lord's work through the ministry, not necessarily through us. When we can give up the demand to receive the credit and rejoice in the fact that the work was accomplished, we have taken a giant step forward in our spiritual growth.

Most successful sports teams are so because they work as a team. They may have a superstar, but without the supporting cast around them, they will not succeed. We need to focus on building the Kingdom of God and not our own.

3. Steer people towards the greater goal and the greater good. If we as leaders will model point two, we will be in a better place to expect those that follow us to do the same.

There is a goal beyond our personal self worth and fame. There is a Kingdom that we are supposed to be building that transcends us and our vision. We are to seek His Kingdom, His will, His plans, and our plans should line up within and under His. Whatever the overall vision for our ministry is, His will should take precedence over our own goals and desires.

If we desire to spread this concept throughout the ministry, it needs to begin with us, be modeled through us, and be spoken of often. Our work is centered in Christ's, and His will matters more than ours.

4. Be open to more than one way to get the job done. If we hope to be successful, we will learn to delegate and appreciate the gifts in others. As leaders, we tend to think we are correct and that we know the best way to accomplish just about anything. The truth is there may be many ways to accomplish the goal, and some may even end up being better than what we would have done. We will only discover this, as well as allow others to use their gifts and talents, if we remain open to new ideas.

Like marriage, if we will quit fighting the differences between us and our spouses, and begin to enjoy them, life will go much smoother. God has created each of us uniquely, and we need to embrace those differences instead of fighting them. The goal is to accomplish the work for Christ, regardless of who does it or how.

Because we are probably gifted in some way, we could do the job better and perhaps even quicker than someone else...at least initially. If we will allow others to learn, grow, and even do a "poorer" job than we would have done, in the long run the ministry will expand. With time and training, many around us can help us accomplish the task we have been given if we will allow them to help.

5. If it is illegal or immoral, you have to take a stand. In all other things, show love. One person can make a difference. In many cases, just one person refusing to go along with the majority in some immoral scheme has derailed the entire plan. We have our integrity, and we must not sacrifice it.

We need to ask questions and not assign motives to others, however. Most of our decisions are made on a great deal less information than we need. We often make 100% conclusions on 1%

information and many times regret it afterwards. Asking someone why they did or said something is much better than simply assuming you know the reason. If, after asking, a moral or illegal issue arises, then take a loving stand praying for redemption.

There are many areas in the Scriptures that are crystal clear which virtually all Christians agree upon. There are many more that almost no one agrees upon. In the matters that are clear we need to be very clear and on the other issues, we need to show deference and love. We need to learn how to disagree agreeably over disputable matters.

The early Church argued over a great deal, but they also agreed to disagree as well. Acts 15 presents a discussion regarding Jews and Gentiles, and Romans 14 and 15 explain how to handle differing value systems. We would be wise to study these chapters and see how the early Church was successful in settling their disputes.

If loving one another is the calling card to the lost (John 13:35), which it is, then we need to learn how to love those that disagree with us over disputable matters. It is easy to love those we agree with; it is supernatural love to do the same towards those who do not.

6. Extend a little grace; you may need some in return. However we wish to be treated is the way we should treat others; so states Jesus in the Golden Rule. Paul said we would reap what we have sown in Galatians 6:7, and Jesus said whatever we give to others we will receive back in a larger amount in Luke 6:38. Most of us would like to reap and receive great quantities of grace!

As leaders we are often a bit older, more experienced, and often scarred by the years. However old and wise we are today, we were not the same way earlier in our life. We all have sinned, spoken out of line, made mistakes, and grown up some. Will we allow others to do the same?

God has worked in and on our lives; will He not do the same to and for others? Maybe the people who irritate us so much do so because they are like us. Perhaps we too were a major pain to someone else when we were younger and didn't even know it. We need grace. So do they. If we want to receive grace, we need to give it freely.

There was only one perfect Man, and He was the Savior of the world. Everyone else is in various stages of spiritual growth. As we lead, we need to extend grace to those who follow us. God is not finished with us, and He is not finished with those we lead. Always look for ways to extend grace; you will not regret it.

An Important Perspective

As we finish this chapter on how to lead a meeting and leading with grace, let's consider one final aspect regarding our leadership philosophy — control vs. accountability.

Control is typically defined in this way:

"To exercise restraining or directing influence over, to have power over, to reduce the incidence or severity to innocuous levels."

Accountability is defined as:

"To account for one's actions"

As leaders, we need to aim for accountability without suffocating, paranoid controls. Too often because of a prior, bad or hurtful experience, leaders and churches attempt to control everything so the event can never happen again.

Mistakes will happen because we live in a sin saturated, fallen world. We cannot place enough controls on anyone or any ministry to guarantee that there will never be another mistake. In fact, it is harmful to do so.

The Pharisees attempted to "enhance" and protect God's Law by adding thousands of controls to assure purity. By the time Jesus arrived, the God-given Law through Moses was unintelligible. We too can lose sight of the mission and vision we have through excessive control.

We cannot control everything, but we can hold ourselves and those we work with accountable for their actions. We cannot achieve perfection on this side of death, but we can reach excellence. No amount of control will ever completely remove the possibility of failure. We need to deal with the failures when they happen and not be trapped by them or allow them to cripple the work.

Leading is important. We want to walk alongside those we lead holding them accountable, but we do not want to control them. A neck massage is different from a strangle hold. A wise leader will know that one relieves tension and increases productivity, and the other one can kill. Strangling others through endless controls, anger, domination, or unrighteous displays of power will only lead to mutiny and not harmony. Leadership is a skill that can be learned, and should be practiced to mature.

Questions to Ponder

1. What do I think about leading meetings? Are they enjoyable or simply a nuisance?

2. If I implemented the "4 D's" approach to my meetings, would they enhance them? Why or why not?

3. What would those who work with me say about my listening skills? My integrity? My openness to new ideas or ways to accomplish tasks?

4. What would those who work with me say about me regarding grace?

5. What would those who work with me say about me regarding control?

20 Eight Navigational Tips

Are there rocks ahead?
If there are we will all be dead.

With a combined ministry experience exceeding a century, we have picked up a few insights over these decades that we love to share. Many wounds, hurts, painful introspections, and even joys can be found in these eight tips. By sharing them with you, we hope to help you avoid some of the mistakes we have made. Many times wisdom is shown by simply knowing where not to go.

Some of these have been touched upon in other chapters, but as we all know, just because we said or read it once, does not mean it was heard or embraced in its fullness.

Before sharing these eight points, let's consider a freeing, foundational understanding — Who it is that will build the Church and see to it that she succeeds.

As leaders in the Church, we sometimes feel that we are personally responsible to assure the success or even the continuation of Christ's Bride. While we have been granted a role to play, we must not take on a position we were never intended to carry.

> **And I tell you, you are Peter, and on this rock I will build my church, and the gates of hell shall not prevail against it. (Matthew 16:18 ESV)**

Jesus said a great deal to Peter about his revelatory statement regarding being the Christ, and we cannot develop all of the truth here. What we can see is that Jesus assured Peter, and by implication all believers of every age, that He would build the Church. In addition, the gates of hell will not prevail against it. That should be great comfort to us when we become overwhelmed with our perceived condition of Christ's Bride. Jesus will complete the task, and the enemy will fail. Jesus can handle it.

To date, Jesus has never lied, failed or misled. If Jesus has promised something, He has done or will do it. We bank our eternal souls on this truth. Yet, we sometimes become obsessed over what we observe in His Bride. We worry about the condition of the Church and the direction She is heading. We can pray, but worry is not an option. Jesus said He would build the Church, and He does not fail, ever.

Another foundational understanding that can bring peace to a troubled mind and soul is found in theses comforting words:

> **O Lord, my heart is not lifted up; my eyes are not raised too high; I do not occupy myself with things too great and too marvelous for me. But I have calmed and quieted my soul, like a weaned child with its mother; like a weaned child is my soul within me. (Psalm 131:1-3 ESV)**

It is easy to become overwhelmed when we are attempting to carry a burden never intended for us. Jesus will fix the Church. Jesus will purify Her, protect Her, and complete Her. Our job is to work within the confines of what we have control and influence over. The range of our influence will vary, but only Christ is in charge of everything. We are not, and that should be freeing.

We have been called to be faithful in our own realm, and becoming fearful, full of doubt, or obsessed over something we have no control over will simply lead to needless distraction and heartache.

These two concepts — Jesus will build the Church, and we do not need to worry about matters that are too great for our understanding — if understood and believed, will lead to greater peace and joy in our ministries.

With that foundation, let's delve into the eight important navigational pointers that we have learned as helmsmen.

1. Some things must remain the same. As we plant a church or begin a season of ministry at a church, we must discover what our vision is. The familiar passage often quoted is, "Without a vision the people perish." (Proverbs 29:18) Some translations read, "the people run unrestrained."

At some point in the process, the church will identify their vision thus stating — this is why we exist. We will "take a bullet for this point." These foundational views will not change, ever. Each church is a unique expression of the Body of Christ and every congregation will have foundational cornerstones that will not or should not change. This is what we were called to do as a group. Understanding this truth will help bring direction and stability to the church.

2. Some things must change. Governance, leadership, management, staff, pastors, budgets, programs, ministries, methods, buildings, and locations can and should change and adapt as necessary. Items in this category run their course, or live their normal life cycle of usefulness, and churches that refuse to acknowledge and take action in these areas tend to suffer a slow death.

Change is a part of life. We age, decay settles in, and everything temporal has an expiration date. It seems sometimes we ignore this reality. Many seem to avoid change like the plague; however, change comes to all. We must prepare for it and embrace change if we want to grow.

A wise pastor will help lead the leadership and congregation through the seasons of change. Some changes will happen quickly and are unavoidable, such as a death of a key leader, or a building burning down. Most changes are slower and require planning to help overcome the objections that will arise. Helping people embrace change is a required skill for every leader.

As a general principle, slow change helps people adapt easier than violent change. A five degree turn is easier to navigate than a ninety degree one. If the turn is too sharp, many of those following will simply crash into the wall and not make it through the change. A gradual, well-thought-out program to implement change will greatly assist those in our wake.

3. The future is uncertain and contains risks. Regardless of prayer, our best laid plans, and human efforts, things happen. We must realize that God is in control. People change, they make mistakes, they stumble, and sometimes they fall, but God remains the same. A certain amount of risk will be required to grow and expand God's Kingdom.

In an earlier chapter we discussed the necessity of insurance for the church. The underlying presupposition for insurance is that there is a need, or at least the potential need. Disasters strike, fraud happens, sin is still happening on planet Earth, and the Church is not immune to the consequences of its destruction.

There are news stories abounding of pastors stealing funds and committing adultery and people shooting other people in church. We cannot control such events, but we know Who will redeem them. Paul gave us this truth:

> **And we know that for those who love God all things work together for good, for those who are called according to his purpose. (Romans 8:28 ESV)**

Many of us have taught this verse, yet it is often difficult to embrace when tragedy strikes. The verse is either true or not, and when considering the risks of the future, we must embrace it as correct, or we will lose hope.

We know that in this world there will be sin, heartache, tribulation, and even rejection. We also know that this world is not all there is. The temporal, earthly future is uncertain and full of risks, but the eternal one is not, and for that we are eternally grateful.

4. There will be failures. Churches that are moving forward and impacting the community will encounter friction and occasional failures. If your car never leaves the garage, you can be relatively certain you won't get in a wreck; however, the car is not fulfilling its intended purpose.

The Church is composed of humans from the leadership to the newest member, and therefore is subject to failure. There are not perfect humans, only a perfect Savior. Sin, failure, disappointment, and death will impact every ministry. Stumbling and falling are common to everyone:

> **For the righteous falls seven times and rises again, but the wicked stumble in times of calamity. (Proverbs 24:16 ESV)**

The righteous person will fall, but they get back up and keep on walking. Every church will have failure somewhere, and to think it will not is to set yourself up for disappointment.

In addition to the inevitable human failings, there will be ministry failures. Not every program, event, or dream will work. A great deal of what we learn to be true comes through trial and error. We cannot reach perfection this side of eternity, and to expect to or, worse yet, to demand it will increase the frustration level of everyone.

We do not look for failures or even necessarily enjoy them, but we can learn from them if we do not let them destroy us. We learn from them, and we get back up and walk on in obedience to what we were called to accomplish.

5. We cannot do everything. Let God be God, and be obedient to what He has called you and your church to do. No more and no less. If the devil can't destroy your ministry, dilution is the next best strategy.

We were born for this time and this age. We are called to accomplish works that God has specifically planned for us to do:

> **For we are his workmanship, created in Christ Jesus for good works, which God prepared beforehand, that we should walk in them. (Ephesians 2:10 ESV)**

We are responsible for what we're called to do. Every church has an identity and a vision. When we operate within those two, we will accomplish what we were intended to do. No one church has been called to accomplish what only the entire Body of Christ can do together. Learning what we are *not* supposed to do is as freeing as discovering what we were called *to* do.

At a personal level, it is freeing to focus on our gifts and to delegate away those tasks that we are not called to do. It may come as a shock to some of us, but we really are not gifted in everything. In addition, there is probably someone around us that is gifted in exactly what we really don't like to do. What we dread, they receive life from.

Why should we struggle to gain mediocrity in an area outside of our gifting? It would be far wiser to allow someone else who actually enjoys the task and is much better at it than we, to move into their gifting. Everyone benefits from this decision. We cannot do everything, nor should we.

6. God's will, will be done. While not venturing into controversial doctrines surrounding God's Sovereignty and man's free will, there is truth in the above sentence. God will accomplish His purposes. and no one will stop Him.

There are seasons and opportunities for individuals and for churches. We will either take advantage of them or not, but God's will is going to be accomplished even if we fail on our part.

Esther was told by her wise uncle that deliverance would come from somewhere if she failed the Jews, and he was correct. Mordecai also said that the reason you were chosen queen might just be because of the hardship facing the Jewish people. While our God-given works will probably not rise to this level of importance, they are nonetheless critical for the Body of Christ.

If we fail to fulfill the works we are given to do, and if God so deems it that they need to be accomplished, they will be performed by someone else. We will probably suffer regret for not walking in obedience, but God's will, will be accomplished.

Our desire must be to walk in daily obedience to the revealed will of our Father. We are told to seek His will, pray that it will be accomplished on earth as in heaven, and put the Kingdom first and foremost in our hearts and mind. If we do the above, we will do well.

7. Quality brings quantity. Our goal should be helping to produce the best quality fruit through our ministry and not necessarily a large amount of poor quality plants.

You don't try to grow fruit before you grow a strong trunk, healthy branches, and corresponding leaves. All of those help create healthy fruit. You need to feed the tree, not the fruit! By providing quality ministries, people will be added, they will grow spiritually, and finances will most likely increase.

Big crowds and large facilities are not the overall goal or defining characteristics of success. Healthy, effective, reproducing disciples should be. There are many large groups of lost, deceived people. Money, buildings, staff, and busyness is not necessarily indicative of success. If these things are the only or primary measurement of success, then Jesus, Paul, and in fact most of the churches in America, are failures.

Jesus invested primarily in the twelve. Within that group it seemed that He spent additional time with Peter, James, and John. While Jesus ministered to the crowds, He mainly invested in the few who would take up His ministry after He left. We would be wise to do the same.

We all know that if we skip laying a good foundation, whatever we build will eventually fall. We must build carefully and wisely, and then if the Lord brings growth, what we have built will stand the test of the inevitable storms.

Our goal must be centered in obedience, faithfulness, and quality, not the endless pursuit of growth. Only God has enough information to properly evaluate the effectiveness of our lives and ministry. We will be judged upon our faithfulness, not the quantity of our talents.

8. Stay the course. "To him who overcomes, I will grant..." is an often-used phrase in the final book of the Bible. Throughout the Scriptures we are encouraged to be faithful, to not give in or up, to overcome, and to be faithful even unto death. We will reap a reward if we do not give up!

Pastoral Helmsmanship

Many studies have been undertaken on the longevity of pastors in their calling. One component is common to all of the studies — most pastors quit before retirement age. There are a variety of valid reasons of course, but giving up should not be one of them.

There are real challenges, and we have already discussed some of them. Sin issues, discouragement, disillusionment with people, hurts, betrayals, family pressures, and many others, but we are called by God to stay the course. We must not quit unless given permission by the Master.

The Scripture encourages us to continue on in spite of the struggles:

> **And let us not grow weary of doing good, for in due season we will reap, if we do not give up. (Galatians 6:9 ESV)**
>
> **As for you, brothers, do not grow weary in doing good. (2 Thessalonians 3:13 ESV)**
>
> **Consider him who endured from sinners such hostility against himself, so that you may not grow weary or fainthearted. (ESV Hebrews 12:3)**

We all want to hear, "Well done, good and faithful servant, enter into the joy of your Master." We will if we don't quit! There is a reward for those who endure. It will be worth it when we step out of this life and see our Lord face to face.

Before we end this chapter let's consider one more thought. Most of us love to read or perhaps watch a good mystery movie. What makes the story interesting is the tension the main character(s) endure. If there were not plot turns, tension, and seemingly impossible difficulties, the story would be boring.

Our lives are often like those stories we love to read. On page 37 of our life, the future looks bleak if not impossible. If we don't give up though, on page 50, perhaps the miracle will arrive. A sudden plot twist occurs, and all ends well. How boring our lives would be if everything worked out just like we planned? How uneventful would our testimony be and how unable would we be to assist others in their trials if our lives never took a turn for the worse.

In truth, most of us do not have enough information to decide if a particular event really is good or bad. Not near enough time has passed in most cases to make a final judgment. Some of life's greatest difficulties end up being the brightest moment after the passage of time. A job loss, while a seeming defeat, ends up opening wide doors elsewhere. A crime committed against us or someone we love is eventually redeemed into a worldwide ministry offering healing to thousands.

The truth is that in most situations we have a very narrow view. God, and God alone, is the One with sufficient information to understand the outcome of the event. Our view is too limited, and we make our judgment calls way too early.

Most of us have heard of Joni Erickson Tada and are acquainted with her huge ministry. We know her story of diving into shallow water and breaking her neck. For multiple decades, she has had a massively effective ministry touching millions of people for Christ. One question to consider is; if she didn't break her neck, would we even know her name?

Questions to Ponder:

1. What would Jesus say to me about His Church, and what would He tell me to quit worrying about?

2. What would be some of the vision of your church that will never change? Why?

3. What is my view of failure? In myself? In others?

4. Are there some areas of my ministry that everyone would be better off if I delegated them? What do I really love to do? What do I hate to do?

5. How close am I to giving up? What could I do to ensure that I won't?

21 Enjoying the Journey:
Final Thoughts from Seasoned Sailors

*Ride the wave, enjoy the splash,
don't get sea sick.*

The vocational life of a pastor is different from most others. In our journey together we have explored some of those unique differences. Those of us who make our living from pastoring are greatly blessed. We also deal with a great amount of pain, heartache, suffering, and spiritual warfare.

During our time together we have explored the tensions our family must deal with, the occupation hazards faced, and the joys and sorrows of working closely with others to further the work of Christ's Kingdom. We have delved into administration and leadership and the pastor's personal life. We trust that there have been some helpful tools provided for you to navigate the sometimes choppy waters of ministry.

Before we end our journey together, we want to encourage you. Don't give up, and don't give in. The vast majority of people that begin their pastoral career end it prematurely. Many lose their way, become disillusioned, and simply quit. We will never regret staying the course, but we almost certainly will regret giving up prematurely. The

Lord may tell us to quit, but we must make sure it is His voice and not simply our frustration.

Peter writes to his fellow leaders and reminds them of an important truth.

> **So I exhort the elders among you, as a fellow elder and a witness of the sufferings of Christ, as well as a partaker in the glory that is going to be revealed: shepherd the flock of God that is among you, exercising oversight, not under compulsion, but willingly, as God would have you; not for shameful gain, but eagerly; not domineering over those in your charge, but being examples to the flock. And when the chief Shepherd appears, you will receive the unfading crown of glory. (1 Peter 5:1-4 ESV)**

Peter partook of the glory at least in part when he saw Jesus in His glorified state upon the mount of transfiguration. In that moment, the veil between our two universes was ripped open. Peter saw glory. No matter what else ever happened in Peter's life, this memory would surely remain. There is a real future, eternal glory, and it is centered in Christ.

As Peter is writing to his fellow elders in this letter he reminds them of this truth. Peter also adds an incentive — unfading crown of glory. We of course don't know exactly what Peter meant by those words, but we do know who that crown is intended for — pastors. Whatever that crown is or may represent, it will be worth whatever struggles we endure here. The Chief Shepherd will give to His undershepherds something that will never fade if we don't quit.

The joys of serving our King far out-weigh the pains suffered. Those of us who are paid to be pastors are paid to pray, teach, worship and serve! We are allowed to spend time reading and soaking in God's Word. There are many others who would love to have the privilege we often overlook.

Paul wrote through the inspiration of the Holy Spirit these words referring to us:

> But grace was given to each one of us according to the measure of Christ's gift. Therefore it says, "When he ascended on high he led a host of captives, and he **gave gifts** to men." And he gave the apostles, the prophets, the evangelists, the **shepherds and teachers**, to equip the saints for the work of ministry, for building up the body of Christ, until we all attain to the unity of the faith and of the knowledge of the Son of God, to mature manhood, to the measure of the stature of the fullness of Christ, so that we may no longer be children, tossed to and fro by the waves and carried about by every wind of doctrine, by human cunning, by craftiness in deceitful schemes.
> (Ephesians 4: 7-8, 11-14 ESV)

We are referred to as gifts, given to the Church. We don't always feel like a gift, but we must align our thinking with the Word of God. Part of the gifts given to the Church includes you.

Pastors have been given the task from the Chief Shepherd to equip the saints for work. We are called to help bring the Church to maturity. We are gifted to help prevent deceitful schemes invented by our foe. What an amazing task we have been called to! We partner with God Almighty to help prepare the Bride of Christ for eternity.

Sometimes in the midst of the daily grind, we lose sight of the glory! God does not, however. There is an unfading crown that awaits God's faithful pastors.

Yes, the voyage can become rough, tedious, even boring at times; yet, we are part of something way beyond our full comprehension. God has called us and equipped us, and He will give us grace to finish the task assigned. That task is noble and eternal in focus. Pastors serve a vital role in helping the Body of Christ mature, and someday we believe that we will know in full what all that means.

For now, we walk on. Day by day we draw near to the Lord and attempt to fulfill the calling He has given us. Don't give in. Don't give up.

Many years ago there was a song by a group named Dogwood. This bluegrass group sang a song that is still applicable today. Some of the lyrics might speak to you as well:

> Keep on walking, you don't know how far you've come,
> Keep on walking, for all you know it might be done,
> And the Father might be standing up right now to give the call to end it all,
> So keep on walking

We don't know when the end will come for any or all of us. We do know it is much closer today than when the Bible was written, and nearer than even yesterday.

We've probably told others, "to not give up." "It's always darker right before the dawn," and a host of other cliché sayings. But, within each of these well-worn thoughts is a kernel of truth. Sometimes we need to listen to our own preaching and receive our own counsel.

Dear pastor, don't quit. Don't give in. Don't throw away your ministry through sin, frustration, or fatigue. Keep on walking. Keep being faithful. There is a reward, and the Great Shepherd is preparing yours.

Questions to Ponder

1. If you are close to giving up and leaving the ministry, why are you considering it? Are the reasons valid?

2. What do you think Peter meant by "the unfading crown of glory?" Will it be worth winning?

3. If we have been called by the Chief Shepherd, do we believe He will empower us to finish His calling? Why or why not?

4. Will you keep on walking or will you quit? Why?

Section Four
Resources

Pastoral Helmsmanship

Treasure Chest:
Helpful Articles, Samples, and a Bit More:

In this fourth and final section of the book, we wanted to provide you with some articles for thought, sample forms and policies, and reading and web resources to help you continue to grow on your journey. Before you plow into the resources, stop just a moment and smile at some true stories.

****

As the pastor was looking at the body in the casket, he confidently stated, "We know that this body is just an empty shell, the nut has gone home to be with the Lord!"

As the pastor lay in the bottom of the freshly dug grave having wandered too close to the edge, he refused to get out — "Just throw the dirt in on top of me" he quipped with an edge in his voice.

A young pastor was waxing eloquently about being circumcised in the Spirit when the illustration took an unexpected turn. The pastor's son had just been circumcised at the hospital so the image was fresh in his mind. "There is cutting, bleeding and hacking away at the flesh, just like in human circumcision, and afterwards, what is left?" asked the pastor. No answer was needed or provided.

The sister was emphatically sharing her story about a man on a Sunday morning during the testimony time. She meant to say the man should be castigated based on his behavior, what she really said had every man instantly crossing his legs.

Treasure Chest

Articles of Interest

Scaffolding Members — Understanding why some people begin with us, but do not stay with us long term.

Ministerial Compensation Package — How to put together a pay package for pastors.

The Pastor's Pay — Some thoughts about the structure of the salary package to maximize tax savings.

Ministerial Housing Allowance — How to compute it, what is deductible, and a sample form to help keep track of it.

Keeping the Ship Afloat: The Administrative Role of the Interim Pastor — Stepping into this situation requires grace and insight, so be prepared before accepting this role.

How to Ride a Dead Horse — A tongue-in-cheek look at keeping outdated and unneeded programs.

How to Navigate the Social Media Waterways — With the rise of social media opportunities for connectivity, there is also the increase of litigation and risks. We must become aware of how to deal with these tools correctly.

Why Not Lead with Integrity? — A call for pastors to set the standard for leadership in integrity within their community.

The Importance of Church Board Minutes — ECFA published an excellent article on board minutes and every pastor should read it to understand why they are needed.

When Should the Church Postpone or Cancel Church Events - A guide to assist pastors on when to make the dreaded call to cancel a service.

Scaffolding Members
Dr. Rodney Harrison

Most pastors have or will experience the pain of members and friends who jump ship. These are often the individuals or couples who made a significant contribution to the church and ministry during the early, tenuous season of your ministry. Often, the contribution was a special talent, abundant generosity or going the second mile with support and encouragement. Steve Sjogren and Rob Lewin address this reality in their book, *Community of Kindness*:

> ... there are two kinds of people--many are there for just a season, and a few are there to stay long-term. This is a vital lesson to learn, because as a leader it is easy to become caught up in the nurturing of what we lovingly call the "scaffolding people." Builders of physical structures use a set of scaffolding to erect a building. The scaffolding is not the building, but it is necessary for the construction of the building that will eventually emerge. As the building nears completion, the scaffolding falls away, leaving the permanent building standing.[13]

Although Sjogren and Lewin address this phenomenon primarily as it relates to church planters, we have observed scaffolding members are also attracted to new pastors and churches that are in transition. Scaffolding members are best understood as home missionaries. Their contributions to the ministry are often just what is needed, and often involve a significant sacrifice of time and resources. As a pastor, these members seem invaluable, so when they call announcing they are leaving, the unsuspecting pastor is caught off-guard. A common response is to try and convince them to stay. This is where a word of warning is merited, as emotions are running high at this juncture.

---

[6] Steve Sjogren, Rob Lewin, *Community of Kindness*, Gospel Light Publishers, 2003, 35

Scaffolding members can often be best identified in hindsight. However, here are some characteristics we have observed over the years:

- They show up already saved, and ready to serve
- They bring a long résumé of former church affiliations
- They show loose denominational fidelity. It is not uncommon for a scaffolding member to work with a liturgical church, then go to a charismatic church, then a Baptist Church and so on
- They show above average hospitality or generosity
- They frequently speak of the need and importance of belonging

The last characteristic is interesting, because when they leave, scaffolding members will often say, "I don't feel important" or "I need to find a church where I belong." Instead of letting scaffolding members send you to the funny farm, consider the following response when they announce they are leaving:

1. Thank them for their friendship and service to Christ and the church
2. If possible and appropriate, publicly acknowledge their contribution and future plans to the congregation. Once I understood the scaffolding principle, I was able to mitigate some of the potential problems by publicly recognizing their contributions and commending them to their next assignment.
3. Do not try to hold on to them. The danger here is that you may be successful, for a season. Imagine leaving the scaffolding up after the building is completed. Scaffolding members who stay will become antagonists and vision hijackers. Let them go, or you'll be the one who either walks the plank or jumps ship.

Ministerial Compensation Package
Glenn A. Miller

We are often asked how a church properly constructs a compensation package for its senior and/or associate pastor.

- Is it a question of how much the church can afford?
- Is it about what it will take to get them to come?
- Is it about what the average congregant makes?

All of these are good questions, but we recommend a different approach. It begins with a biblical understanding of the position of pastor and an understanding of biblical compensation. The Bible tells us in Luke 10:7 "...the laborer is worthy of his wages." It goes on to say in Titus 5: 17 -18 "Let the elders who rule well be considered worthy of double honor, especially those who work hard at preaching and teaching. 18 For the Scripture says, "YOU SHALL NOT MUZZLE THE OX WHILE HE IS THRESHING," and "The laborer is worthy of his wages." (NASB)

The short answer is that pastor's compensation should be viewed as a biblical imperative, and we should exercise grace and generosity as we construct the package. We also believe in accountability, and there are some "earthly" criteria that may help create the appropriate package listed below.

We recommend that the basis for a pastor's compensation package should begin by evaluating, to the best extent possible, the candidate's three "Es":

- Education – the higher the level of professional education and preparation, the higher the package. We strongly recommend checking credentials and placing more weight on accredited degrees and accredited educational institutions.

- Experience – the more relevant experience, the higher the package. Be sure to double check the experience listed to ensure accuracy.

- Expertise — expertise is defined here as the level of proven skills and competencies. The higher level of proven success, the higher the package. Once again, double check information for accuracy.

A proper evaluation of the three "E's", then church budget, surrounding area market conditions, previous pay scale for the church and/or the candidate, along with a study of comparable jobs in the area will all help to formulate the package.

We are asked on a regular basis to discuss our opinion regarding pastors' compensation packages and the payment of FICA tax (Social Security). The following is an attempt to clarify the decision-making criteria that churches may want to consider when formulating pastors' compensation packages.

The standard we recommend when formulating pastors' compensation is to be certain that there is a level playing field among all church staff. When paying custodians, secretaries, and other non-ordained staff, the church treats those people as "regular" employees. FICA tax of 7.65% is deducted from their paychecks, and the church is then required to match 7.65% and pay that in to the federal government with what was deducted from the employee's check.

Ordained pastors are considered "dual status" employees. They are employees for *benefits* purposes and *self-employed* for taxation purposes. We believe that the special status should not alter the amount of compensation. We further believe pastors, regardless of what they chose to do with their retirement or benefits, should be compensated on an equal basis, just like all other employees.

Although the church is not permitted to directly pay in matching FICA funds for pastors, they should be given the matching amount, just as all other employees are receiving through the mandatory matching FICA that the church pays on behalf of the employee. This would equate to a pastor receiving 7.65% of their salary and housing as added compensation to his/her paycheck. It will be considered taxable income, but it should not be considered a part of their wage package unless the employer FICA contribution is considered a part of a Secretary or Custodian's compensation package. The church is simply giving matching FICA tax directly to the pastor instead of to the government. At this point, all staff would be treated equally.

Another commonly held opinion is that if a pastor elects, for religious objection reasons, to opt out of the Social Security system, then why should the church have to give them the 7.65%?

Again, we believe that what a pastor chooses to do with their personal finances is not related to the decision of treating employees equally. The pastor, after receiving equal compensation, is then responsible for providing benefits and retirement income for his/her family. If they choose, for religious reasons, not to participate in the Social Security system, then it is still their responsibility to find and implement benefits and retirement income for themselves and/or their family. This decision should not impact how the church compensates them.

It is not uncommon to place salary, housing, auto, insurance, retirement, books, discretionary funds, and meals and entertainment all into a single package and "let the pastor work out the details." Often times the package number, say $50,000.00 looks impressive against a congregant making a 50,000.00 salary, but it is not the case.

The "50k" congregant salary does not show employer taxes (10% additional minimum) health insurance, retirement etc. that often all total 30-40% additional compensation above the 50k.

We recommend that items such as books, discretionary funds, meals, and entertainment be setup in the budget, with separate line items as reimbursables. If a legitimate expense is charged to the church and approved by someone other than the purchaser, it can be charged directly to that account. If it is purchased by the pastor, receipts and request for reimbursement are submitted and charged to the correct account. This keeps the amounts legally out of compensation, thus reducing confusion and potential tax burden.

Treasure Chest

They are also then more visible, accountable, and controllable. If not handled this way as under an accountable plan, the business expenses have to be reported as taxable income to the pastor.

Please visit www.instituteforchurchmanagement.com for free forms and more information.

The Pastor's Pay
Dr. Jeff Klick

Render unto Caesar what he is due, but not one cent more

Clergy have been given some wonderful opportunities to structure their pay in such a way as to limit their income tax bill. The IRS provides multiple tax shelters for the pastor, and knowing them can save thousands of dollars per year.

Fear often creeps in when we consider tax planning. The thought of sitting before an IRS agent defending our expenses sends chills down our spine. If we do a good job of recordkeeping, this fear is unfounded. Most IRS agents do not have fangs, and are simply attempting to reconcile your receipts with your tax return. Fear not!

We are a self-taxing country so in many ways, our 1040 tax return is simply an offer to settle our tax bill. If accepted, then we will call it even. If rejected, then we will meet to further discuss our initial offer. There is nothing to fear if you keep good records and provide receipts. Using the legal tax shelters is part of our privilege built into the tax code and is no different than itemizing our deductions or writing off the interest payment on our home.

We covered the housing allowance in a previous chapter so we won't spend very much time here. Remember to designate the percentage or designated amount before the end of the previous year.

Over estimating is preferred to under estimating because any amount spent over the designated housing allowance is not allowed to be deducted. Any unused housing allowance is simply added back in to the taxable amount with no penalty, so aim higher than lower to maximize the shelter. Keep track of your receipts throughout the year, and you might be pleasantly surprised when you prepare your tax return.

Anything related to the home is deductable — home owners insurance, furniture, maintenance, cleaning supplies, improvements, hired labor, yard improvements, etc. are all acceptable expenses. Interest and property taxes are also deductable even though they are also taken as an itemized deduction.

In addition to the blessing of the housing allowance, pastors can move many expenses to a reimbursement type plan and avoid any tax consequences. Books, reasonable expenses for meals, travel, further education, cell phones, computers, and miles reimbursements can all be provided tax free to the pastor.

Insurance should be part of the pay package of any pastor. Health, life, dental, and disability insurance should be included. In addition, retirement plans should be considered, and there are many ways to structure these plans to greatly reduce the tax expense. The IRS tax code allows churches and pastors to contribute to a 403(b) retirement plan, which has many benefits for the pastor.

There is more to the pastor's salary than just the paycheck, though that is important. With careful planning a pastor can save a great deal of money on taxes and the church leadership can provide nicely for the pastor.

Resources are plentiful for detailed descriptions and techniques to help with this process. Insurance companies like Guide One that specialize in churches have free tools to help the pastor plan carefully. The National Association of Church Business Administrators offer resources as do many financial planners.

Spend some time planning and discussing these issues to assure that you are being the best possible steward of the resources spent on pastoral pay packages.

Ministerial Housing Allowance
Glenn A. Miller

MMS, LLC position papers are a compilation of our staff's research, education, training classes and seminars attended, 25 years field experience, and interpretation of current laws as we understand them. The information contained in this paper is not legal advice and is intended to be used as general information to help formulate your organization's guidelines. It is understood that your organization is legally responsible for all policies and procedures and their legal basis.

What is a housing allowance? A housing allowance is an annual amount of compensation that is set aside by the church to cover the cost of housing related expenses for its ministers. The amount spent on housing reduces a qualifying minister's federal and state income tax burden.

Who qualifies? To be classified as a minister for federal tax purposes and thus be able to claim a housing allowance, there is one primary requirement along with a set of secondary requirements:

Primary Requirement: a person must be ordained, commissioned, or licensed as a minister by a church, body of churches, or a religious order.

Secondary Requirements: an ordained, commissioned, or licensed minister must meet most of the following
- administer sacraments (provide communion, water baptism, and/or solemnize marriages)
- conduct religious worship
- have management responsibility in a local church or religious denomination
- be considered a religious leader by his or her church or denomination

The IRS applies the secondary requirements as a "balancing test" to determine if the job duties of the individual are ministerial in nature. Although some case law indicates that the IRS may allow a minister to meet only one or two of the secondary requirements, other case law suggest that at least three points are needed to qualify a person to receive the tax benefits of a housing allowance. Based on our interpretation of the law, we feel it is difficult to meet "most" of the secondary requirements without including at least three of them. Therefore, we recommend a minister meets at least three of the secondary requirements in addition to the primary requirement to safely satisfy the requirements.

How does it work? Each year, the minister estimates the amount of eligible housing expenses to be incurred during the following year. This amount is submitted to the governing body of the church for approval. When paid to the minister the following year, that housing amount is <u>excluded</u> from the taxable federal and state compensation that is reported in box 1 and 16 of the W2. The housing amount is instead reported in box 14 for informational purposes.

How to establish the correct amount? We have formulated the attached worksheet to aid your ministerial staff in the process of estimating an appropriate housing allowance for the year. *It should be stressed that this form is intended to assist in the estimation process; it is not a guarantee of what taxes will be owed.* Each minister is responsible for tracking actual allowable, documented housing expenses during the year and reporting that amount to their tax preparer. Any amount of paid housing allowance that was not used on actual housing expenses has to be reclassified as taxable for federal and state income taxes on the minister's tax return. Because of the complexity of ministerial taxes, we strongly recommend that ministers consult with tax preparers who specialize in church and clergy taxes.

Timing? IRS guidelines stipulate that all housing allowances are approved by an appropriate governing body of the church <u>in advance</u> of paying it to the minister. Housing allowances cannot be approved or changed retroactively for housing expenses already incurred. We recommend that all housing allowances are approved no later than December 31, for the upcoming year. Approval should be recorded in the formal minutes of the governing body.

Annual Ministerial Housing Allowance Worksheet

Church: _____ Pastor's Name: _____
Date: _____

Estimated Monthly Expenses:

Monthly house payment : * principle   * interest * pmi
* taxes * insurance   _____

Monthly electric bill (12 month average)   _____

Monthly natural or lp gas bill (12 month average)   _____

Monthly water/sewer bill (12 month average)   _____

Monthly trash collection/recycling bill   _____

Monthly phone bill, (one land line phone only,
not including long distance)   _____

           Sub-Total   _____

           Times 12 month   x   12

Annual total of Estimated Monthly Expenses =   _____

Treasure Chest

Estimated Annual Expenses:

General maintenance & upkeep
  * Cleaning supplies related to house maintenance
  * Lawn care- all related expenses, equipment, gas, trim string,
   etc.
  * Any plumbing, electrical, roof, or
   general repairs   _____

Home additions, remodeling, new fence,
new carpet, painting, etc.   _____

New furniture, equipment, or appliances   _____

Closing costs, down payment, extra equity payment,
or refinancing costs   _____

Total Estimated Annual Expenses: _____

Total Annual Estimated Monthly Expenses

                      _____

Total Estimated Annual Expenses   +_____

* **Grand total of Estimated Annual
Housing Expense:**   _____

Pastoral Helmsmanship

Keeping the Ship Afloat: The Administrative Role of the Interim Pastor
Dr. Rodney Harrison

An old rancher is talking about politics with a young man from the city. He compares a politician to a "post turtle." The young man doesn't understand and asks him what a post turtle is.

The old man says, "When you're driving down a country road and you see a fence post with a turtle balanced on top, that's a post turtle. You know he didn't get up there by himself. He doesn't belong there; he can't get anything done while he's up there; and you just want to help the poor, dumb thing down."

Although this political joke has been used by former Commander in Chiefs, to describe presidents and as an acceptance speech at the Country Music Awards, it aptly describes the congregational situation an interim pastor will be immersed into when coming to a new church. While an understanding of the administrative role of the interim pastorate should be established at the beginning, planned discussions regarding administrative observations can provide critical insights for the church and leadership. In addition, a great deal of heartache can be avoided by discussing these matters before the hire rather than during the firing process when unspoken expectations are unmet.

An apt description of the Interim Pastor is articulated by Transforming Ministry, which states "The Interim Pastor is one who, on short notice, can step into a pastor-less church by providing the necessary leadership and assistance enabling the church to maintain its program, act as a buffer between pastors, perform a healing ministry [when necessary], and prepare the way for the coming pastor." The guidelines go on to note that the interim should place everything the church does into one or more of the following categories, which in turn become the ministry objectives for the interimship:

- CLEAN UP: Messes that need to be cleaned up; things broken that need fixing.
- SHORE UP: Things in decline that need to be stabilized and re-energized.
- KEEP UP: Things now okay needing to be maintained at the same level.
- RAMP UP: Things going okay that can be improved and make even more impact.
- START UP: Things that don't exist [at the present time] needing to be started.[14]

My first interim pastorate was simple. Fix everything. The congregation was down to under 15 adults and felt they had nothing to lose and everything to gain by providing total administrative control. The agreement provided the congregation the right to terminate my services, and ensured that the confessional statement would be honored and maintained. That first Sunday, all 22 committees were disbanded and every office was declared vacant. Over the next twelve months, every aspect of the church was re-invented, every policy rewritten, and every member re-affirmed. Twelve months later, the church called a full-time pastor, who is now in his 21st year of service to the church. Although I did not have the benefit of the bullet points above, the objectives of comprehensive assessment and refinement were accomplished during that year.

Of course, not every congregation wants, or needs, an interim pastor who serves as a consultant, and comprehensively evaluates every aspect of the ministry. My current interim pastorate involves preaching on Sunday morning and not much else. These two extremes illustrate the varying expectations congregations may have for the interim pastor. The problem comes when the expectations of the congregation, the church leadership and/or the interim pastor are not

---

[14] Transformation Ministry, *Guidelines for the Calling and Role of the Interim Pastor*, http://www.transmin.org/files/TM%20Documents/Calling%20and%20Role%20of%20Interim%20Pastors%202012.pdf, Accessed March 14, 2014.

clearly understood. This section serves as a guide for writing an interim pastor contract.

Expectations:

Will the interim be expected to join the church?
Has a copy of the church constitution and bylaws been provided to the interim?
Which services will the interim be expected to preach or teach?
- Sunday School (class and time)
- Sunday Morning Worship
- Sunday Evening Worship
- Midweek Service (type, i.e., pray meeting, Bible study, discipleship training, etc)

What other meetings or activities are expected?
- Deacon/Elder Meetings
- Staff Meetings
- Other meetings
- Community Activities

Weddings
Funerals
Pastoral Counseling
Leadership Consultations
Office Hours
Pastor Search Committee
Outreach and Evangelism
Home visitation
Hospital visitation

By clearly identifying the expectations, most churches experience positive interim pastor experiences. The dangers often hide in the unspoken expectations such as having the sermon outline submitted by a certain time or day. Be sure that worship leaders and administrative staff are provided input prior to developing the interim covenant or contract.

Administrative responsibilities

The size of the church will often determine which pastoral roles and responsibilities the interim pastor will fulfill. In the smallest churches (those under 50 in worship), lay leaders generally assume the administrative and care-giving roles. These churches often secure an interim pastor primarily for their pulpit service. Large churches with a full complement of staff will also tend to secure interim pastors primarily for their pulpit service. Congregations running 50-500 are the most likely to seek out an interim who can provide leadership from the pulpit as well as administratively.

Pastoral Need by Level

Some congregations benefit from determining their need by level.

Level One: The interim pastor provides leadership at all services, including Sunday morning, Sunday evening, midweek, weddings, funerals, and calendared events such as revivals, concerts and holy day services. Visitation of members, prospects, those in the hospital and visitors is expected, as is pastoral counseling. The interim is also available for meetings with the elders, deacons, church council and search committee.

Level Two: The interim is less involved administratively and pastorally. Major responsibilities include pastoral oversight of the preaching services, on-call availability for weddings, funerals, and consultation as it relates to the work of committees, staff and general administrative issues.

Recommended Reimbursement for Interim Pastors

A rule of thumb for interim pastor reimbursement is 25-60% of a full-time senior pastor's salary package, depending upon the duties and responsibilities of the interim. In some cases, church may opt to secure the services of an intention interim or transitional pastor, whose compensation may be higher.

An interim pastor is not merely pulpit supply. His role is to coordinate and fulfill the pulpit ministry of the church, thus allowing the church staff and committees time to discern God's man for senior pastor. The interim pastor should be available to provide counsel and guidance as requested by the church.

If the interim pastor is expected to provide level one service, preaching the morning, evening services, and mid-week service, plus providing limited pastoral ministry, a package of approximately 33-60% of the senior pastor's salary/housing (not including insurance/annuity) is appropriate. For example, if the interim will be staying over the weekends (being on the field each weekend) and providing all or most of the level one services, it would be appropriate to use the high end of this scale.

For an interim pastor providing only level two services, 25% is appropriate for Sunday morning only and 33% for Sunday morning and evening. Remember, just like the senior pastor's package, consideration should be given to the interim's experience, education, travel and need. For a church that is grieving, experiencing significant conflict or attendance changes more than 10% in the previous year, securing the services of an experienced interim with a proven history is advised, as doing otherwise is penny wise, but pound foolish.

If the interim is traveling from out of the area, mileage should be negotiated as a part of the package, especially for tax purposes. If the interim pastorate is not their primary employment, the travel to and from the church can be accounted as mileage reimbursement, and is non-taxable. However, additional travel does not result in additional compensation.

Final Thoughts

The interim pastor brings his gifts, talents, abilities and experiences to the church. It is up to the church leaders to avail themselves of these benefits. The benefit to the congregation includes continuity in the pulpit and a familiar face during a season of change. The church and leaders benefit from the insights gained and shared from the interim's week to week observations. Securing and interim also removes the challenging task of securing weekly pulpit supply. Clearly, the utilization of an interim pastor is a wise and prudent action. Nevertheless, it is imperative to remember Christ is the Head of His church, and to seek Him first, and foremost during the pastoral search process.

Pastoral Helmsmanship

How to Ride a Dead Horse
Unknown

Ancient Rabbinic wisdom states that when you discover you are riding a dead horse (or camel), the best strategy is to dismount. However, church boards and committees often try other strategies with dead horses, including the following:

- Buying a stronger whip.
- Changing riders.
- Saying things like "This is the way we always have ridden this horse."
- Arranging to visit other sites to see how they ride dead horses.
- Increasing the standards for those who ride the dead horse.
- Appointing a committee to study the dead horse.
- Waiting for the horse's condition to improve from this temporary downturn.
- Providing additional training to increase riding ability.
- Passing a policy declaring, "This horse is not dead."
- Blaming the person who sold you the horse.
- Acquiring additional dead horses for increased speed.
- Declaring that "No horse is too dead to beat."
- Providing additional funding to increase the horse's performance.
- Commissioning a study to see if lay-leaders can ride it cheaper.
- Removing all obstacles in the dead horse's path.
- Taking bids for a state-of-the art dead horse.
- Declaring the horse is "better, faster and cheaper" dead.
- Revising the performance requirements for horses.
- Saying the horse was cheaper than one that was "alive."
- Asking for increased donations (any excuse will do).

And if all else fails:

Declare that resurrecting the dead horse is the congregation's primary mission.

Treasure Chest

How to Navigate the Social Media Waterways
Dr. Jeff Klick

With the advent of the internet, social media has become a normal part of our lives. Facebook, Twitter, Google+, and dozens more are visited and updated multiple times a day by most church folks. There are still a few holdouts, but in most churches the majority of people are online.

Pastors, churches, church staff, and those speaking for the church need to consider what they post in social media. The illusion that e-mail is private and no one would ever read my personal posts, should have been dispelled by now. Once written, it is recorded and has the potential to be read by millions.

There is of course a distinction between personal and professional social media, but within the church, those lines are often blurred. A pastor that writes a blog or makes a Facebook post that reveals a secret discovered during a counseling session could still be sued. So could the church. Social media is a wonderful tool to communicate quickly and it also can be a nightmare out of control.

Reputations can be destroyed in a moment, and pictures, prayer requests, and videos can go viral instantly. While there are dangers involved, that does not mean we should not use these tools. However, we must be wise, and a well thought out policy will help. In addition, most insurance companies have developed a Cyber Liability Insurance policy that is inexpensive but necessary. If your church has a website, the pastor has a blog, or you broadcast your sermons online, you need this policy.

There are multiple sites to visit to see what other groups have put together regarding social media guidelines. We really don't have to reinvent the wheel with ours. Here are some links that are worth exploring to help you being to develop a specific policy for your church and staff:

http://socialmediagovernance.com/policies/ - A large listing of policies by organization category.

http://justinwise.net/social-media-policies-churches-ministries
Another large listing of social media policies broken down by denominations.

http://pastors.com/the-ultimate-list-of-social-media-policies-for-churches-ministries/ - As stated, the ultimate list for policies.

Spending some time on these sites should trigger some thoughts regarding your own policy. In addition, a discussion with your church insurance agent would be profitable to explore what their company may offer.

Here is a sample policy suggested by Guide One Insurance:

Social Media Policy - Sample

If anyone on your staff has a social networking web page (Facebook, MySpace, Twitter, Plaxo, LinkedIn and similar sites) and they write about any work-related activities, they need to agree to the following terms and conditions:

1. You agree to write under your own name, unless you notify the church in writing of the name under which you are writing and the applicable networking site.

2. You may write about the church, your job, or some aspect of our business on a regular basis, but you cannot write while you are on duty at the church unless that writing is part of your job description.

3. You agree to include the following disclaimer on your site: "The opinions expressed on this site are the opinions of the participating user. _____ Church acts only as a passive conduit for the online distribution and publication of user-submitted material, content and/or links and expressly DOES NOT endorse any user-submitted material, content

and/or links or assume any liability for any actions of the participating user."

4. You agree not to attack fellow employees, members, or vendors. You may disagree with the church and its officers, provided your tone is respectful and you do not resort to personal attacks.

5. You agree not to disclose any sensitive, proprietary, private, confidential, or financial information about the church, other than what is publicly available.

6. You may comment on other churches, but you agree to do so respectfully without ridiculing, defaming, or libeling them in any way.

7. You agree not to post any material that is obscene, defamatory, profane, libelous, threatening, harassing, abusive, hateful or embarrassing to another person or any other person or entity. You agree not to disclose any private information about others.

8. You agree not to post advertisements, solicitations and/or market and/or promote any business or commercial interest, chain letters, or pyramid schemes.

9. You agree not to post anyone's copyrighted or trademarked materials.

10. You agree not to make promises that you cannot keep.

11. You agree to provide the church with your identity and website url if you choose to write about the church. You also agree to make anyone designated by the church as your "friend" so that the church may monitor your postings.

Pastoral Helmsmanship

Name: _____
Date: _____

Source: *Frank Sommerville, JD, CPA, Weycer, Kaplan Pulaski & Zuber, P.C*
(10.01.2010)

© 2010 GuideOne Center for Risk Management, LLC. All rights reserved.

This material is for information only and is not intended to provide legal or professional advice. You are encouraged to consult with your own attorney or other expert consultants for a professional opinion specific to your situation.

As you can see, polices can be broad and personally tailored to the individual church or ministry. Given the frequency of social media usage, it would be prudent for every church to create and share a social media policy soon.

Treasure Chest

Why Not Lead With Integrity?
Dr. Jeff Klick

It is interesting that God called His people, better stated, commanded His people, to be holy. Holy is a word that can be defined as "different" or "set apart." In both the Old and New Testament, the command is clear.

> **For I am the Lord your God. Consecrate yourselves therefore, and be holy, for I am holy. (Leviticus 11:44 ESV)**

> **But as He who called you is holy, you also be holy in all your conduct, (1 Peter 1:15 ESV)**

If a man on the street poll was taken, I doubt holiness would be the top response to this question:

> **"When you think of a Christian leader, what is the first word that comes into your mind?"**

While discouraging, it is even more so when we consider the public black eye received when a church leader steals or commits some other form of fraud. The news outlets seem to love freely sharing the sins of the Christian. When a well-known Christian is exposed as a cheat, thief, immoral or unfair in their dealings, the news receives above the fold exposure.

The Institute of Church Management was created by a good friend of mine. Glenn Miller saw a need for the Church and Christian ministry arena to step up in their financial integrity. Glenn often asks those attending the workshops offered by the Institute the following question:

> **"Is there any reason why the Church cannot, or should not be, the financial integrity leaders in our communities?"**

Pastoral Helmsmanship

The truth is that we all are an example to those around us. Will our behavior be a benchmark or an excuse? When we fail to lead in financial integrity, we provide an excuse for those that do not know Christ. Every time a Christian leader is caught in fraud, the Church suffers shame. Why can't the other side be true? If we would learn to lead with exemplary integrity, our light would shine brighter in the darkness.

The good news is that we can limit the potential damage of fraud through our procedures, and by gaining the appropriate knowledge. The Church does not need to continue down the same old path of failure. There is a movement beginning to change the way the Church does business. At least there should be. If there isn't one yet, then let's you and I begin one today.

The Church of Jesus Christ should be leading the way in financial integrity. Pastors and Christian leaders should be providing answers regarding how to handle money and not gaining headlines through practicing unethical behaviors. We serve the King of Kings. We work as unto the Lord, so why shouldn't we be the best in the industry?

Every church or ministry receives and spends money. How we do those two primary activities will reflect our financial integrity. Do we have the proper controls in place to discourage fraud? Do we even know what controls are necessary? If not, we are unarmed in a gun battle, and that is always unwise. (Can I still write gun in our current political climate?)

The Church is populated with humans. Humans are subject to temptation. Money, and often large quantities of it, is a major temptation to many humans. What are we doing to help those that deal with money to resist or overcome this temptation? How do we know if they are being successful in their struggles? Financial integrity demands that we answer these questions. If we fail to do so, we may find our ministries on the front page of the newspaper, or the subject of thousands of tweets. We may lose them entirely.

Do not despair, there is good news! Churches and Christian ministries can implement policies and procedures that will keep honest people honest. These practices do not have to cost much. In fact, most of them cost nothing at all. Okay, there is the cost of time, and perhaps overcoming the resistance to changing improper behaviors, but these are not financial in nature.

Where do we begin to change? First, there must be a desire to *want to* change. Will you embrace Glenn's challenge to become the leader in financial integrity in your community? Even if no one ever asks you a question about how you handle your finances, you can and should excel. We serve the King of the Universe and anything less than our best is too little and unacceptable.

Second, will you pursue education to learn how to become an excellent leader in financial integrity? No one knows everything, so we all need help. Glenn is a Certified Fraud Examiner. The fact that we have to have such people in the Christian world is disheartening, but leaving that aside for a moment, he, and those like him, have a lot of wisdom to share.

In the interest of full disclosure, I help teach along with Glenn at The Institute of Church Management. I have been in full time, paid ministry for over thirty years. For eleven of those years I was the administrator of a large church in my city, and for about the last twenty years, I have served as a senior pastor of my own church. I am therefore somewhat familiar with the inner workings of the church.

While serving as an administrator, I studied and passed the CFP (Certified Financial Planner) professional designation exam. Since becoming a senior pastor, I have completed my Masters degree, a Doctorate and a Ph.D. I know a little bit about studying and learning as well. When I challenge people to keep on learning I am speaking from a position of experience. We must study and we must grow, learn and adapt.

So, back to my second point; will you pursue the education necessary to learn what needs to be accomplished to protect your ministry? If you will not, who will? If you will not become the leader in integrity in your ministry who will? Who should be if not you?

There are tools available to assist you in your pursuit of excellence in integrity. The Institute of Church Management has plenty of them. The National Association of Church Business Administrators and The Evangelical Council for Financial Accountability do as well.

Pastoral Helmsmanship

Regarding financial accountability and integrity, Jesus' words still remain true – ask and you will receive, seek and you will find. Lead with integrity and you soon will be followed. I know the last words are not Jesus', but they are true nonetheless.

I will leave you with two questions of my own – Will we lead in integrity? If not, why not?

Treasure Chest

The Importance of Church Board Minutes

The ECFA (Evangelical Council for Financial Accountability) recently released an important article establishing why board minutes are so important. We would recommend that you visit their website and view this article in its entirety. (See below)

Here is a quote highlighting just some of the matters addressed:

> "Minutes not only provide an indispensable record of the deliberations in annual membership meetings, board meetings, and board committees, but they also offer a valuable history that reflects a prudent and responsible board. Minutes also can protect the board from litigation or other administrative proceedings. Additionally, board minutes may be one of the first places the IRS and other oversight groups look during an audit."

One can quickly see how important detailed minutes of official meetings may become. Establishing a procedure, according to the approved church documents is critical. Frequency, detail depth, the person(s) responsible for recording them, and some sort of review and approval process should be considered.

The ECFA article details what to include, which type of meetings to record, specific actions that the leadership board should or has agreed upon to take, and notations of dates, dollars, and deadlines. All of these important matters should be included in the minutes in case there is ever a difference of opinion at a future date. Memories fade, but the written word, agreed upon and entered into record will restore them.

In addition, the article includes a detailed sample that is extremely helpful to the leadership board. The article is available at the ECFA website here:

http://www.ecfa.org/Content/TopicCHURecordingChBdMin

Pastoral Helmsmanship

When should the Church Postpone or Cancel Events?

Dr. Rodney Harrison

As a pastor in California, weather cancelations were rare. In ten years of service in the Golden State, the only two changes I can recall were for services following the Northridge earthquake and 9-11. However, as a pastor in Minnesota and Missouri, snow, blizzards, ice storms, and tornados were annual events. Although some weather events result in power outages and weather emergency declarations, the challenge for the pastor and church administration is more than likely the hype preceding the storm. As media outlets seek to gain audiences, the desire to turn weather into a news event results in many "misses" when it comes to the actual outcome. At the same time, pastors have a responsibility to mitigate risk to members.

Recently, my church hosted a Saturday night event advertised as "rain or shine." That afternoon, a snowstorm dropped enough snow to cause every church in town, except ours, to cancel Sunday services by 6:00 pm that night. Despite the weather, the special event drew a record crowd (resulting in the headlines "Miracle at Main Street"). The next day, the church saw many visitors, some whom worshipped with us because their church was closed. This "win" was wrought as a result of having implemented a clear policy on weather cancellations. The following are the foundations on which these policies are built.

Cancelling a Sunday morning service on Saturday night, based on "what may happen," is a bad idea

Don't cancel or postpone an event if your only worry is the *chance* of bad weather. Recently, a major snow warning for the upcoming weekend was hyped in the local media for nearly a week. By Saturday night, the list of metro area church cancellations was well into the hundreds. By Sunday morning, however, the storm moved south of the city, resulting in nary a flurry. The minority of churches, that were not "quick to cancel," experienced normal attendance and little or no disruption of their programs.

Follow the local and state government suggestions

If the local officials have declared a state of emergency and told people to stay home, then you should cancel. In most states, official warnings to stay home and not travel can trigger a cancellation of services. Just remember, local schools generally cancel services based on different data, so don't consider school cancellations as the same as official state or local government "stay home, don't travel" warning.

Utility Outages

If the power or water is out, services should be cancelled. Not having a safe environment with working restroom facilities is almost always cause for cancelling services and church events.

Have well understood communication methods

Using a combination of email blasts, website postings, and social media is a good starting point. For churches in some metro areas, local media outlets will also post cancellations. For those who may not use technology, strategic phone calls are a good solution. Many churches use the same communication for cancellations as they use for a "prayer chain" update. It is also important that you "share the policy until it is shared policy." If the power is out all over town, members will know, "no church tonight." If the mayor has declared a weather emergency or stay home warning, the services are cancelled. It is also important that the process for posting cancelations is clearly understood. Trying to find the email that outlines the process for calling the media outlets, the phone chain contact list, or changing the website is hard to do once the internet is out.

Pastoral Helmsmanship

Consider an alternative service in lieu of the canceled one.

Matthew Mead notes that with good communication, you can cancel one service and replace it with an alternate one. This is essentially what our church did after 9-11. Instead of the usual Wednesday and Sunday services, we held a pray meeting on Wednesday night and a joint service with four other congregations on Sunday. When the weather is bad, consider holding a service for those who can attend in a smaller, more intimate room. Instead of a praise team, consider singing a cappella, especially if the worship team is unable to play. Being open to alternative ways of worship is wise. This can become a meaningful opportunity for worship for those who love to brave the elements.

Put your policy in writing.

Once you develop a policy, put it into writing. The policy should demonstrate not only the process by which services will be cancelled; it should also provide instructions for communicating the change. Ideally, the key points of the policy will be shared with all members, and incorporated into the new member class.

Storms happen. Having a weather cancellation policy will reduce the urgency of making difficult decisions when the storms are on the horizon.

Resources:
Sample Ministry Descriptions:

ABC Church
Ministry Position: Pastor, Youth Ministry

Position Status: Full time, exempt   **Employee**
Classification: Pastor

Regular Work Hours: Monday – Thursday ….9:00am – 5:00 pm, Sundays 8:00 – 4:00 pm Days off: Friday & Saturday (It is understood that when evening or weekend meetings are needed, that comp-time will be taken in that same week to off-set those hours)

Accountable to: Senior Pastor

Accountable for: Building a strong discipleship based youth ministry under the vision and missions of the church.

Position Overview:
The Pastor of Youth Ministry is responsible for all aspects of Youth ministry. Ages include students from 7th grade through 12th grade. Students include current church members and those in the community who need to know, grow in and serve the Lord.

Overview of Responsibilities:
1) Recruit, train, and otherwise lead teams to lead Junior and Senior high school age kids in a quality, meaningful weekly worship experience. The integration of parents is essential to a viable youth ministry.

2) Identify, recruit, train and otherwise raise up leaders to be available for assisting you, subbing in for you and for appropriate succession planning.

3) Provide regular discipleship and growth opportunities for Jr. and Senior high kids including, but not limited to, small groups, special events, retreats, camps etc.

4) Provide regular service opportunities for Jr and Senior high kids including but not limited to: short term missions trips, local community projects, servant evangelism opportunities, serving at food pantries etc.

5) Work with other staff and ministry areas to integrate youth into other ministries as needed.

6) Work with all staff and volunteers to fulfill the vision and mission of the church.

Budget Authority:
This area will have it own departmental budget. It is expected that financial resources will be managed with accuracy, prudence and accountability and operate within the established parameters. Any unapproved budget overage will be the personal financial responsibility of the Pastor.

Evaluation:
Evaluation will be on an ongoing basis in weekly staff meetings and in private conversations. A more formal written evaluation will be completed once each year. Performance will be based on degree and quality of completing the job description plus any additional goals agreed upon at the beginning of the evaluation year. Compensation adjustments will be based on quality and quantity of work performed and the overall value that the individual brings to the organization.

Conduct:
It is understood that every employee will make a good faith effort to conduct themselves in a friendly and professional manner at all times. Biblical standards are the overarching guidelines we will adhere to in our private and professional lives.

Resources

ABC Church
Ministry Description: Nursery Coordinator

Position Status: Part time, non-exempt
Employee Classification: Management Staff

Regular Work Hours: Monday – Thursday ….as needed
Sundays 8:00 – 1:00 pm
Days off: Friday & Saturday

It is understood that when evening or weekend meetings are needed, that comp-time will be taken in that same week to off-set those hours.

Not permitted to schedule events for more than 3 nights in any one week, must be home ministering to family at least four nights per week. Not to exceed a total of 20 hours per week

Accountable to: Children's Ministries Pastor

Accountable for: Overseeing and administering all facets of nursery ministry from birth to age 5

Position Overview:
The Nursery Coordinator is responsible for managing and directing nursery ministries. This includes a heavy emphasis on working with parents of the children to help them minister more effectively to their kids.

Overview of Responsibilities:
1) Recruit, train, develop and otherwise supervise staff (paid and volunteer) of all nursery ministries. Establish annual goals, assist where needed, and review and assess progress each year. Emphasis is on recruiting and training of others, not doing everything yourself.

2) Coordinate all Sunday nursery ministries. This includes providing high quality, safe and organized nurseries for all kids of that age group.

3) Coordinate to provide periodic support for other events in need of child care.

4) Train and equip parents to shoulder the main responsibility of growing and raising their children in a biblical manner.

5) Work with other staff and ministry areas to help integrate all areas managed into the church-wide vision and mission.

6) Work with other staff and ministry areas on special projects or events as needed or assigned.

Budget Authority:
The children's ministry will have it own departmental budget. It is expected that financial resources will be managed with accuracy, prudence and accountability and operate within the established parameters. Any unapproved budget overage will be the personal financial responsibility of the Pastor of this area.

Evaluation:
Evaluation will be on an ongoing basis in weekly staff meetings and in private conversations. A more formal written evaluation will be completed once each year. Performance will be based on degree and quality of completing the job description plus any additional goals agreed upon at the beginning of the evaluation year. Compensation adjustments will be based on quality and quantity of work performed and the overall value that the individual brings to the organization.

Conduct:
It is understood that every employee will make a good faith effort to conduct themselves in a friendly and professional manner at all times. Biblical standards are the overarching guidelines we will adhere to in our private and professional lives.

Resources

Sample Counting Agreements/Forms:

Biblical Ministry Description for Offering Counters

Responsible To: _____ (name), _____ _____ (title)

Purpose of Ministry:
The purpose of the Offering Counter Team is to provide accurate, consistent, confidential and timely processing of all donations and monetary gifts to the church.

Duties:
Follow offering counting procedures as outlined in a separate document, including:
- Pre-service setup of supplies
- Collect offerings during service
- Sort, count, and record offerings and donation credit
- Maintain names/lists for special offerings
- Take deposit to bank
- Provide contribution report and documentation to _____ as required

Desired Results:
- Feeling of trust / security / confidence from church members and visitors
- Good, accurate financial records
- Confidentiality of donor records
- Assist the Treasurer by ensuring good information is fed into the General Ledger

Time Commitment:
- ____ to ____ minutes per week

Gifts, Skills, Talents, & Qualifications:

Qualifications:
- An active Church Member for ____ months
- Regular, consistent giver

Gifts, Skills, Talents:
- Spiritual gift of administration
- Responsible
- Organization skills
- Attention to detail

Pastoral Helmsmanship

- Financial integrity on a personal level
- Ability to *consistently* maintain confidentiality
- Assertiveness to bring up anything that "doesn't feel right" to the lead counter or senior church leader

Offering Team Confidentiality Agreement
(Church / Organization Name)

Thank you for agreeing to serve in the ministry position of Offering Counting Team member. We are honored that you are willing to use your spiritual gift of administration to assist the Church. It is our goal to strive for the highest level of integrity as we are entrusted to be stewards of the Lord's finances in the local body of Christ.

This agreement serves to clarify expectations of confidentiality in your role as a member of the Offering Counting Team. Confidential information is defined as: all information obtained through performing offering counting and related administrative duties. This includes, but is not limited to, names and addresses of donors, amount of any individual donations, individual giving patterns, bank account information, etc. By signing below, I agree that I will strictly maintain the confidentiality of all information as defined above.

_____   _____   _____

Printed Name   Signature   Date

Resources

Cash Counting Sheet - Counter #1

Type of Count: ☐ Loose ☐ Envelopes ☐ Activities/Fees

Date:_____

CURRENCY			COIN		
$100.00			Dollars		
$50.00			Fifty Cent		
$20.00			Quarters		
$10.00			Dimes		
$5.00			Nickles		
$1.00			Pennies		
TOTAL			TOTAL		

TOTAL _____

Counter Signature:_____

------------------- Fold Here -------------------

Cash Counting Sheet - Counter #2

CURRENCY			COIN		
$100.00			Dollars		
$50.00			Fifty Cent		
$20.00			Quarters		
$10.00			Dimes		
$5.00			Nickles		
$1.00			Pennies		
TOTAL			TOTAL		

TOTAL _____

Counter Signature:_____

Pastoral Helmsmanship

Loose Check Log
(for Contribution Credit Only)

Date:

Name	ID Number	Check Number	#3110 Gen.Offering	Other Description (Acct. #)	Other Amount	Total

Counter Signature: _____

Sample Accounting Forms

For additional counting, budgeting and many other helpful and free reporting forms please visit:

http://www.mmsmidwest.com/resources/

Pastoral Helmsmanship

Best Practices Organization
Statement of Financial Position
12/31/2013

Assets

Current Assets

1010	Checking	$ 127,751.09
1020	Money Market	90,079.92
1050	Financial Investments	120.97
1210	Prepaid Expenses	-
	Total Current Assets	**$217,951.98**

Fixed Assets

1510	Land & Building	1,207,043.00	
1590	Construction/Renovation WIP	9,772.74	
	Total Fixed Assets		1,216,815.74

	Total Assets	$ 1,434,767.72

Liabilities & Net Assets

Current Liabilities

2005	Accounts Payable	$ -	
2010	Federal Withholding Tax Payable	2,128.18	
2020	State Withholding Tax Payable	298.00	
	Total Current Liabilities		2,426.18

Long Term Liabilities

2105	Building Loan - Liberty Bank		971,590.79
2110	Line of Credit - Building Renovations		-
	Total Long Term Liabilities		971,590.79

Net Assets
Temporarily Restricted
Social Responsibility

2310	Social Responsibility	50.00	
	Total Social Responsibility	50.00	

Ministries

2410	Children's Ministry	612.39	
2420	Children's Ministry Projects	72.10	
	Total Ministries	924.41	

Facilities

2510	Building Fund Contributions	229,205.47	
2515	Disbursed for Building Purchase	(128,743.00)	
2520	Disbursed for Building Renovation	(9,772.74)	
2525	Disbursed for Furniture & Equipment	(25,109.82)	
	Total Facilities	65,579.91	

	Total Temporarily Restricted		66,554.32

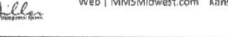
Web | MMSMidwest.com   Kansas City | 816.382.3050   Springfield | 417.708.8237

Resources

Best Practices Organization
Statement of Financial Position
12/31/2013

Unrestricted
2990	Unrestricted - Prior Years	3,409.21	
	Unrestricted - Current Year	390,787.22	
	Total Unrestricted		394,196.43
	Total Net Assets		460,750.75
	Total Liabilities & Net Assets		$ 1,434,767.72

Cash Available for General Operations		
Total Cash and Cash Equivalents		$ 217,951.98
Less:		
Current Liabilities	2,426.18	
Temporarily Restricted	66,554.32	
Total Unavailable	**68,980.50**	
Total Cash Available for General Operations		$ 148,971.48

 Web | MMSMidwest.com Kansas City | 816.382 3050 Springfield | 417.708.8237

Pastoral Helmsmanship

Best Practices Organization
Statement of Activities
For the Period Ended 12/31/2013

		Current Month			Year-to-Date				
		Actual	Budget	Variance	Actual	Budget	Variance	11-month Budget	Budget Remaining
	Personnel								
5110	Salaries & Benefits	21,094.37	21,785.00	(690.63)	195,771.07	196,400.00	(628.93)	196,400.00	628.93
5190	Payroll Taxes	840.88	1,000.00	(159.12)	6,686.84	8,799.00	(2,112.16)	8,799.00	2,112.16
	Total Personnel	21,935.25	22,785.00	(849.75)	202,457.91	205,199.00	(2,741.09)	205,199.00	2,741.09
	Administration								
6110	Accounting Services	984.00	1,000.00	(16.00)	12,088.00	12,000.00	88.00	12,000.00	(88.00)
6120	Advertising / Marketing	-	-	-	-	-	-	-	-
6130	Bank / Other Fees	479.80	-	479.80	1,690.49	-	1,690.49	-	(1,690.49)
6140	Communication	60.94	-	60.94	60.94	-	60.94	-	(60.94)
6150	Insurance	1,265.00	-	1,265.00	2,403.00	1,284.00	1,119.00	1,284.00	(1,119.00)
6160	Supplies	3,478.38	4,000.00	(521.62)	22,450.51	33,420.00	(10,969.49)	33,420.00	10,969.49
	Total Administration	6,268.12	5,000.00	1,268.12	38,692.94	46,704.00	(8,011.06)	46,704.00	8,011.06
	Facilities								
6210	Building Rent / P&I Payment	7,065.46	6,750.00	(1,684.54)	59,240.46	68,467.50	(9,227.04)	68,467.50	9,227.04
6220	Furniture & Equipment	-	-	-	-	-	-	-	-
6230	Maintenance	2,016.20	500.00	1,516.20	3,126.20	2,500.00	626.20	2,500.00	(626.20)
6240	Utilities	404.64	3,000.00	(2,595.36)	1,829.64	15,000.00	(13,170.36)	15,000.00	13,170.36
	Total Facilities	9,486.30	12,250.00	(2,763.70)	64,196.30	85,967.50	(21,771.20)	85,967.50	21,771.20
	Total Expenses	38,198.36	46,035.00	(7,836.64)	341,462.23	392,575.50	(51,123.27)	392,575.50	51,123.27
	Net Balance from Operations	$ 30,030.47	$ 3,965.00	$ 26,068.47	$ 252,271.48	$ 215,424.50	$ 36,846.98	$ 215,424.50	$ (36,846.98)
	Other Income / (Expense)								
8110	Net Assets Released from Restriction	9,772.74	-	9,772.74	138,515.74	-	138,515.74	-	(138,515.74)
	Total Other Income / (Expense)	9,772.74	-	9,772.74	138,515.74	-	138,515.74	-	(138,515.74)
	Net Balance	$ 39,803.21	$ 3,965.00	$ 35,838.21	$ 390,787.22	$ 215,424.50	$ 175,362.72	$ 215,424.50	$ (175,362.72)

Resources

Best Practices Organization
Revenues & Expenses Comparison
For the Period Ended 12/31/2013

	Weeks	Revenues	Expenses
January	4	$ -	$ -
February	4	57,306	14,892
March	5	53,149	15,081
April	4	45,177	29,494
May	4	48,005	42,527
June	5	51,239	31,399
July	4	123,827	31,647
August	4	40,655	32,880
September	5	46,479	32,532
October	4	31,410	43,329
November	4	28,249	29,474
December	5	68,229	38,198
YTD Totals	52	$ 593,724	$ 341,452
Weekly Average		$ 11,417.76	$ 6,566.39

Pastoral Helmsmanship

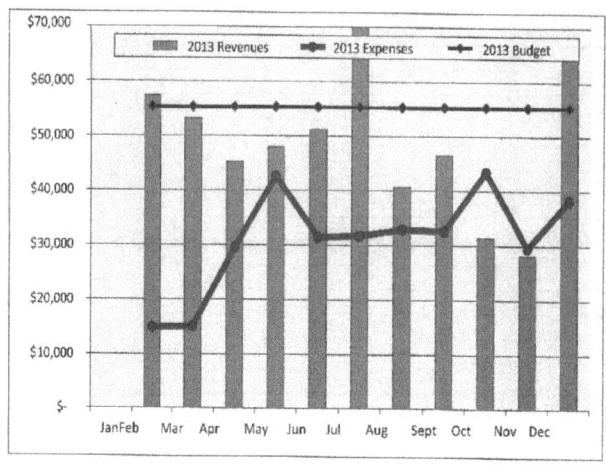

Resources

Sample Policies:

Sample Whistle-Blower Policy

GENERAL POLICY STATEMENT

Church/Ministry name is responsible for establishing the cultural environment, training employees, volunteers, and board members regarding whistle-blower policies in support of the church's anti-fraud policies and conflict of interest policies. This whistle-blower policy is intended to provide parameters, definition, procedures and protection to those involved in the discovery and or subsequent reporting of violations of the church's anti-fraud or conflict of interest policies.

It is the church's policy that there is zero tolerance for actions that subvert, decrease or otherwise prevent or impairs this policy to fulfill its intended purpose.

DEFINITION OF A WHISTLE-BLOWER

A whistle-blower is defined as any individual, inside or outside the organization, who provides substantiated information regarding an employee, volunteer, vendor, contractor, consultant, board member or other organization doing business with or who is associated with the church and is in violation of stated church's anti-fraud or conflict of interest policies.

WHO IS INCLUDED IN THE WHISTLE-BLOWER

Any employee, volunteer, vendor, contractor, consultant, board member or other organization doing business with or who is associated with the church.

REPORTING RESPONSIBILITIES AND SAFEGUARDS

Any known or suspected violations of the church's anti-fraud or conflict of interest policies should be reported immediately upon discovery to the Senior Pastor and the Chairman of the Board.

It is the responsibility of every board member, employee or volunteer to report, preferably in writing, discovered or suspected violations of the church's anti-fraud or conflict of interest policies.

No reporting party, who in good faith reports such a matter, will suffer harassment, retaliation or other adverse consequences. Any board member, employee or volunteer who harasses or retaliates against the party who reported such a matter in good faith is subject to discipline up to and including termination of employment, or removal from board. Any allegation that proves to have been made maliciously or knowingly to be false will be viewed as a serious disciplinary offense against the accuser.

Confidentiality

Discovered or suspected matters can be reported anonymously or on a confidential basis. Anonymous allegations will be investigated, but consideration will be given to seriousness of the issue, its credibility and the likelihood of confirming the allegation from other reliable sources. In the case of allegations made on a confidential basis, every effort will be made to keep the identity of the reporting party secret, consistent with the need to conduct an adequate and fair investigation.

Allegations will not be discussed with anyone other than those who have a legitimate need to know. It is important to protect the rights of the persons accused, to avoid damaging their reputation should they be found innocent and to protect the organization from potential liability.

Investigation Procedures

Resources

The Chair of the board or their delegate will investigate all allegations on a timely basis. The investigation may include but is not limited to examining, copying and/or removing all or a portion of the contents of files, desks, cabinets and other facilities of the organization without prior knowledge or consent of any individual who may use or have custody of such items or facilities when it is within the scope of the investigation.

The reporting party must not attempt to personally conduct investigations, interviews or interrogations related to the alleged fraudulent activity.

Resolution Procedures

The results of the investigation will be reported to the Board of Directors. Actions taken against the perpetrator of alleged policy violations will be determined by the Board with potential consultation with legal counsel.

Current Contact Information

Senior Pastor:

Xxxxxx
Xxxxxxxx
xxxxxxxxxx

Chair of the Board:

Xxxxx
Xxxxxxx

Pastoral Helmsmanship

Sample Credit Card Policy & Agreement

By issuing you a credit card, we are demonstrating our trust in you. You are empowered as a responsible agent to safeguard our assets. Your signature below is verification that you have read and agree to comply with the following responsibilities. It also acknowledges that you have received card #XXX-XXXX-XXX.

1. I understand the card is for organization approved purchases only and I agree not to charge personal purchases.

2. Improper use of this card can be considered misappropriation of funds. This may result in disciplinary action up to and including termination of employment.

3. If the card is lost or stolen, I will immediately notify the bank. I will confirm the telephone call by written correspondence to the program administrator.

4. I agree to surrender the card immediately upon termination of employment, whether for retirement, voluntary or involuntary reasons.

5. The card is issued in my name. I will not allow any other person to use the card. I am responsible for any and all charges against the card.

6. All charges will be billed directly to and paid directly by our organization. The bank cannot accept any monies from me directly; therefore any personal charges billed to the organization could be considered misappropriation of funds.

7. As the card is not my own, I understand that I may be required to comply with internal control procedures designed to protect assets. This may include being asked to produce the card to

Resources

validate its existence and account number. I will be required to produce receipts and statements to audit its use.

8. I will receive a monthly statement, which will report all activity during the statement period. Since I am responsible for all charges (but not payment) on the card, I will work with the program administrator to resolve any charge discrepancies.

9. To meet IRS and our organization's standards, original corresponding receipts will accompany each credit card statement and include in that documentation the following substantiation requirements: business purpose for the expense, names or titles if paying for others, dates of travel.

10. I understand a credit card is not automatically provided to all employees or volunteers. Assignment is based on my need to purchase materials for the organization and/or to provide for organization travel. My card may be revoked based on change of assignment, need or violation of this agreement. I understand that the card is not an entitlement nor reflective of title or position.

_____ _____
Cardholder Signature   Program Administrator Signature

_____
Cardholder Printed Name   Date

_____
Program Administrator Printed Name Date

SAMPLE Anti-Fraud Policy

GENERAL POLICY STATEMENT

Church/Ministry Name is responsible for establishing the cultural environment, training employees, volunteers, and board members, assessing fraud risks, implementing internal controls and monitoring activities designed to prevent and detect misappropriation of organization's assets and intentional material misrepresentation of organization's financial or other data or other actions constituting fraud. It is management's responsibility to communicate this policy to all board members, employees and volunteers and their responsibility to comply with this policy.

It is the church's policy that there is zero tolerance for actions constituting fraud.

DEFINITION OF FRAUD

Actions defined as fraud include but are not limited to:

- Theft of cash, securities, merchandise, equipment, supplies or other assets.

- Unauthorized use of organization employees, property, credit cards, cell phones or other resources.

- Submission of personal or fictitious employee expenses for reimbursement or fictitious or inflated vendor invoices or payroll records for payment.

- Receiving kickbacks or other unauthorized personal benefits from vendors or others.

Resources

- Forgery or fraudulent alteration of any check, bank draft, statement, billing, record, form, report, return or other financial document.

- Intentional material misclassification or misrepresentation of revenues, expenses, costs or other data in financial statements, reports, regulatory returns, applications or other communications.

- Intentional failure to disclose material related party transactions, noncompliance with lender requirements or donor/grantor restrictions or other required disclosure matters.

- Intentional improper use or disclosure of confidential donor, client/customer, employee or organization proprietary information.

- Any violation of copyright or licensing laws.

- Any other illegal or unethical activity

WHO IS INCLUDED IN THE ANTI-FRAUD POLICY

The anti fraud policy applies to fraud or suspected fraud by board members, employees, volunteers, vendors, contractors, consultants and others doing business with the church or its subsidiaries.

REPORTING RESPONSIBILITIES AND SAFEGUARDS

It is the responsibility of every board member, employee or volunteer to report, preferably in writing, discovered or suspected unethical or fraudulent activity <u>immediately</u> to the Senior Pastor and/or the Chairman of the Board.

No reporting party who in good faith reports such a matter will suffer harassment, retaliation or other adverse consequences. Any board member, employee or volunteer who harasses or retaliates against the party who reported such a matter in good faith is subject to discipline up to and including termination of employment, or removal from board. Additionally, no board member, employee or volunteer will be adversely affected because they refuse to carry out a directive which constitutes fraud or is a violation of state or federal law.

Any allegation that proves to have been made maliciously or knowingly to be false will be viewed as a serious disciplinary offense against the accuser.

Confidentiality

Discovered or suspected matters can be reported anonymously or on a confidential basis. Anonymous allegations will be investigated, but consideration will be given to seriousness of the issue, its credibility and the likelihood of confirming the allegation from other reliable sources. In the case of allegations made on a confidential basis, every effort will be made to keep the identity of the reporting party secret, consistent with the need to conduct an adequate and fair investigation.

Allegations will not be discussed with anyone other than those who have a legitimate need to know. It is important to protect the rights of the persons accused, to avoid damaging their reputation should they be found innocent and to protect the organization from potential liability.

Investigation Procedures

The Chair of the board or their delegate will investigate all allegations on a timely basis. The investigation may include but is not limited to examining, copying and/or removing all or a portion of the contents of computers, computer files, disks, tapes, other electronic storage devices, files, desks, cabinets and other facilities of the organization without prior knowledge or consent of any individual who may use or have custody of such items or facilities when it is within the scope of the investigation.

The reporting party must not attempt to personally conduct investigations, interviews or interrogations related to the alleged fraudulent activity.

RESOLUTION PROCEDURES

The results of the investigation will be reported to the Board of Directors. Actions taken against the perpetrator of alleged fraud will be determined by the Board with potential consultation with legal counsel.

CURRENT CONTACT INFORMATION

Senior Pastor:
Xxxxx
Xxxxxx
Xxxxxxxx

Chair of the Board:
Xxxxx
Xxxxxx
Xxxxxxxx

Pastoral Helmsmanship

Sample Short-Term Missions Trip Letter:

(CHURCH LETTERHEAD)

Potential donor
Name
& Address

Date

Dear _____,

This coming summer, I have the opportunity to participate in a mission trip to Jamaica with First Community Church. I look forward to seeing how God will open doors of ministry and use us to minister to the people of a small community called Harmons, Jamaica.

The mission agency we're partnering with, *Won By One To Jamaica*, will put us to work constructing a greenhouse that will provide a source of food and employment for several people
in the community. In addition to this, a few members of our group will assist some teachers in the local grade school while others will help in a medical clinic.

To participate in this wonderful missions experience, each person wanting to go is asked to raise or contribute $1,425. I would be very grateful if you would make a contribution to First Community Church to help me raise the needed funds. If you're able to help, I'm asked to communicate the following:

- Checks must be made payable to First Community Church and sent directly to the church.
- On a church offering envelope or the envelope enclosed with this letter, please indicate
  that this contribution is helping me (David Smith) raise money for the Jamaica mission trip.
  By doing this, the church will credit my involvement in raising the required funds.

Resources

- If, for any reason, I cannot participate in this mission trip (due to illness, etc.), the Church
  will probably use your gift to help cover the overall costs of the Jamaica mission trip or it
  could be used for the church's general missions budget. Contributions cannot be refunded. Contributions are solicited and received with the understanding that First Community Church has complete discretion and control over the use of all donated funds.

The Church is leading several training and orientation classes so we'll be fully prepared for the trip. When we return, the group plans to share some videos and stories of how God worked through us. Wow – I can hardly wait!

Thank you for taking the time to read this letter and for praying about how you can partner with us for this mission trip.

Sincerely,

David Smith
Soon-to-be Missionary to Jamaica

General Guidelines for Record Retention

Nonprofit organizations are often confronted with the challenge of records management and retention. It is not unusual for convenience and limited space to drive these decisions; however, a variety of government regulations and best practices should be considered and lead to a formal policy that is consistently followed. Such a policy should be understood and approved by the organization's governance board and leadership. Organizations have a responsibility to protect records in both the retention and destruction processes. Companies that specialize in the destruction of documents should be consulted to properly shred and dispose of paper copies as well as purge electronic files from the server and backup devices.

In some situations, a records retention policy covering the disposal of records should be immediately suspended. The destruction of records should cease when:

- the organization is served with any subpoena or request for documents
- the organization is subject to a governmental investigation or audit
- at the commencement of any litigation against or concerning the organization

Miller Management Systems, LLC (a/k/a MMS, LLC) offers the following recommended time frames that each of the listed records and documents should be retained. The following guidelines apply to both physical and electronic documents:

Resources

	3 years	7 years	Permanently
Accounting Records			
Invoices (after payment)	X		
Monthly financial reports	X		
Budgets	X		
Accounts payable/receivable ledgers & schedules		X	
Employee Expense reports & logs		X	
Bank statements and reconciliations		X	
Cancelled checks		X	
General Ledgers			X
Audit reports			X
End-of-year financial statements			X
Checks used for important payments, such as taxes, property, etc.			X
Contribution Records			
Contribution envelopes	X		
Donor contribution receipts		X	
Contribution ledgers & schedules		X	
Payroll and Personnel Records			
Employment / Personnel Records		X	
Payroll Registers		X	
W-2 and W-4 forms		X	
Proof of deductions		X	
Property Records			
Leases			X
Service contracts (after termination)	X		
Property Insurance			X
Real Estate Records			X
Tax Records			
Tax bills, receipts, statements		X	
Payroll Tax Records		X	
Sales/use tax records		X	

Pastoral Helmsmanship

Tax exemption letter	X
Tax and information returns	X
IRS examinations	X

Corporate Records

Contracts	X	
Committee minutes and bylaws		X
Articles of Incorporation		X
Insurance records		X

E-mail, PDF files, electronic document files	**Retention depends on the subject matter.**

Resources

Sample - Fellowship Church

Vision Statement:
"Fellowship Church exists to celebrate the presence of the living God"

Mission Statement:
"Our mission is to celebrate the presence of the living God by:
<u>*Gathering*</u> *people from all walks of life into a caring Christian community,*
<u>*Equipping*</u> *people with a practical faith that impacts their daily lives,*
<u>*Sending*</u> *people to serve Christ in our community and around the world"*

Core Values:
"As we labor together to accomplish the God given vision and mission of this organization/ministry, we will endeavor to:

Bring glory and honor to God in all that we do and say
Exercise Hospitality to all of God's people
Seek to support social justice for all
Serve our community with love and compassion
Practice good stewardship individually and corporately
Continually pursue knowledge and truth"

Suggested Reading:

Doing Good Even Better: How to Be an Effective Board Member of a Nonprofit Organization - Edgar Stoesz

Extraordinary Money: Understanding the Church Capital Campaign - Michael Reeves

Kicking Habits: Welcome Relief for Addicted Churches - Thomas Bandy

Leadership Axioms: Powerful Leadership Proverbs - Bill Hybels

Next Generation Leader - Andy Stanley

Redneck Dictionary - Jeff Foxworthy

Revolution in Generosity: Transforming Stewards to be Rich toward God - Wesley K. Willmer, Editor

The Peace Making Pastor; A Biblical Guide to Resolving Church Conflict - Alfred Poirier

Team Players and Teamwork - Glenn M. Parker

When Not to Build - Ray Bowman

Helpful Links:

The Institute of Church Management - Provider of the "Fireproofing Your Ministry" DVD workshop and other Christian Management training. Provider of many of the forms in this book

http://www.mmsmidwest.com/ - Accounting, Payroll, Operational Audits, Consulting and Training for Non-profits and churches

http://www.acfe.com/ - The National Association of Certified Fraud Examiners - Great place for additional resources in learning about and combating fraud.

http://www.ecfa.org/ The Evangelical Council of Financial Accountability - the Good Housekeeping seal for Christian ministries in how they handle money.

http://www.nacba.net/Pages/Home.aspx - The National Association of Church Business Administrators - Excellent resources for all things related to church administration.

http://www.churchmutual.com - All manner of insurance for churches

https://www.guideone.com/ - Church insurance

http://www.mbts.edu/ - Midwestern Baptist Theological Seminary

http://www.jeffklick.com - Blog, books, etc.

Index:

1099's, 132, 133, 134, 135, 136, 137, 138, 139, 140, 177
Accountability, 6, 51, 92, 103, 127, 142, 143, 145, 152, 155, 234, 261, 265, 286, 309, 310, 313, 315, 342
Accounts payable, 118
Administration, 1, 6, 33, 71, 162, 165, 346, 349
Administrative, 3, 4, 5, 6, 12, 37, 126, 160, 296, 297, 298, 299, 311, 317
Anti fraud, 332
Audit, 179, 338
Authority, 3, 4, 5, 39, 64, 76, 119, 186, 211, 212, 229, 230
Auto allowance, 120, 132, 133
Board member, 4, 150, 201, 326, 327, 332, 333
Body of Christ, 40, 227, 269, 272, 279
Budget, 6, 29, 30, 31, 76, 141, 142, 154, 313, 315
Budgeting
  Budgeting, 70, 140, 141, 142, 145, 147, 152, 155, 190, 320
Budgets, 145, 151, 155, 338
Cash, 103, 104, 105, 106, 107, 109, 110, 111, 112, 115, 119, 139, 153, 154, 177, 178, 229, 331
Change Management, 7
Charles Spurgeon, 25, 48
Check signers, 118, 176
Checks, 107, 175, 335, 338
Children, 8, 28, 35, 36, 37, 38, 39, 40, 41, 42, 43, 52, 53, 54, 73, 79, 89, 122, 165, 171, 187, 189, 199, 237, 279, 314, 315, 347, 348
Church, 2, 3, 4, 8, 2, 3, 4, 5, 6, 7, 8, 9, 11, 12, 13, 14, 15, 17, 18, 19, 21, 22, 23, 24, 25, 26, 35, 36, 38, 39, 40, 43, 44, 45, 50, 53, 54, 61, 62, 63, 64, 65, 66, 67, 68, 69, 70, 73, 74, 83, 104, 105, 106, 109, 110, 111, 113, 114, 115, 118, 119, 121, 122, 123, 124, 128, 129, 130, 131, 132, 133, 134, 135, 136, 138, 140, 141, 142, 145, 146, 147, 148, 149, 150, 151, 152, 153, 154, 155, 156, 157, 158, 159, 160, 161, 162, 164, 165, 167, 168, 169, 170, 171, 172, 174, 179, 180, 181, 184, 185, 186, 188, 189, 190, 205, 206, 222, 227, 228, 229, 230, 231, 236, 237, 240, 253, 257, 268, 269, 270, 271, 272, 275, 284, 285, 286, 287, 288, 291, 292, 293, 294, 296, 297, 298, 299, 300, 302, 303, 304, 305, 306, 307, 308, 309, 311, 312, 313, 315, 316, 317, 326, 327, 331, 332, 335, 336, 342, 347, 349
Church discipline, 69
Church planting, 8, 43
Clergy, 48, 119, 120, 121, 122, 123, 124, 125, 127, 185, 186, 293
Committees, 7, 227, 228, 231
Compensation, 283, 286, 313, 315
Compensatory time, 125, 126
Confidentiality, 316, 317, 327, 333
Conflict Resolution, 7, 205
Constitution, 69, 211, 298
Contribution, 338
Contributions 109, 114, 336
Credit_Card, 329
Custodian, 73
Cynicism, 54, 55
Debit cards 119
Delegation, 7, 227, 228
Denomination, 59, 68, 292
Deposit, 106, 107, 108, 153, 176, 316
Devil, 67
Documentation, 110, 221

Resources

Donated stock, 110
Donations, 103, 105, 109, 111, 115, 117, 141, 176, 302, 316, 317
Donor 103, 106, 109, 110, 111, 112, 113, 229, 316, 332, 335
EFT's, 119
Employee, 76, 124, 170, 177, 312, 314, 338
Evangelism, 2, 298
Expenditures, 6, 115, 117, 119, 128, 129, 144, 150, 152, 156
Facilities, 6, 157, 160, 165
Federal income tax, 122, 123
Feedback, 90, 91, 92, 93, 94, 97, 99, 100, 223, 233, 234, 235
FICA, 121, 122, 123, 124, 135, 136, 287
Finances, 6, 141
Firing, 14, 70, 96, 184, 190, 296
Forms, 316, 320
Fraud, 67, 95, 104, 108, 152, 153, 169, 172, 173, 174, 175, 176, 177, 178, 179, 270, 307, 308, 326, 327, 331, 332, 333, 334, 342, 349
General Ledger, 338
Goods or services, 109, 110, 111, 112
Governing body, 119, 293, 294
Hazards, 6, 47
Helmsman, 4, 6, 141
Hiring, 14, 37, 70, 73, 74, 75, 77, 78, 80, 85, 87, 123, 171, 179, 184, 190
Holy Spirit, 3, 4, 36, 67, 201, 278
Housing allowance, 120, 121, 122, 140, 290, 291, 292, 293
Humility, 57, 59
Illegal, 126, 263, 264, 332
Institute, 307, 309, 342, 347
Insurance, 122, 170, 180, 291, 303, 304, 338, 339
Integrity, 24, 70, 81, 91, 103, 104, 107, 108, 118, 140, 141, 154, 155, 171, 190, 263, 266, 283, 307, 308, 309, 310, 317
Interim pastor, 61, 62, 296, 297, 298, 299, 300
Internet, 5, 53, 118, 125, 154, 181, 303
IRS, 109, 110, 111, 113, 114, 118, 120, 122, 127, 128, 130, 131, 132, 133, 134, 135, 136, 137, 138, 140, 177, 178, 188, 290, 291, 293, 294, 311, 330, 339
Jesus, 3, 2, 7, 9, 16, 17, 19, 21, 25, 34, 35, 44, 47, 54, 55, 56, 57, 58, 59, 60, 77, 189, 193, 234, 262, 264, 265, 268, 269, 271, 273, 275, 278, 308, 310
Kingdom, 3, 8, 6, 33, 36, 57, 58, 60, 115, 131, 149, 150, 189, 202, 227, 231, 234, 257, 262, 263, 270, 273, 277, 348
Kubernesis, 2, 4
Leaders, 2, 4, 2, 3, 4, 6, 14, 25, 32, 40, 42, 43, 50, 55, 57, 64, 68, 77, 89, 146, 148, 154, 167, 172, 189, 194, 202, 242, 254, 261, 262, 263, 264, 265, 267, 278, 298, 299, 300, 302, 307, 308, 312, 347, 349
Leadership, 2, 3, 4, 11, 18, 22, 24, 39, 40, 44, 55, 59, 61, 62, 63, 68, 69, 79, 91, 141, 143, 144, 146, 147, 148, 149, 150, 153, 154, 184, 185, 195, 201, 203, 234, 240, 241, 243, 247, 252, 253, 261, 265, 269, 271, 277, 283, 291, 296, 297, 299, 311, 337
Legal, 5, 70, 78, 97, 118, 126, 135, 171, 177, 183, 185, 187, 190, 290, 292, 306, 328, 334
Management, 6, 7, 23, 157, 172, 239, 306, 307, 309, 314, 337, 342, 347
Meeting, 7, 29, 30, 31, 165, 167, 257, 259
Members, 11, 13, 14, 17, 18, 37, 38, 61, 64, 65, 67, 68, 69, 93, 97, 98, 105, 106, 118, 127, 131, 138, 147, 149, 161, 165, 169, 171, 199, 227, 229, 230, 231, 232, 233, 235, 240,

246, 250, 251, 284, 285, 299, 305, 312, 316, 326, 331, 332, 335
Ministry, 2, 4, 8, 2, 5, 6, 11, 12, 14, 18, 19, 22, 26, 28, 35, 36, 38, 40, 41, 42, 43, 44, 45, 47, 48, 49, 50, 51, 52, 54, 59, 64, 65, 66, 69, 70, 73, 74, 75, 76, 77, 78, 79, 80, 81, 84, 85, 87, 90, 91, 92, 95, 103, 106, 113, 114, 115, 118, 119, 121, 140, 142, 143, 144, 145, 146, 147, 148, 149, 150, 151, 153, 154, 157, 158, 171, 172, 175, 176, 177, 178, 179, 180, 181, 184, 189, 190, 193, 200, 202, 206, 210, 211, 219, 222, 225, 226, 227, 228, 236, 239, 242, 248, 253, 254, 255, 262, 263, 265, 267, 269, 271, 273, 275, 277, 279, 280, 284, 296, 297, 300, 306, 307, 308, 309, 312, 313, 314, 315, 317, 335, 340, 346, 347
Mission trips, 105, 112, 113, 114, 115
Money, 12, 14, 21, 28, 38, 48, 58, 60, 89, 103, 104, 105, 107, 108, 113, 115, 117, 118, 134, 141, 142, 144, 149, 150, 151, 152, 153, 155, 172, 173, 174, 175, 179, 211, 291, 308, 335, 342
Moral failure, 50, 52, 53
Nonprofit organizations, 337
Offering, 73, 77, 79, 84, 103, 104, 105, 106, 107, 108, 115, 138, 275, 316, 317, 335
Pastoral, 1, 2, 3, 4, 2, 76, 121, 298, 299, 347
Pastorate, 5, 37, 296, 297, 300
Paul, 3, 4, 25, 48, 49, 52, 67, 69, 103, 206, 207, 222, 264, 270, 273, 278
Payments, 117, 122, 123, 133, 135, 137, 138, 139, 338
Payroll, 119, 121, 124, 177, 338, 342
Peter, 36, 42, 57, 268, 273, 278, 280, 307
Planning, 5, 14, 28, 33, 74, 120, 141, 151, 156, 161, 162, 163, 169, 212, 229, 254, 257, 269, 290, 291, 312

Prayer, 4, 9, 13, 14, 15, 21, 25, 26, 28, 34, 41, 47, 49, 73, 142, 146, 161, 207, 210, 254, 270, 303
Pride, 57
Priorities, 4, 43, 44
Program, 31, 52, 106, 158, 167, 250, 270, 271, 296, 329, 330
Publication, 5, 304
Receipts 112, 114, 120, 129, 140, 288, 290, 330, 338
Record keeping, 23, 127, 132, 133
Records retention, 337
Reimbursement
    Reimbursement plan, 127, 128, 129, 131, 132, 288, 291, 299, 300, 331
Relationships, 25, 40, 49, 73, 84, 184, 194, 199, 203, 207, 222, 242
Report, 6, 141
Reporting, 23, 70, 110, 111, 117, 127, 138, 140, 141, 155, 185, 186, 187, 190, 293, 320, 326, 327, 328, 332, 333, 334
Reviews, 76, 88, 91, 93
Risk, 6, 169, 306
Salary
    Salaries, 24, 83, 120, 122, 123, 124, 128, 135, 138, 139, 283, 287, 288, 291, 299, 300
Schedule, 28, 33, 42, 43, 45, 73, 127, 314
Secretary, 73
Seminaries, 5
Sermon, 22, 49, 52, 93, 144, 210, 298
Severance pay, 99, 100
Social media, 40, 77, 92, 171, 180, 181, 283, 303, 304, 306
Spouse, 8, 36, 37, 40, 41, 42, 50, 53, 122, 174, 175
Staff, 3, 5, 11, 12, 13, 22, 25, 31, 36, 62, 70, 73, 74, 75, 83, 89, 91, 92, 93, 94, 95, 96, 98, 100, 101, 102, 105, 109, 118, 123, 124, 126, 127, 128, 129, 130, 131, 133, 148, 151, 171,

172, 180, 181, 190, 194, 195, 201,
202, 206, 212, 234, 236, 242, 246,
269, 273, 287, 288, 292, 293, 298,
299, 300, 303, 304, 313, 314, 315

Tax, 5, 68, 109, 110, 111, 112, 113,
114, 120, 121, 122, 123, 124, 131,
134, 135, 136, 140, 153, 185, 188,
189, 283, 287, 288, 290, 291, 292,
293, 300, 338

Tax deductible, 113

Tax exemption, 339

Taxes, 13, 120, 121, 123, 136, 174,
178, 183, 288, 290, 291, 293, 294,
338

Terminate, 102, 297

The Evangelical Council of Financial Accountability, 342

The National Association of Certified Fraud, 342

Time Management, 6, 27

Two signatures, 118, 176

Vision, 15, 18, 19, 20, 21, 22, 23, 24,
25, 26, 33, 34, 41, 55, 56, 57, 60, 81,
91, 142, 143, 144, 145, 146, 147,
149, 150, 151, 154, 155, 156, 158,
161, 162, 168, 230, 236, 243, 247,
252, 253, 261, 263, 265, 269, 272,
275, 285, 312, 313, 315, 340

Volunteer, 6, 73, 76

W-2, 129, 132, 133, 135, 138, 139, 177, 338

Author Bio's

Rodney Harrison

Dr. Rodney A. Harrison has been in full-time and bi-vocational ministry since 1984. He currently teaches Church Administration at Midwestern Baptist Theological Seminary in Kansas City, where he serves as Vice President for Institutional Effectiveness, Dean of Online Education, and Director of Doctoral Studies. Dr. Harrison holds the D.Min. in Mission Administration and MACE from Golden Gate Seminary and has done post-doctoral studies at Oxford University and post-graduate studies at Southwestern Baptist Theological Seminary. Harrison and his wife, Julie, have 3 grown children, Joshua, Cassandra, and Gabrielle. In addition to his academic role, he is a frequent conference speaker on church revitalization, conflict mitigation, and issues in church health.

Jeffrey A. Klick

Dr. Jeff Klick has been in fulltime ministry for over thirty-four years (since 1981). He currently serves as the senior pastor at Hope Family Fellowship in Kansas City, Kansas, a church he planted in 1993. Dr. Klick married his high school sweetheart, Leslie, in May of 1975. They have three adult children and ten grandchildren. Dr. Klick loves to learn and has earned a professional designation, Certified Financial Planner, earned a Master's degree in Pastoral Ministry from Liberty Theological Seminary, a Doctorate in Biblical Studies from Master's International School of Divinity, and a Ph.D. in Pastoral Ministry from Trinity Theological Seminary. In addition to serving as senior pastor at Hope Family Fellowship, Dr. Klick is a consultant with The Institute for Church Management, and also serves on the Board of Directors for The Council for Gospel Legacy Churches. Dr. Klick is a frequent blogger on several websites and has published multiple books.

Glenn A. Miller

Glenn has served the Church in multiple capacities since the mid-1980's. Glenn has been a church administrator with two different ministries, a director of Financial and IT Services, a CFO of a seminary, and currently is the president of Miller Management Systems, LLC in Kansas City, Missouri. In addition to assisting over 1,000 churches and other non-profit organizations with accounting, administration, and consultation, Glenn founded the Institute for Church Management which has trained hundreds of leaders in effective administration. Glenn is a highly awarded senior adjunct professor for Baker University since 1991, and also taught at Sterling College and Avila University. Glenn is a Certified DiSC Personality Assessment Trainer, a Certified Fraud Examiner, has completed his MBA from The University of Missouri- KC and is currently completing his Doctorate. Glenn has been married to Kim since 1981 and has four adult children - Chris, Jon, Beth and Ben. And, Anysia, the first granddaughter!

Thank you for reading our thoughts and we trust that God will use this tool to further the work of His Kingdom.

If you liked this book, make sure to purchase our new book scheduled to be released in June 2015 - *Confessions of a Church Felon: Protecting Your Ministry from the Flames of Fraud.*

Books and Video by the Authors:

Rodney's Books:
Seven Steps for Planting New Churches - One of the first books on church planting written from the perspective of the sponsoring church Seven Steps is a practical guide for pastors and church leaders committed to church multiplication.

Spin-Off Churches: How One Church Successfully Plants Another - is a comprehensive resource for sponsoring new congregations, and is available in print and e-book formats

Jeff's Books: (Amazon.com - Print/Kindle)
Courage to Flee: Second Edition - How to achieve and keep moral freedom
Generational Impact: A Vision for the Family - God's plan for the family explained from a Biblical perspective
The Master's Handiwork - God is not finished with any of us yet and He never fails so don't give up or in.
Reaching the Next Generation for Christ: The Biblical Role of the Family and Church - Detailed research on faith impartation to the next generation.
The Discipling Church: Our Great Commission - An in-depth study and training guide on the Great Commission
A Glimpse Behind the Calling; The Life of a Pastor - Written to help both pastors and those who love them.

Glenn's Video's - Available at
http://www.mmsmidwest.com/institute-for-church-management

3 Hour HD - Workshop DVD's
Fireproof Your Ministry!
Installing affordable internal controls to prevent fraud and increase credibility - Every church needs this information, now!
Church Administrator/Treasurer 101
Understanding the Basics of Effective Church Administration - a perfect complement to this book.